Terence Fisher

On the set of *Frankenstein Must Be Destroyed* (1969)

Terence Fisher

Horror, Myth and Religion

PAUL LEGGETT

McFarland & Company, Inc., Publishers
Jefferson, North Carolina, and London

To my family
S.D.G.

Library of Congress cataloguing data are available

Leggett, Paul, 1946–
    Terence Fisher ; horror, myth and religion / Paul Leggett.
      p. cm
    Filmography: p.
    Includes bibliographical references and index.

    ISBN 0-7864-1167-8 (softcover : 50# alkaline paper) ∞

    1. Fisher, Terence, 1904–1980 — Criticism and interpreta-
tion. 2. Horror films — History and criticism. 3. Motion
pictures — Religious aspects. I. Title.

PN1998.3.F58 L44 2002
791.43'0233'092 — dc21   2001056267

British Library cataloguing data are available

Manufactured in the United States of America

On the cover: Peter Cushing in the 1958 film *The Horror of Dracula*

McFarland & Company, Inc., Publishers
 Box 611, Jefferson, North Carolina 28640
  www.mcfarlandpub.com

TABLE OF CONTENTS

ACKNOWLEDGMENTS

I was eleven years old standing on a street corner in Asbury Park, New Jersey. It was the summer of 1957. A van was slowly driving by, pulling a large billboard which screamed, "*The Curse of Frankenstein* will haunt you forever!" A giant reddish face, horribly scarred, stared out from the poster which also included the polite suggestion, "please try not to faint." This was quite simply the most vivid movie advertisement I'd ever seen in my life. I quickly asked my parents if I could go see the film. I don't remember their exact words but it was something to the effect of, "Don't even think about it." Such was my introduction to the cinematic world of Terence Fisher, the British director whose films dominated world markets in the 1950s and '60s.

This book is the product of many years of fascination with the films of Terence Fisher. In bringing it to completion I am indebted to many, many people. It would be impossible to list all who have helped and influenced me but the following have each had a major impact on me.

To begin with, I wish to acknowledge many friends who over a number of years not only viewed films with me but offered numerous helpful insights and comments. My friend, Tim Gregson, first alerted me in the late 1950s to the significance of Fisher's films (we knew them generically then as only "Hammer Films"). Our disappointment at seeing *The Evil of Frankenstein*, a film Fisher did not direct, first indicated to us that it wasn't enough simply to have a Hammer film starring Peter Cushing. For the first time I began paying attention to the director's name. Tim's brothers Dave, Wes and Dan all played a role in the viewings (not to mention his younger sister, Janet, a good friend of my sister's, who had to put up with the various vampires, werewolves and monsters). Tim and Dave first helped me see the strong Christian emphases of Fisher's films. Their father, the Rev. E. Wesley Gregson, was one of the most formative influences on my life and the first minister I knew who enjoyed Hammer films.

My oldest and best friend, Sandy Samson, sat through endless hours with me viewing many of these films, as did my close friends and college and seminary roommates, Steve Deckard, Glenn Weaver and Glenn Fields. Diane Meslar Alimena not only sat through many films with me over many years but furnished me with copies of several of the BBC-TV Sherlock Holmes series starring Peter Cushing. To call that invaluable would be a gross understatement.

I am also indebted to many teachers and professors who encouraged me to think and write about the religious and theological significance of motion pictures. Among these I especially wish to mention Professor Diogenes Allen of Princeton Theological Seminary and Professor Tom Driver of Union Theological Seminary in New York City. I also wish to mention the late William K. Everson who served on my dissertation committee and the late Chris Steinbrunner, both of whom were authorities in the field of mystery, fantasy and horror.

I am especially thankful to the faculty and students at the Latin American Biblical Seminary in San Jose, Costa Rica, where I first explored some of these ideas in a class I taught on "God and Satan in Contemporary Film." I also wish to thank the editors of *Christianity Today*, particularly Harold Lindsell, Cheryl Forbes, Kenneth Kantzer, and Stephen Brown, who published my first articles on Fisher. The Rev. Stephen Brown deserves special mention here for telling me that if I didn't write this book God would judge me! Among more recent editors I am indebted to the Rev. Sue Cyre, editor of *Theology Matters*, who published several articles of mine which dealt with the themes of this book. In the area of film publications I particularly wish to thank Allen Eyles for publishing several of my articles in the past, including one on Sherlock Holmes films.

John Skillin of the Montclair Public Library has been invaluable to this project. He has offered numerous helpful suggestions as well as much encouragement. He has also been enormously helpful in obtaining stills, posters and other visual materials. Special thanks must also be given to Ron Borst, Richard Klemensen, Bruce Hershenson and Rich Allen for graciously supplying me with stills, posters and other helpful materials.

A special word of gratitude must go to the members of Grace Presbyterian Church who provided much support and opportunity to explore the areas of religion and myth which form the backdrop of virtually all of Fisher's work. I especially wish to thank Terryl Anderson for her constant prodding, prayers and encouragement and Jimmy Elliott for many helpful editorial suggestions.

This book could not have been written without the help of the staff of Grace Presbyterian Church. Our music director, Donald Du Laney, has probably sat through more horror films with me than any other living person. Enduring some of the later Hammers like _Lust for a Vampire_ was certainly going beyond the call of duty. My former associate pastor, the Rev. Lori Kallgren, offered several valuable suggestions. My current associate pastor, the Rev. Brandi Wolf Drake, and her husband, Dr. Evan Drake, have also been extremely helpful and supportive. And to put the matter bluntly, without our church secretaries— Susan Richards, Esther Bader, Kay Jensen, and Karen Rankin — this book would never have been completed.

There have been many people throughout the years who played incalculable roles in my religious development and cultural interests. I wish to mention especially Dr. Sigurd Johnsen, Alex and Helen Samson, Samuel and Dorothy Allcorn, Jay and Betty Poppinga. These, along with "Aunt" Joyce Farrell and her husband, Bill, have mentored me my whole life. Joyce, with her background in publishing, played a decisive role in the shaping of this whole project.

Finally, and most importantly, I must thank my family to whom this book is dedicated. My parents have provided me with more support, love and guidance than I can ever measure. They had no idea of the long range impact when on an autumnal night many years ago, in answer to my pleadings, they drove me some distance to the last theater in the area showing _The Hound of the Baskervilles_. My sister Pam has learned far more about the Gothic tradition, myths and horror films than she perhaps ever intended. She has played a decisive role in my understanding of Christian faith and cultural expression. My daughters Elisabeth and Gwendolyn have faithfully sat with me through film after film and have helped me decipher the theological implications of even the weakest examples. My son James is a little young yet but he has already been initiated into the Christian fantasy tradition with his enthusiasm for C.S. Lewis' _The Lion, the Witch and the Wardrobe_.

My wife Beth has given me greater love, support and encouragement than I could ever imagine. She has been my greatest asset and continues to give me the most help and encouragement I could ever have. When I first met her she had never seen a Hammer film or any film with Peter Cushing or Christopher Lee, to say nothing of Fisher's films. After hundreds of viewings she can now easily quote lines from scores of these films around the house. Talk about love and devotion! I could never thank her enough for all she is and does.

In conclusion, I must thank Terence Fisher for his unique cinematic vision. To quote the closing dialogue from _The Devil Rides Out_, "Thank God," "Yes, He is the One we must thank." _Soli Deo Gloria_. To God alone be the glory.

Montclair, New Jersey • October 2001

INTRODUCTION: THE IMPORTANCE OF TERENCE FISHER

Terence Fisher's death in 1980 hardly received much notice in the general press.[1] This was despite the fact that some prominent critics in England and France had already maintained that he was one of the greatest directors of fantasy films in history.[2] One of the reasons for Fisher's relative obscurity was that he was mostly known as a director of so-called "horror films," a term he himself despised. Even in 1980 this was seen as a less than serious film genre. Yet since 1980 Fisher's reputation has steadily grown.[3] With the advent of videocassettes more and more of his films were available for reappraisal. The films he made for Hammer Studios in Great Britain were beginning to be shown in museums and art theaters. He was the subject of a major biography by film scholar Wheeler Winston Dixon and his films were increasingly described as major works by mainstream critics.[4] Like many artists Fisher was more celebrated after his death than at any time during his life.

Fisher's films have clearly been a major influence on contemporary cinema. One can see this in examples which range from Roger Corman's American International pictures, which were the training ground for directors like Francis Ford Coppola and Martin Scorsese, to George Lucas' *Star Wars*. Fisher has done more to establish the conventions and styles of the modern horror film than any other director. (John McCarty, in a listing of the 50 most influential modern horror films, included no less than nine representatives of Fisher's work.[5]) Yet Fisher's importance cannot be summed up in terms of the fantasy and horror film genres. Fisher's work can be truly appreciated only when his primary motion pictures are recognized as spiritual allegories. Fisher's work presents a Christian worldview

1

in which evil is subtle, beautiful and deadly. Evil is real and it is ultimately supernatural. It can only finally be defeated by the cross of Jesus Christ. Fisher's films abound with spiritual symbols and references. This is all the more evident considering that Fisher rarely worked with original material. Most of his films are remakes of familiar stories and themes. It is Fisher's treatment that is strikingly original. He begins his long running Frankenstein series with the scene of a priest who comes to offer spiritual comfort to a condemned Baron Frankenstein. Frankenstein's first words in the film are, "Keep your spiritual comfort for those who think they need it," thereby establishing both his atheism and the reason for his self-destruction. Fisher gives us a Robin Hood who prays and crosses himself, a Sherlock Holmes who defines his role, not as a detective, but as one who "fights evil," and an assortment of doctors and scientists who quote Scripture and profess their faith in God. Fisher's symbolic world is comprised of crosses which often appear out of nowhere, holy water, running streams, mystical light and even animals who oppose the forces of evil. One of Fisher's most dominant images of evil is the serpent goddess, an ancient mythical figure whose origin probably predates the written word.[6] Fisher is a cinematic version of a longstanding group of British Christian apologists who used fantasy and mysticism to convey the Christian message. This group includes classic literary figures like Edmund Spenser (*The Fairy Queen*), John Milton (*Paradise Lost*), and John Bunyan (*Pilgrim's Progress*) as well as such twentieth century writers as C.S. Lewis, J.R.R. Tolkien, Charles Williams and Dorothy L. Sayers.[7]

These claims may sound extravagant but they hold up under critical scrutiny. From the perspective of the twenty-first century it can be seen that Fisher's approach to familiar film material was nothing short of revolutionary. Unlike his more lauded European contemporaries Ingmar Bergman, François Truffaut, Jean-Luc Godard and Federico Fellini, he was never considered a film *auteur*, that is, the author of a major body of artistic work. The fact that Fisher worked in routine genre films in an unpretentious studio should not blind anyone to the depth and force of his work. Fisher did not set out to revolutionize a part of the film world. He did not expect to be the focus of detailed analysis nor would he ever have defined himself as a Christian apologist. These things came naturally to him as he was catapulted quite unexpectedly to success. Before we look at some of his films in detail we need to see Fisher's two critical stages of development. The first is his developing identification with Hammer Studios. The second, and more significant, is his unique involvement with gothic horror, or as he preferred to call it, "fairy tales for adults."[8]

Terence Fisher came up through the British film industry in a way that was far from remarkable. He originally worked as a film editor. His first experience as a director was on several routine pictures including a short public affairs film on road safety. His career took a giant step forward shortly after World War II when he worked at one of Britain's major studios, Gainsborough films. Here he co-directed two major films in 1949, both of which offered some insight into his future work. The first was an adaptation of a Noel Coward play entitled *The Astonished Heart*. The film's story focuses on a psychiatrist (played by Coward himself) who is seduced away from his wife by a younger and sexier woman. The doctor's adultery ultimately leads to his death. The second film, *So Long at the Fair*, tells of an English brother and sister who attend the Paris World Fair at the end of the nineteenth century. To the sister's utter dismay her brother vanishes overnight completely. Even his hotel room no longer exists! After a series of suspenseful encounters in which she is aided by an English artist living in Paris, she discovers that her brother had contacted the bubonic plague. The authorities, fearful of a possible panic which would shut down the World Fair if the news ever got out, arrange the elaborate deception to suggest that he had never even been in Paris. Reportedly, even Alfred Hitchcock expressed admiration for this film.[9] Both these films deal with themes which will later occupy Fisher extensively. The deadly attraction of evil often in a sexual form, a conspiracy of silence around a mysterious infection and of course the classic fantasy device that reality is not what it seems all suggest major themes in Fisher's later work. These two pictures brought Fisher together with some key figures in English drama and film including Noel Coward, Celia Johnson, Jean Simmons and Dirk Bogarde.[10]

These modest but significant successes led to a second major step in Fisher's film career. In 1951 he was given the opportunity to direct a mystery thriller for a small studio which had just established an arrangement with an American theater owner named Robert Lippert to have their films distributed in the United States and Great Britain. The studio's name was Hammer Films, now identified with a legendary output of fantasy and horror films, but in the early 1950s it was a barely known, tiny film studio. Hammer's originators, back in the 1930s, had been a Spanish born theatrical entrepreneur named Enrique Carreras and an equally industrious Englishman, William Hinds. Hinds had appeared on the stage as "Will Hammer." The result of their collaboration, which would be continued by their sons and even Carreras' grandson, was a modest film distribution studio which took the name of Hammer Films. Early film productions in the 1930s included a musical with famed American singer Paul Robeson and a mystery starring Hollywood's Dracula star, Bela Lugosi.

By the early 1950s Hammer Films had bought a small country estate in Bray, near Windsor. This was to serve as the studio's headquarters for the next 17 years. Over the years all fans of Hammer would easily recognize the familiar halls, rooms and staircases of this same country estate which variously served as Frankenstein's home, Castle Dracula or Baskerville Hall, ingeniously modified each time by set designer Bernard Robinson. Hammer saw their future in the early '50s in making inexpensive mystery thrillers with a dash of sex. They were hardly competing with MGM or Paramount who were having their own troubles with the advent of television. Their formula called for a recognizable American actor who, while hardly being a star, was nonetheless familiar to U.S. audiences and a blend of atmosphere, mystery and a suggestion of sex, at least as tolerated by the strict attitudes of the period. An early example of this was a mystery thriller scripted by Frederick Knott, author of *Dial M for Murder*. The film, which reportedly dealt with blackmail, seduction and murder, starred Hollywood actor George Brent and included Diana Dors, who would come to be known as England's version of Marilyn Monroe. The film's title in England was *The Last Page*. Its American title was the somewhat more sensational sounding *Man Bait*. This was Terence Fisher's first film for Hammer, a studio where he was to work, on and off, for more than twenty years.

Fisher's next film for Hammer was another thriller called *Wings of Danger*, this time starring American actor Zachary Scott. The impact of television had led the Hollywood studios to cut back, and many familiar character actors of the 1930s and '40s were now more than happy for any work that was available, including working in Great Britain. Fisher's third film for Hammer followed the same formula but for the first time invoked a metaphysical twist. This film, titled *Stolen Face*, starred Paul Henried (Ingrid Bergman's husband in *Casablanca*) and American actress Lizabeth Scott. The film tells of a plastic surgeon who, spurned by the woman he loves, attempts to copy her face on to that of a scarred woman criminal who he then tries to woo as if she were the woman who spurned him. More than one critic has noticed the similarities of this story to Hitchcock's *Vertigo*, filmed seven years later. In its modest way the film touches on the themes of beauty and its relationship to evil, dual identity, and a human being's attempt to play God, all subjects which would concern Fisher in his more mature work.

By this time Hammer was expanding its horizons and becoming attracted to the commercial possibilities of science fiction stories. By the mid–1950s Hammer would be filming radio plays and other stories dealing with aliens from outer space, radioactive forces and earthbound mysteries like the abominable snowman.[11] Before any of these would go into production new director Terence Fisher would both co-write and direct a science fiction film with the intriguing title, *Four Sided Triangle* (the American title was *The Monster and the Woman*). The film opens with a quote from the Bible: "God hath made man upright; but they have sought out many inventions"— Ecclesiastes 7:29.

The film tells the story of three childhood friends: two boys, Rob and Bill, and a girl, Lena. The two boys, Rob and Bill, grow up and become scientists. Lena tries various pursuits as an adult and returns home disillusioned and suicidal. She reestablishes her relationship with her two childhood friends. Both Rob and Bill fall in love with her. Lena (played by American actress Barbara Payton, another Marilyn Monroe look-alike) chooses Rob (John Van Eyssen) and becomes engaged to him. All three remain friends although Bill (Stephen Murray) is clearly brokenhearted at losing Lena. The two scientists are working on a duplicating machine (which would also show up six years later in Hollywood's first version of *The Fly*). Their experiments are successful and, of course, Bill now wants to duplicate Lena. They proceed to clone her. The problem however is that being an identical duplicate, the new Lena also loves Rob. The potential complexities quickly become overwhelming. Bill now struggles with a second rejection from Lena's double and the original Lena is none too happy having an identical rival for her husband. The film does not fully develop these intriguing premises and the whole issue is resolved in a *deus ex machina* fire in which the cloned Lena dies.

More than any other early film, *Four Sided Triangle* introduces a number of key themes which will be developed throughout Fisher's career. The first is his belief in a definite God-ordained moral and spiritual order. This is established in the opening biblical quote and referred to throughout the film. The second is the deception of beauty. Bill is committed to having Lena yet she is seen as a deeply troubled and even suicidal woman, not the ideal choice to clone. The third is the danger of playing God. This latter theme is even more timely given the current debate and, indeed, reality of cloning. The film does not present a negative view of science as much as a warning (repeated by various characters) of the pride potentially inherent in seeking to control the natural order. What is also striking is that this is the only Hammer film where Fisher receives a script credit. It is known that later films did not follow their scripts in the final resulting film. It is safe to assume that Fisher continued to play a role in his film's stories as well as their direction.

From 1952 to 1956 Fisher continued to make thrillers and occasional science fiction films for Hammer. Few of these are available today despite such interesting titles as *Face the Music, Blood Orange, The Stranger Came Home* and *Murder by Proxy*. At the same time he directed a number of television episodes for such shows as *Colonel March Investigates, Douglas Fairbanks Presents* and *The Adventures of Robin Hood*. More importantly, other developments were taking place at Hammer which would have a major impact on Fisher's career. By the mid–1950s science fiction films in both England and America had become extremely popular.[12] Hammer began to cash in on this fascination with two films based on another popular radio program. The two films dealt with the adventures of an eccentric but brilliant scientist named Dr. Quatermass. *The Quatermass Xperiment* (*The Creeping Unknown* in the U.S.) released in 1955 was followed by the equally successful *Quatermass II* (*Enemy from Space* U.S. title). Following their pattern for American export both films starred a former Hollywood character actor, Brian Donlevy. Their success led Hammer to think in terms of something bolder and even more exciting.

The result was the epochal *Curse of Frankenstein*, one of the most successful films in British history and a milestone in the modern development of the horror film, as important in the 1950s as Boris Karloff's version had been in the 1930s. Several important decisions were made regarding this film. First, the film was to be shot in color and in genuine nineteenth century period (unlike the earlier Hollywood films). Second, the cast was to be an all–British one, eschewing the former policy of casting a recognizable Hollywood face in the lead. Beyond this, having Peter Cushing in the lead (apparently initiated by the actor himself) brought the film a distinction well beyond any of Hammer's previous efforts. While Cushing was unknown to American audiences, he had already established himself in Britain as a distinguished Shakespearean actor (having worked with Laurence Olivier), well known to BBC-TV audiences. The choice of casting Christopher Lee as the monster was no less propitious.

The idea of remaking *Frankenstein* in 1956 was a far from obvious one. Hollywood had run its Frankenstein series into the ground less than a decade earlier with *Abbott and Costello Meet Frankenstein*. Boris Karloff, seeing the way things were heading, had bowed out of the series a decade earlier. The story of *Frankenstein* belonged to the literary genre of gothic romance (or gothic horror). *Frankenstein*, written in 1818 by Mary Shelley, teenage bride of poet Percy Shelley, belonged to the early Romantic, premodern period of English literature. By the 1950s these stories and the films based on them in the 1930s were considered passé, especially with the burgeoning interest in science fiction brought on by the atomic age and the emerging dawn of space travel. In hindsight such assumptions regarding gothic literature are quite naive. Nonetheless, they were widespread in the mid–1950s. Hammer though was willing to take a chance on the scientific aspects of the story. By 1956 Terence Fisher had become Hammer's most accomplished director. It was not surprising then that he was chosen to direct *The Curse of Frankenstein.* The unforeseen enormous success of the film changed the status of Fisher and Hammer Studios forever.

In directing gothic horror films Terence Fisher found the ideal outlet for expressing both his personal beliefs and his distinctive approach to film. His relationship with Hammer Studios had its share of conflict since his goals did not always fit the more commercial ones of the studio. Despite Fisher's fame in the horror film genre he claimed he was seeking to make "fairy tales for adults." Therefore his nonhorror films with characters as diverse as Robin Hood and Sherlock Holmes are equally important as an expression of his beliefs. Yet there are unique features in the gothic Romantic tradition which ideally suited him. If, as many would contend, Fisher is the most accomplished fantasy film director in history it is because his distinctive Christian outlook accords very well with the flourishing of gothic literature in the eighteenth and nineteenth centuries.[13]

The first gothic novels appeared in England in the latter part of the eighteenth century. While being quite popular they were also novels of social protest. The eighteenth century in Europe was the era of the so-called Enlightenment. Alternately known as "the age of reason," this was a period of unrestrained confidence in human ability and, specifically, in the power of the mind to comprehend the universe. Science was believed to be the gateway to all truth and to have the capability of solving all problems and answering all questions. Religious dogmas tended to be dismissed as little more than mythology. In particular, the Christian doctrine of original sin was scorned in the face of a belief in the perfectability of human beings. Much of the modern era was shaped in the Enlightenment. It was the period that saw both the American and French Revolutions as well as a number of advances in the physical sciences. It also saw the birth of modern feminism. The most critical concept of the Western European Enlightenment was its confidence in human autonomy. Human being were both free and capable of shaping their own destiny. Ancient beliefs in "gods and monsters" were passé. The supernatural simply did not exist. While reasoned people might believe in a Supreme Being, he was seen as a distant figure, no more than a cosmic watchmaker. The natural world was all there was to reality and science was more than able to explain it. It was against this secular naturalism that the early gothic novels protested.

The characters in gothic novels were often clearly sinful figures whose self-confidence and pride created disaster. They suffered for rebelling against a very real supernatural God. Confidence in human rationality in the gothic novel was presented as an illusion which inevitably led to tragedy. Very few of the gothic novels of the eighteenth century (e.g., *The Castle of Otranto, The Mysteries of Udolopho, The Monk*) are known or read today. These works are important primarily as precursors to Mary Shelley's *Frankenstein*. Mary Shelley wrote *Frankenstein* when she was barely nineteen years old. Her father, William Godwin, was a classic Enlightenment figure. An early socialist, he had such confidence in reason that he believed human beings could live without laws or social institutions provided they simply followed the dictates of their own reason. He was heavily influenced by the Swiss philosopher Jean Jacques Rousseau, possibly the most significant European figure of the eighteenth century.[14] Godwin's wife, and Mary's mother, was Mary Wollstonecraft, whose *Vindication of the Rights of Woman* was one of the early statements of modern feminism. Unfortunately, Mary Wollstonecraft died giving birth to her daughter who was given her mother's name. Mary Wollstonecraft Godwin knew her mother only by reputation. Exposed at an early age to her rather domineering father's strong confidence in human reason and rebellion against social convention, she became involved with some of the most prominent figures in English letters in the early nineteenth century. For a period she was mistress to Lord Byron. Later she ran off with Percy Bysshe Shelley and became his second wife.[15]

The theme of Mary Shelley's *Frankenstein* essentially contradicts the views of her father and other Enlightenment thinkers. It is tempting to see Mary's work as a young feminist protest against the ideals of middle-aged men. There have indeed been several studies of Mary Shelley from a feminist perspective.[16] Nevertheless, *Frankenstein* is particularly striking as a novel with clear theological and philosophical implications. The book's protagonist, Victor Frankenstein, is a young scientist who believes he can create a perfect man. The result is a knowledgeable but tormented creature whose murderous frustration finally destroys Frankenstein and all those close to him. The subtitle of the book is *The Modern Prometheus*. The implication is clear. Frankenstein, like the mythical Prometheus and the biblical Adam, has rebelled, not against social convention or human views of morality, but against heaven itself. It is noteworthy that the novel includes several references to John Milton's *Paradise Lost*.

Frankenstein, like Lucifer, has committed the ultimate blasphemy. He has rebelled against God by usurping God's place and he pays a terrible price for his sin. All the central themes of the Enlightenment — the basic goodness and perfectability of human beings, the trust in science, the identification of god with the natural order — are severely questioned in *Frankenstein*. The novel is far more than a horror tale. It is an allegory about the spiritual dangers of unlimited confidence in human reason, goodness and science. It is hard to imagine a single work of fiction which more completely predicts the coming crises of the twentieth century.

The influence of *Frankenstein* in the century just ended is more evident in film than in literature. The story has been filmed in every decade of the twentieth century beginning with a 1910 version by Thomas Edison and continuing up through Kenneth Branaugh's striking 1994 adaptation. What is even more notable is the way the filming of *Frankenstein* has coincided with motion picture versions of four other nineteenth century gothic novels. Remarkably, in a fifteen year period of the late Victorian era in Britain, 1886–1901, four immensely popular, influential novels were written with strong gothic themes. These include Robert Louis Stevenson's *The Strange Case of Dr. Jekyll and Mr. Hyde,* Oscar Wilde's *The Picture of Dorian Gray,* Bram Stoker's *Dracula* and Sir Arthur Conan Doyle's *The Hound of the Baskervilles.*[17] What is striking about these four British gothic tales is that they appear at a time when Enlightenment assumptions about modernity were largely unquestioned. It is also important to note that Terence Fisher is the only director in film history to have filmed all of these stories (if one grants that *The Man Who Could Cheat Death* is a loose adaptation of *Picture of Dorian Gray*).

At the dawn of the twentieth century optimistic beliefs in human goodness and perfectibility, along with widely held views about the utopian benefits of science and technology, were virtual assumptions. Yet such beliefs were severely questioned in these late Victorian novels. These novels were by and large Christian allegories, this despite the fact that most of their authors, like Mary Shelley before them, claimed to have left orthodox Christianity behind them. The fact was that Christian faith was a clear ally in critiquing Enlightenment views. Stevenson's *Jekyll and Hyde* abounds in biblical quotes and, like Wilde's *Dorian Gray,* strongly questions the dominant view of the essential goodness and perfectibility of human nature. *Dracula* explicitly challenges a rational view of reality that seeks to deny the supernatural and indeed places a strong emphasis on the power of the cross to defeat the forces of evil. *The Hound of the Baskervilles,* the most famous of Conan Doyle's Sherlock Holmes stories, likewise combines an atmosphere of intense human cruelty with an emphasis on the supernatural. Despite the story's rational ending, it is the one occasion when Holmes, the master of deductive logic, admits that he is perhaps being asked to take on "the Father of evil himself."

What is especially intriguing about these classic gothic novels is that they have been filmed often within close proximity of each other throughout the twentieth century. The first example of this cycle takes place in

Germany beginning just before the First World War and continuing into the late 1920s. While *Frankenstein* is not filmed by name during this period, the story *Der Golem,* which is strongly similar (a Jewish rabbi brings a statue to life which quickly embarks on a destructive rampage), appeared twice on the German screen, once in 1914 and again in 1920. Including *Der Golem,* all five English gothic classics were filmed in Germany in less than a decade, from 1914 to 1922. Film scholars such as Siegfried Kracauer and Lotte Eisner have noted that these films and others with similar gothic themes (such as the highly influential *Cabinet of Dr. Caligari*) prefigure many of the social and political themes of Nazism.[18] These films do this at the same time that they also critique the dominant Enlightenment assumptions of the twentieth century.

The same prophetic impact of the filming of these stories can be seen at other critical points in the century. Hollywood's classic gothic horror cycle began in 1931 at the onset of the Depression and continued until the end of World War II. Save for a brief hiatus during a short-lived optimistic period in the years 1937 and 1938, gothic horror films were produced yearly with every major studio in Hollywood taking part. Both *Frankenstein* and *Dracula* were filmed along with numerous sequels. *Dr. Jekyll and Mr. Hyde* was filmed twice. *The Picture of Dorian Gray* and *The Hound of the Baskervilles* were each given lavish treatments. Many other horror films were made during this period; most of them, including *The Phantom of the Opera, The Mummy* and *The Wolf Man,* are clearly gothic in style and subject matter (supernatural, anti-rational, anti-scientific). Others range from science fiction (several films based on the work of H.G. Wells) to routine or not so routine thrillers involving everything from circus freaks to loose adaptations of Edgar Allan Poe. Yet, as in Germany two decades earlier, the five gothic classics set the tone and direction for the fantasy and horror films of the period.

As previously mentioned, these stories were considered old fashioned at mid-century when Hammer films seems to have stumbled on to them. The success of *Curse of Frankenstein* led the studio to follow the same paths that have been traversed in earlier periods of film history, turning not only to the classic gothic stories but to the related themes of *Phantom of the Opera, The Mummy* and *The Wolf Man.* All of these, including various sequels, were directed by Terence Fisher in a relatively brief span of time from 1957 to 1973. Conventional wisdom, espoused even by some at Hammer itself, might indicate that their formula wore thin in the wake of more intense forms of horror, beginning with *The Exorcist* and continuing with *Halloween, Night of the Living Dead, Carrie* and *Nightmare on Elm Street* on up to such recent examples as *The Silence of the Lambs* and *The Blair*

Witch Project. But such thinking misses the point as to just how distinctive the classic gothic tradition is. The public's fascination with Frankenstein, Dracula, et al. continues in spite of alternative forms of horror. Consider that in the 1990s there were no fewer than three versions of *Frankenstein*, an elaborate remake of *Dracula* by no less than Francis Ford Coppola, another adaptation of *Dr. Jekyll and Mr. Hyde (Mary Reilly)* as well as new versions of the Wolf Man (*Wolf*) and *The Mummy.* Andrew Lloyd Webber's musical version of *The Phantom of the Opera* is slated to be filmed sometime in the near future. Britain's Granada Television series of Sherlock Holmes with Jeremy Brett continues to be shown, including a two hour version of *The Hound of the Baskervilles.*

In the 1970s it was not the gothic horror tradition that was dead, but rather Hammer's indifferent treatment of it. Age and sickness had taken their toll on Terence Fisher. Moreover, following disputes over the 1969 film *Frankenstein Must Be Destroyed,* Fisher was increasingly alienated from Hammer Studios. Without Fisher, Hammer's Frankenstein and Dracula films degenerated into self-parody and crude exploitation. (Three interesting versions of *Dracula* were filmed in the 1970s, none of them however by Hammer Films.[19])

The gothic subject matter remains viable, as its long history shows, but only when it is taken seriously. The gothic tradition is rooted deeply in a Christian view of the world. It expresses itself in the form of a modern morality play in which objective forces of good and evil are in conflict always with the assurance that good will ultimately win out. God is in control but it is clearly the God revealed in the cross and resurrection of Jesus Christ. Therefore suffering can have a redemptive quality to it. Life has a purpose that is ultimately supernatural but also knowable. The world is neither purely rational nor irrational. It is finely suprarational, or beyond rational. Life has a higher purpose than can be found either through the mind or the physical senses. Existence has a spiritual dimension which alone can give it meaning.

Terence Fisher was not raised an orthodox Christian but as a Christian Scientist.[20] As a young man he converted to the Church of England. Interestingly, Christian Science does not believe in the reality of evil. This accounts perhaps for Fisher's longstanding fascination with the nature of evil and the illusions surrounding it (what Wheeler Winston Dixon has called "the charm of evil"). Fisher's spiritual orientation is a mixture of myth, fairy tale and Christian doctrine. In this he is a kindred spirit with the British "Inklings": C.S. Lewis, Dorothy L. Sayers, Charles Williams and J.R.R. Tolkien. It is particularly fascinating to compare Fisher with C.S. Lewis. Their primary difference is really cultural. Lewis was a professor of

Renaissance literature at both Oxford and Cambridge. He had a prodigious knowledge of myth and did in fact write fairy tales (the famous "Chronicles of Narnia" series). Fisher had no such academic background yet was equally intrigued by myth and saw himself, in his famous quote, as a filmmaker of "fairy tales for adults." Lewis actually wrote a science fiction trilogy as a Christian allegory.[21] His hero in the series, John Ransom, is a mystical Christian scientist not unlike many of the heroes in Fisher's films. Unfortunately, Lewis's space trilogy has never been filmed. Terence Fisher would have been the ideal director for it.[22]

Terence Fisher is important because he was the director best suited in film history to deal with the gothic tradition and its related field of Christian allegory. His own personal worldview was essentially the same as that underlying the gothic novels. He shared the same concerns about human autonomy and the illusions of perfectibility and science. He was also fascinated by classic mythical figures like the serpent-goddess and the redeemer hero. His films do not follow their mythical or literary sources literally. Fisher developed his own approach, complete with a near repertory company of actors and technicians, which drew heavily on the gothic sources. There is a continuity to the films that Fisher made at Hammer as well as several he made at other studios which demonstrate his particular cinematic worldview. Truthfully, his liaison with Hammer was a brief one. While he served their commercial goals he was free to work. Over the course of the 1960s his Christian allegorical view began to clash with the studio. By 1970 their interest in gothic horror was clearly different from his. For a period though he flourished at Hammer. Fisher remains one of the few directors in cinema history with a clear, spiritual outlook.[23] To appreciate that distinctive outlook this work looks at some of his films in detail.

Notes

1. According to a letter published in *Little Shoppe of Horrors* my article in *Christianity Today* may have been the only obituary article on Fisher published in the U.S. *Little Shoppe of Horrors*, No. 10/11 July 1990, p. 6.

2. Actually, French critics in general were far more receptive to Fisher than their British and American counterparts. Murphy, Robert. *The Sixties British Cinema.* p. 162.

3. Wright, Bruce Lanier. *Nightwalkers*, p. 13.

4. Examples include not only David Pirie's groundbreaking *A Heritage of Horror* but also Robert Murphy (*The Sixties British Cinema*) and Marcia Landy (*British Genres: Cinema and Society, 1930–1960*). One need only consult listings of Fisher's films in the *Blockbuster Entertainment Guide to Movies and Videos* and *Time Out* to appreciate the rising stature of many of Fisher's films.

5. McCarty, John. *The Modern Horror Film.*

6. Campbell, Joseph. *The Masks of God: Occidental Mythology,* pp. 9–41. Baring, Anne, and Cashford, Jules. *The Myth of the Goddess,* pp. 64ff .

7. This group published a number of apologetic Christian works, the most famous being C. S. Lewis' *Mere Christianity* and Dorothy L. Sayer's *Creed or Chaos?*

8. Fisher, Terence. "Horror Is My Business," in *Films and Filming* (July, 1964).

9. Cited in the video history, *Flesh and Blood.*

10. Noel Coward both scripted and starred in *The Astonished Heart,* co-directed by Fisher.

11. The most famous and influential of these films were the two Quatermass pictures.

12. Hardy, Phil. *The Overlook Film Companion: Horror,* p. 98.

13. Pirie, David. *A Heritage of Horror,* pp. 50ff.

14. Russell, Bertrand. *A History of Western Philosophy,* pp. 684–699.

15. Florescu, Radu. *In Search of Frankenstein,* pp. 77ff.

16. The "Mary Shelley" website on the internet provides a number of resources including *Literary Women* (1978) by E. Moers, published by Women's Press; *Mary Shelley* (1993) by M. Spark. London, Constable and Company, Ltd.; and *Approaching Literature: The Realist Novel* (1995), edited by Denise Walder, London, Routledge.

17. It is striking that all four men apparently had some knowledge of each other. Wilde's *Picture of Dorian Gray* came out of a publishers' meeting which also produced Conan Doyle's *The Sign of Four.* Stevenson told Sherlock Holmes stories to the natives in Samoa. Bram Stoker was actor Sir Henry Irving's business manager and in that capacity moved freely in some of the same circles as Wilde and Doyle.

18. Cf. Kracauer, Siegfried, *From Caligari to Hitler* and Eisner, Lotte, *The Haunted Screen.*

19. Those include two made for television versions starring Jack Palance and Louis Jourdan respectively and a theatrical version with Frank Langella. This is not to mention Werner Herzog's *Nosferatu,* a remake of F. W. Murnau's 1922 silent version.

20. Wheeler Winston Dixon has illuminating comments about Fisher's Christian beliefs throughout his fine biography, *The Charm of Evil: The Life and Films of Terence Fisher.*

21. The three titles are *Out of the Silent Planet, Perelandra,* and *That Hideous Strength.*

22 . This is all the more remarkable considering that Lewis' science fiction novels have sold well for over fifty years. They remain in print to this day.

23. Pirie, David. *A Heritage of Horror,* p. 51.

Chapter One

THE FAILURE
OF FRANKENSTEIN

The first, and most sustained, character in Terence Fisher's gothic film series is Baron Frankenstein. The Baron, as ably portrayed by Peter Cushing, appears in five films over a 17-year period (1957–73). Fisher's Dr. Frankenstein character is arguably the director's greatest and most disturbing achievement. Fisher's interpretation of Frankenstein is unlike any other in film history, as different from James Whale's in the early thirties' *Frankenstein* films as from Hammer's other attempts at Frankenstein movies. In many ways Fisher's conception is noticeably different from Mary Shelley's Dr. Frankenstein in the original (and often neglected) novel. There is nothing in Fisher's previous career to prepare one for such an unsettling and dominant figure.[1] Fisher inaugurates the character at mid-century and continues to portray him throughout the period of unprecedented social change which occurs in the 1960s and early 1970s.

In Frankenstein Fisher develops an original and penetrating symbol of Western cultural goals, beliefs and values at a time when those standards were passing through a period of profound crisis. It is only now, two decades after Fisher's death, that we can begin to get some perspective on one of the most complex and insightful portrayals in modern cinema. Fisher's Frankenstein epitomizes a civilization in dissolution, a culture witnessing the collapse of its own tottering belief system. To appreciate the full impact of Fisher's work we must consider the specific films in this remarkable series.

Much has already been written on the original impact of Fisher's *The Curse of Frankenstein* in 1957.[2] The point has been made that the gothic horror film was going through a rebirth simultaneously that year in different parts of Europe (though not in the United States).[3] Yet *Curse of Frankenstein* stands as a unique work in many ways. It is the first real

Paul (Robert Urquhart) comforts a distressed Elizabeth (Hazel Court) in *The Curse of Frankenstein* (1957).

gothic horror film made in England (British fantasy films previously had fallen into such categories as mystery thrillers or ghost stories, but nothing to rank with German cinema in the twenties or Hollywood in the thirties and forties). Second, it was made in color with graphic depictions of body parts, dismembered eyes and blood. In terms of style alone this film opened the door to a modern film approach still prevalent today which emphasizes explicit blood and gore (though used in ways far different from Fisher's films). Third, Fisher's narrative approach was more controlled and literary than many of his predecessors. The excessive melodrama and flamboyant fantasy of Hollywood's classic horror pictures was eschewed in favor of a somewhat more realistic style. Fisher's shocks tend to be conveyed through action and camerawork rather than through purple prose dialogue, bizarre sets or shrieking actors.

These observations are valid though somewhat superficial. To appreciate *The Curse of Frankenstein* and indeed Fisher's whole Frankenstein saga, we must examine the character of Baron Frankenstein himself. *The*

Curse of Frankenstein is told in flashback. Frankenstein is introduced through the eyes of a priest who has come to hear his final confession as he awaits execution in a jail cell. He is a dishevelled, wild-eyed figure who implores the priest to hear his "tale." What follows is the account of an utterly amoral person obsessed with the pursuit of knowledge. For Frankenstein, knowledge is power, a power that ultimately can control life and death.

Frankenstein's whole perspective is devoid of moral scruple. He murders a former professor to obtain the old man's brain. He impregnates a servant girl and then has her killed. He deceives both his assistant and his fiancée. In reality he is a pathological liar. The "perfect man" he attempts to create is to have the body of an athlete, the hands of an artist and the brain of a genius. The result of this experiment, however, is a pathetic creature who is both dim-witted and fearful. After the creature is shot in the head and killed, Frankenstein insists on bringing it back to life. This second action is more obsessive than purposeful since Frankenstein knows the creature is a far cry from a perfect man. In one of the film's most memorable scenes Frankenstein shows the restored creature to his former teacher Paul Krempe and delights that the creature can respond to simple commands such as "stand up" and "sit." The assistant icily asks if this is Frankenstein's conception of the "perfect man," a creature who cannot even speak, much less solve mathematical problems. Frankenstein has an answer. It is Paul's fault since he tried to prevent Frankenstein from stealing the brain of the murdered professor. Frankenstein has an answer for everything. Eventually the creature escapes again and is destroyed in a vat of acid leaving no trace whatsoever. Paul forms a collusion with Frankenstein's fiancée, Elizabeth, to deny that there ever was a creature. As Frankenstein concludes his story to the priest he is about to be executed for the murders committed by the monster. The film ends with Frankenstein insisting that he wasn't responsible for any crimes. Paul and Elizabeth refuse to come to his aid. His story of a "creature" remains unproven, leaving him the only suspect for the creature's murders. In the final scene, still unrepentant, he is led out to the guillotine.

The Curse of Frankenstein unnerved both audiences and critics when first released. In retrospect its blood and gore look quite moderate. What remains fascinating is the approach to Frankenstein himself. Fisher has said that all of his gothic films are commentaries on the fall of humanity as recorded in the Bible's Book of Genesis.[4] Another way of describing what is theologically summarized as the Fall is to see it as an unjustified and destructive attempt to gain the "knowledge of good and evil." Symbolically Adam and Eve are driven out of Paradise into a world of "thorns and thistles."

The importance of Fisher's Dr. Frankenstein is that he is a totally unsympathetic character (as opposed to the original novel and the various Hollywood films). What sustains interest in the series is that he remains a fascinating and contradictory character. Initial attempts at analyzing him have painted him as an early modern, i.e., rational, scientist in a world still shaped by feudal and medieval beliefs. British film critic David Pirie has done some excellent studies on Fisher including the Frankenstein series but he seems to miss an essential point.[5] Fisher's Frankenstein is not a morally complex figure occasionally accomplishing good by improper motives nor is he an early martyr to science or a romanticized "dandy" after the fashion of Baudelaire or Oscar Wilde. Baron Frankenstein, following the image of the Fall, is humanity in sin, "Adam" in the symbolic sense of the apostle Paul in the New Testament opening the gateway to the dominion of sin and death.[6]

The real-life model for Baron Frankenstein both for Mary Shelley and Fisher may well be Jean-Jacques Rousseau (1712–1778). Rousseau, like Dr. Frankenstein, is Swiss and has been called the first truly modern European figure. Rousseau is brilliant and complex yet fatally flawed morally. On one side Rousseau was an able thinker, writer and political philosopher. He is frequently cited as one of the founders of the Romantic movement. He gave vivid expression to the life of the emotions and the reality of a heartfelt, rather than purely intellectual, approach to life. Rousseau was eminently cultured and supremely a man of the world. He speaks of hiring musicians while in Italy to perform favorite pieces of opera for him[7]. Here is a model of Fisher's Frankenstein unique in film portrayals. As interpreted by Peter Cushing, Baron Frankenstein is impeccably dressed, well-mannered and appreciates art, good food and stimulating conversation. The fatal flaw in Rousseau, as in Frankenstein, is the denial of any moral absolutes. Rousseau's sole standard in life was a vague and rather mystical idea of nature. He professed a belief in human equality but was himself vain and intolerant. He denied Christianity to be a revealed religion, rejected totally the doctrine of original sin and yet became Catholic or Protestant as circumstances dictated. He kept a mistress who bore him five children, all of which he abandoned to an orphanage. His political ideas gave verbal tribute to the common person but really took shape as a totalitarian expression of an ill-defined "General Will." Bertrand Russell saw him as the progenitor of the French reign of terror, Stalin's Russia and Hitler's Germany. Rousseau ended his life virtually insane, driven by paranoid fears. Yet Rousseau's influence in morals, literature, theology and politics remains strong to this day. Rousseau was the modern exponent of the ancient creed of Protagoras that "man is the measure of all things."

Fisher's Baron Frankenstein is a figure very much like Rousseau. He is apparently interested in everything but ultimately interested only in himself. His experiments are not designed for any larger good for humanity but really only to call attention to himself. They may appear to accomplish some immediate benefit but they result only in disaster. Fisher followed up *The Curse of Frankenstein* with the superior *Revenge of Frankenstein* (1958). This sequel opens with the closing scene of *Curse*. Frankenstein is being led out to the guillotine. At the last minute however his henchmen substitute the priest (!) for him at the execution. Frankenstein is officially dead but his coffin contains the body of the priest who heard his "confession." Once escaped, Frankenstein is far from repentant. Under the pseudonym of "Dr. Stein" he works in a hospital which gives him free access to body parts. He is still pursuing the goal of the "perfect man." He transplants the brain of a deformed servant into a perfect "body" he has been constructing. Ostensibly the experiment is a success. The man, once misshapen, awakens to find himself handsome and strong. There is no suggestion that Frankenstein has any interest in helping his servant. (In reality he is paying off a debt because the servant helped him escape the guillotine.) The servant is simply the means for Frankenstein to accomplish his self-aggrandizing experiments.

Unfortunately the success is short-lived. In a disturbing and perceptive touch, Fisher shows the "perfect" body reverting back to the original deformity as Frankenstein's assistant suffers a violent attack. The soul in effect breaks through the outer "perfect" shell. In fact the resultant deformity is worse than the assistant's original state. In the wake of violence the newly deformed "perfect man" resorts to cannibalism. In an unforgettable scene the now totally deformed servant breaks through a glass door into an elegant party which Frankenstein is attending. In his dying words he reveals Frankenstein's true identity. Frankenstein attempts to flee but is cornered by the patients in his hospital who, knowing his true identity now, beat him nearly to death. Left to die, Frankenstein gives instruction to an assistant to transplant his brain into yet another body. The scene abruptly shifts from Switzerland to London. We see into the office of a "Dr. Frank." We recognize Frankenstein in a somewhat new form, his hairline barely concealing the scar running across his forehead. The transformation is complete. Frankenstein has become his own monster. The film ends.

There are a number of striking motifs in *The Revenge of Frankenstein*. The figure of Dr. Frankenstein in this second film has been expanded. In *The Curse of Frankenstein* Fisher had juxtaposed the grey charnel house quality of the upstairs laboratory with the elegant decorum of the downstairs living area. This served to symbolize the contrasting elegant exterior of Frankenstein's life with his more gloomy (and perverse) inner self. In *Revenge* the elegant exterior has disappeared and Frankenstein's world is the charity hospital and the laboratory. Other than this he lives (and eats) alone in a small undistinguished apartment. Frankenstein's obsessive pursuit of knowledge has limited his world, not expanded it. In this film Frankenstein comes a step closer to his goal of in effect becoming God. This time he does succeed in creating a "perfect man." However his efforts fail because, as was made clear in the earlier film, Frankenstein is setting himself against nature and ultimately against God. He is a modern atheist. He does not deny the existence of God in any formal way. He simply disregards God and attempts to create man in his own personal image. Unfortunately he succeeds all too well. The final image is his own and it is a seriously flawed one.

Throughout these first two films, made within a year of each other, Fisher is dealing with the classic image of sin as an ever-recurring spiral downward. Humanity in sin, as the apostle Paul argues in the New Testament, cannot break out of the deadly cycle. Sin only leads to more sin. This cannot be understood primarily in moral terms. Paul's image, echoed by Fisher, is fundamentally theological:

> Claiming to be wise, they became fools; and they exchanged the glory of the immortal God for images resembling a mortal human being.... They exchanged the truth about God for a lie and worshipped and served the creature rather than the Creator who is blessed forever! Amen [Epistle to the Romans 1:22–23, 25].

This is an apt description of Fisher's Baron Frankenstein so ably portrayed by Peter Cushing. He is not devoted to truth or science as portrayed in earlier (and later) films. Fisher's Frankenstein is an amoral being bent on his own self-created divinity. It is important to reflect that Fisher's first two Frankenstein films appeared at the time of the first sputnik satellite and the enormous focus on science and technology which followed. Fisher's essential theme in these early films is that knowledge doesn't necessarily lead to goodness. A unilateral pursuit of knowledge can well become demonic if divorced from God and the moral order of the world. Frankenstein's pursuit of knowledge is in reality an attack on Western culture's entire moral and religious base. In this, Frankenstein is an heir to the spirit of Rousseau and a frightening warning to a culture intent on pursuing knowledge apart from God. The theological overtones of Fisher's Frankenstein series would become more pronounced in his next film, *Frankenstein Created Woman* (1967).

Baron Frankenstein (Peter Cushing) contemplates his experiments in *The Revenge of Frankenstein* (1958).

A considerable hiatus occurred between Fisher's second and third film in the Frankenstein series. Fisher's early success at Hammer Studios led to a period of incredible productivity. Following *The Revenge of Frankenstein* and *Dracula*, both released in 1958, Fisher directed a total of nine films for Hammer from 1959 to 1962. This astonishing output included a full range of English fantasy subjects from Sherlock Holmes to Robin Hood to Dr. Jekyll and Mr. Hyde, as well as major reinterpretations of such Hollywood "horror" figures as the Mummy and the Werewolf. Fisher's work throughout this period became increasingly more complex, culminating in an elaborate remake of *The Phantom of the Opera* (1962). Fisher's unabashedly romantic approach to that story (which, as will be discussed subsequently, was closer to the spirit of the original novel than previous film versions) unfortunately doomed the film at the box office. The net result was that Hammer dropped Fisher for a two year period. The next Hammer Frankenstein film, titled *The Evil of Frankenstein,* was not made by Fisher although Peter Cushing reappeared in the role of the Baron. The result was an uninspired Hollywood imitation. Fortunately, the studio later relented and Fisher returned to Hammer to film his best work.

Among these *Frankenstein Created Woman* must rank very highly. Released ten years after *Curse of Frankenstein,* this film shows both a greater maturity and depth of understanding in approaching the Frankenstein theme. As the title suggests, *Frankenstein Created Woman* presents the

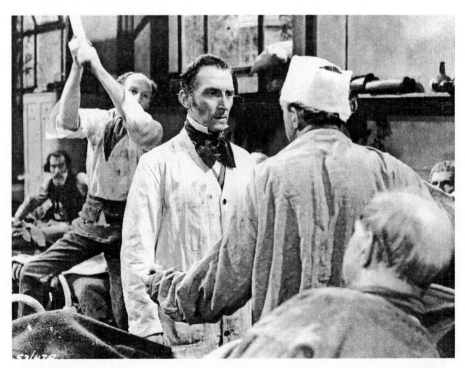

The hospital patients who realize they're being used for experiments rise up against Baron Frankenstein in *The Revenge of Frankenstein* (1958).

Baron as a full developed demagogue, the ultimate blasphemer. Frankenstein says confidently, "I have conquered death." In response to the protestations of yet another assistant that what he contemplates is not right, Frankenstein replies irritably, "Right!? What does 'right' have to do with it?" More than ever Frankenstein regards others as simple pawns for his experiments. In an inspired scene Frankenstein at one point curiously browses through a Bible while waiting to testify at a trial. For him the Bible is both an alien and somewhat intriguing relic. In this film however Frankenstein is not the center of the narrative. He is confronted here with moral and spiritual forces beyond both his reckoning and his control.

The dominant visual image of *Frankenstein Created Woman* is a guillotine. Yet it is not a guillotine designed for Frankenstein. The film opens with a flashback as a young boy watches his drunken father executed on the guillotine for murder. Years later the boy, grown to manhood, works as an occasional helper at Frankenstein's laboratory. This young man, named Hans, is in love with Christine, the daughter of the local innkeeper. Unfortunately Christine's face is disfigured and she walks with a limp. Christine is tormented by three hedonistic young aristocrats who delight in mocking her.

Hans is infuriated by the three young men and gets into a violent fight with them. Hans is almost equally violent with Christine's father who disapproves of their relationship. In this case his violence is verbal including even a rash threat to murder the old man. Soon thereafter he tells Christine that he would also like to kill her three tormentors. While our first exposure to Hans saw him as a pleasant likeable young man, these scenes reveal a violent character which relates him to his father, the convicted murderer. In a subsequent brawl over a bill, the three young aristocrats accidentally kill the innkeeper. They decide to hide their crime by framing Hans since as a murderer's son he would be a likely suspect.

During much of this narrative Frankenstein is absent. He is called on as a character witness at Hans' trial. However the testimony is stacked against Hans since a number of people heard his murderous threat against Christine's father. The three young aristocrats testify against him and are believed. Hans is executed on the same guillotine which killed his father. Christine has been away during the court proceedings. She returns just in time to see Hans' execution. Plunged into despair, she commits suicide by jumping into a river. The three young men who are responsible for her father's death and Hans' execution are thereby implicated in her death as well. They go free and are under no suspicion at all.

The film then returns to Frankenstein. He is engaged in experiments on the "soul." He has determined that the soul does not leave the body immediately at death but remains in the body for an hour after death. Frankenstein manages to obtain both the bodies of Hans and Christine within an hour of their deaths. He transplants Hans' soul into Christine's body and then operates on her body, removing its deformity. The result is the most novel "monster" of any Frankenstein film. Christine emerges as a beautiful, blond young woman. However, she has latent within her the soul of her lover Hans. Basically, though, Christine retains no memory of her previous life. When the "spirit" of Hans takes over she forsakes her peasant dress and demeanor and stalks out into the night transformed into a beautiful seductress. One by one she hunts down each of the three aristocrats responsible for Hans' death, entices them into a lonely setting with the clear suggestion of sexual favors and then brutally murders them.

As part of this grim exercise in revenge she carries Hans' decapitated head with her in a hat box. In a remarkable final scene she kills the third young man in a beautiful forest following an idyllic picnic. All of this has taken place unbeknownst to Frankenstein who, finally suspecting her murderous actions, follows her into the forest. He finds her just after she has killed her third victim, talking in Hans' voice to his head! Following this she rushes to a cliff where she commits suicide a second time by jumping into a river. The closing shot shows Frankenstein walking back through the forest, apparently purposeless and confused.

Frankenstein Created Woman is regarded by some critics as Fisher's best film in the series.[8] The film emphasizes three essential themes which are part of Fisher's most mature work. The first is *the inevitability of sin*. Fisher was a strict follower of St. Augustine in his understanding of original sin as essentially biological. Sin is passed from parent to child virtually through the genes. Hans, despite all efforts to the contrary, acts out the murderous legacy of his father. Sin in this film, however, cannot be seen as a series of immoral actions. It is a complex web which pulls in all the characters. Hans, Christine, her father, Frankenstein, the three young aristocrats, even Frankenstein's somewhat comic assistant Dr. Hertz, all in different ways are tainted by sin. All are guilty at some level. Even the original murder victim, Christine's innkeeper father, is intolerant of Hans and disdainful of his daughter's wishes. The surrounding society is no less sinful, witnessed by the trial which preemptorily condemns Hans to death despite his innocence. Unlike *Curse of Frankenstein* there is no sympathetic character here, no moral spokesperson. The priest who appears briefly ineffectually mumbles the Scripture. The mayor and the chief of police are seen as having legal, not moral, authority. The Bible, while present in the trial scene (and clearly emphasized in Fisher's direction), has no one to proclaim its message.

Susan Denberg and Alan MacNaughton in *Frankenstein Created Woman* (1967).

The second theme in this film is the *beauty of evil*. The one potentially sympathetic figure in the story is Christine. Yet her metamorphosis into a beautiful killer undercuts this even though she is being guided by Hans' spirit. Yet in one of the strangest scenes in the film she is shown pledging herself to Hans' head and thereby his spirit. She is a willing

Baron Frankenstein (Peter Cushing, left) and his Dr. Watson–like assistant (Thorley Walters) prepare to revive the dead Christine in *Frankenstein Created Woman* (1967).

participant. The theme of the beauty of evil is essential in Fisher's gothic horror films. Fisher saw the serpent in the garden of Eden as basically attractive, Satan masquerading as an "angel of light" (II Corinthians 11:14). This theme is reinforced by the fact that the most sadistic of the young aristocrats is also the most handsome. The film itself is shot in lush Technicolor,

An Italian poster for *Frankenstein Created Woman* (*La Maledizione dei Franken-stein*).

A French poster for *The Curse of Frankenstein* (*Frankenstein S'Est Échappé!..*).

culminating in its final scene in a picturesque forest. Sex and violence are more pervasive here than in Fisher's earlier films though these themes are mostly suggested rather than shown.

The third critical theme here is the *power of the spiritual over the material*. If one takes Frankenstein's research into soul transplants literally the film becomes absurd. The focus here of course is on the symbolism. In the earlier Frankenstein films the Baron's experiments dealt with physical phenomena such as brain transplants. In this film the emphasis passes over to the spiritual, the soul. If Frankenstein could not control the results of his physical experiments he can control these "spiritual" investigations even less. The Christine which emerges from his operation is in many ways a mythical figure, the devouring revengeful woman who emerges in late eighteenth century literature and becomes the "fatal woman" of Victorian fiction. If the earlier films showed Frankenstein's unprincipled rationalism leading to destruction (an effective metaphor for the nuclear age) this film shows rational "science" at a loss to even understand the spiritual realities of the merged Hans/Christine character which Frankenstein, like a latter day Pandora, has unwittingly unleashed. The firm material realities of this film, evidenced in Frankenstein's laboratory, the local inn, the law court, even the stark guillotine are eventually displaced by the shadowy, ethereal world of the beautiful but deadly Christine. The forest at the end represents non-rational, even mystical, reality which could not be more different from Frankenstein's laboratory.

The fourth film in the series, *Frankenstein Must Be Destroyed*, was considered by Fisher to be one of his best. The opening scene of this film is one of the more graphic in the series. We see a dark figure in the streets. A murder is committed. The murderer runs through the streets back to a laboratory when he encounters a robber. A fight ensues. The robber flees. The murderer is alone. We see his face. It is ugly and deformed. The murderer proceeds to tear the face off, revealing it to be only a mask. We recognize the familiar face of Baron Frankenstein (Peter Cushing). In an impressive opening shorn of any dialogue Fisher has shown us several crucial things regarding the present status of the Baron. Where he had previously bought body parts from intermediaries or had access to hospital clinics through his medical practice, Frankenstein now must do his own dirty work. Also he is alone. He has no assistant. The grotesque mask he wears reminds us again that he himself is now the monster.

The plot of *Frankenstein Must Be Destroyed* is relatively simple. An associate of Frankenstein's, a Dr. Brandt, has gone mad and is currently in an asylum. Frankenstein needs a formula that Brandt has developed. In order to gain it Frankenstein must first get Brandt out of the asylum and,

A French poster for *Frankenstein Created Woman* (*Frankenstein Crea la Femme*).

second, cure his madness. To assist him in his plans Frankenstein blackmails a young couple, Karl and Anna, whom he discovers using illegal drugs. With their help he kidnaps Brandt from the asylum. Unfortunately Brandt subsequently dies of a heart attack. In an obsessive effort to keep Brandt's brain alive, Frankenstein transplants it into the dead body of another scientist, a Professor Richter. The result is apparently successful. Brandt's sanity and memory are restored yet he exists now in a different body.

In the interim Brandt's wife Ella has become suspicious that Frankenstein has abducted her husband. She traces Frankenstein's current laboratory and confronts him with the crime of kidnapping Brandt. To her surprise Frankenstein freely admits that he stole her husband from the asylum and has him in his laboratory. In a sequence which has been described as "a moment of superb irony," Frankenstein takes her to see her husband. Brandt is just recovering from the brain transplant surgery. He is not yet able to speak. He is completely covered in bandages so neither he nor his wife knows that his brain (or soul) inhabits a different body. Brandt is able to respond with gestures accurately to his wife's questions, so she is convinced that Frankenstein truly has "healed" him. She leaves expressing her gratitude, and Frankenstein assures her she can come again soon when her husband is more recovered. The minute she is out the door Fisher gives us a close-up of Peter Cushing uttering one word to his two young assistants: "Pack!" The next scene shows Frankenstein, the still bandaged Brandt and Karl and Anna hurtling through the night in a carriage.

The following day Ella Brandt returns to Frankenstein's house to find it deserted. She calls the police, and a search of the house reveals her husband's body. She, of course, has no way of knowing that the bandaged figure she met earlier was her husband's brain/soul in a different body. Subsequently Brandt recovers and manages to escape from Frankenstein and his two helpers. He is now in the body of Professor Richter. He is neither deformed nor monstrous. Rather he is sad and pathetic with his shaved head and scarred forehead. He comes back to his wife while she is sleeping. He tries to speak to her behind a screen, knowing she of course would not recognize him as he now is. He tells her of his love for her. Understandably she is unable to deal with him and leaves the house. Frankenstein, meanwhile, is enraged that Brandt has escaped. Accusing Anna of letting him get away, he kills her with a scalpel. Rightly assuming that Brandt has returned to his house, Frankenstein rushes there in a carriage. Brandt is waiting for him. Using Frankenstein's obsessive desire for his formula, Brandt lures him into the interior of the house and then sets the place on fire. When Frankenstein attempts to escape the blaze, Brandt pursues him and carries him back into the flames. The film ends with a long shot of the burning house and Frankenstein's pleas to be set free.

Many agree with Fisher that *Frankenstein Must Be Destroyed* is one of his best films.[9] Unfortunately the film's complexity eluded both audiences

An Italian poster for *The Man Who Could Cheat Death* (*L'Uomo Che Inganno la Morte*).

and critics when it was released in 1969. In this film Frankenstein is more isolated than previously. He has no scientific associate and no established base, like a castle or hospital clinic, from which to work. The only possible colleague in the film is the unfortunate Dr. Brandt who we learn is insane early on in the film. Frankenstein's need of forcing two young people like Karl and Anna to help him shows him to be in a desperate state with regard to scientific assistance. If anything the Baron is more obsessive than ever here and more ruthless. Some critics such as the notable David Pirie see Frankenstein's work in recovering Brandt's sanity as something positive.[10] In reality Frankenstein's purpose is totally self-serving. He wants information that only a "sane" Brandt can provide. Frankenstein's murder of Anna in a fit of rage shows his continuing moral degeneration. It is worth pondering what Fisher is trying to show with such a malevolent figure.

Mary Shelley subtitled the original Frankenstein novel "The Modern Prometheus" after the Greek hero who stole fire from heaven as a gift to humanity and was punished for his presumption. Fisher's development of the Frankenstein character could well be subtitled "The Modern Gilgamesh" after the more ancient Gilgamesh legend of Middle Eastern origin. Gilgamesh was a tyrannical king who embarks on a series of adventures involving dragons and other mythical creatures. Following the death of a friend, Gilgamesh begins a relentless search for eternal life. This search ends in futility with a resigned Gilgamesh returning to his native city summarizing his search with the words, "For whom is my heart's blood spent? I have accomplished no good for myself."[11]

Fisher's Frankenstein series has depicted a tyrannical "king of science" on an obsessive but futile search for the secret of life. Fisher's attitude toward science was predominantly negative. At various points in his career Fisher had made science fiction films. These were not his best work but even their Saturday matinee titles—*The Horror of It All, The Earth Dies Screaming, Island of Terror, Night of the Big Heat*—suggest a view of science as something essentially fearful. In Fisher's world science does not merely go awry, it destroys the world. Frankenstein poses no ultimate threat to the world at large but he destroys himself along with those with whom he comes in contact. Frankenstein represents scientific and medical technology devoid of moral purpose. Fisher shows the elaborate skill of Frankenstein in transplanting a human brain. But no valid purpose is served by this skill. Frankenstein then symbolizes a science which has become a god in itself, a god shorn of any moral restraint or accountability. Fisher's Frankenstein is a prophetic image of genetic engineering, medical experimentation and scientific technology—three disciplines that exist for their own sake in the film.

A second important theme of *Frankenstein Must Be Destroyed* is the ancient question of the relationship between soul and body. The question is raised, "Where is Brandt?" If Brandt's brain inhabits another body then who in reality is "he"? Fisher and his screenwriter Bert Batt pose an interesting question that is never really explored. What is the true self? The poignancy of Brandt's dilemma is seen in his encounter with his wife. She cannot relate to him on any level and therefore abandons him. Fisher succeeds in delivering a powerful impression of Brandt's dilemma. In so doing he touches on the question, "What makes a person truly a person, and to what extent does the soul (or the inner self) affect the body and vice versa?" This is a question as old as Socrates and as modern as Alzheimer's disease. Contemporary British Christian authors such as Charles Williams were fond of exploring these issues in their novels. Fisher's presentation of the theme is quite evocative but is never really developed. As noted in Fisher's approach to other gothic themes, this is one of his drawbacks as an artist. Enticing themes are presented well but are not always explored adequately. Nonetheless, Fisher's direction and Freddie Jones' performance of the changed Brandt result in a moving and disturbing sequence which is not easily forgotten.

Frankenstein Must Be Destroyed was released at a time when Fisher's dominance of the modern "horror film" (a term he hated) was coming to an end. For over a decade Fisher had led the gothic horror film cycle which he had inaugurated with *Curse of Frankenstein*. By the late sixties, however, younger directors who did not share Fisher's Christian or metaphysical convictions began moving the fantasy and horror film genre into very different directions. Foremost among these were Roman Polanski who satirized Fisher's Dracula films with his 1967 *The Fearless Vampire Killers* followed by *Rosemary's Baby* the next year and the Italian director, Dario Argento, whose *Bird with the Crystal Plumage* in 1969 inaugurated the graphic violence "slasher" genre which continues to this day. A third was the little known British director Michael Reeves who died of an overdose of drugs in 1969 after making the disturbing *Witchfinder General* (*The Conqueror Worm* in America) in which good and evil are inextricably linked. These artists were clearly responding to a dominant mood of disenchantment and distrust among young people especially in the late 1960s. By 1969 Western society in both North America and Europe was passing through a major shift in values and beliefs occasioned by the war in Viet Nam, rising racial tensions, protests against materialistic lifestyles, drugs and sexual experimentation. The expression of this shift in popular culture was most clearly seen in rock music and the horror film.

These trends in the horror film will be further discussed in a later context. They are relevant here because they introduce the setting of Fisher's

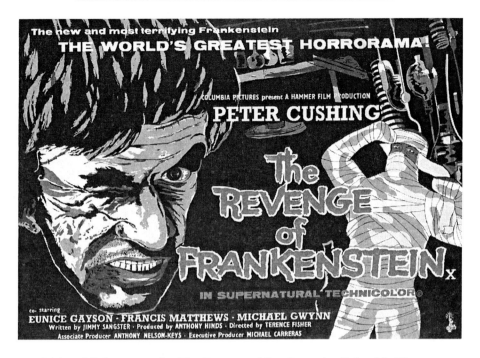

British publicity poster for *The Revenge of Frankenstein*, Columbia Pictures (1958).

last film. By 1970 Terence Fisher was 66 years old, an age associated with the much abused "establishment" then being criticized by those under 30. Hammer Studios had always been essentially commercial in its orientation and they quickly sought to adapt to the changing cultural climate with a more exploitative approach. In 1970 Hammer released a double bill of *The Horror of Frankenstein* and *The Scars of Dracula*. While former Fisher collaborators Jimmy Sangster and Anthony Hinds worked on these films, the movies' content could not have been further removed from Fisher. These pictures featured exploitative violence and sex including nudity. More significantly, the spiritual conflict of good and evil, found in Fisher's work with its rich symbolism and metaphysical overtones, was completely missing. Hammer began a downward spiral which would lead to the studio's collapse before the end of the decade. Fisher as a Christian artist found himself at odds with the studio where he had made his most successful films. To add to his difficulties Fisher had been in two car accidents which laid him up for a significant period. In 1972 he returned to Hammer Studios one last time to direct his final film, *Frankenstein and the Monster from Hell.*

British poster for *Frankenstein Created Woman*, Hammer (1967).

Contrary to virtually all previous critics who have written on Fisher, this writer regards *Frankenstein and the Monster from Hell* as one of his finest films. It is a dark, disturbing picture which was largely dismissed when released in 1973, but with the hindsight of nearly three decades it appears as a near prophetic statement on the crisis of late twentieth century Western culture. In this severely underappreciated film Fisher presents one of his most disturbing parables.

Frankenstein and the Monster from Hell opens in a graveyard after dark. A police officer discovers that a grave has been robbed. The investigation leads quickly to a Dr. Simon Helder (Shawn Briant) who has purchased the cadaver as the only way of doing medical research in nineteenth century Switzerland. Dr. Helder is put on trial for sorcery. His attempts to defend himself based on the importance of medical research are of no avail. He is sentenced to a prison for the criminally insane. Upon arriving he encounters the director of the prison (John Stratton) who takes him at first for a physician assigned to the prison rather than an inmate. The director is seen as a gross pompous figure leering over his private collection of pornography.

Simon soon learns that the real leader of the asylum is none other than Baron Frankenstein (played by Peter Cushing of course) posing as a Dr. Victor. Frankenstein has signed false documents of his own death so technically he is free to leave the asylum in his new identity of Dr. Victor. However he chooses to remain and his knowledge of the corrupt practices of the institution's director gives him the leverage to act with impunity in the asylum. The director, fearing exposure and the loss of a comfortable post, readily complies with the Baron's wishes.

Frankenstein quickly realizes that Simon would make an excellent medical assistant and appoints him to be his helper. Simon is then introduced to the inhabitants of the asylum. One of the first persons he meets is also an assistant of the Baron, an attractive mute girl named Sarah who has been christened "The Angel" by the patients. Her background and circumstances are not revealed except that her loss of speech is due to an earlier trauma in her life. The first patient Frankenstein introduces Simon to is a madman dressed in the guise of an Old Testament prophet whom Frankenstein casually dismisses with the explanation, "He thinks he's god." The irony of this is that this disheveled figure is actually a mirror image of Frankenstein himself who quite definitely thinks *he* is god. Frankenstein's outward poise and elegance masks his disheveled soul within.

The rest of the inmates are essentially a pathetic lot verging on the edge of a caricature of the old *Marat/Sade* play. A striking exception is a mathematics professor named Durendel (Charles Lloyd Pack). The professor is a quiet, amiable person who enjoys playing the violin for relaxation. "What is he doing here?" asks Simon. "He has a murderous temper," answers Frankenstein. "He even attacked the director once," adds Frankenstein. The professor is also quite fond of Angel.

Frankenstein is still pursuing his obsession to create life. His earlier attempts at creating perfection having failed, he now is apparently satisfied to create human life in any form. However the Baron's world is more limited than ever. He no longer has any real contact with the world outside the asylum. In addition to this, his hands are badly burned (presumably from the climax of the previous film) so his ability at surgery is also limited. Until Simon's arrival Angel had attempted to serve as his "hands" during operations, acting under his direction. The result of this is a Neanderthal hulk adapted from the body of a previous inmate, a murderer whose main weapon was broken glass. Simon's advent provides Frankenstein with a trained surgeon to perform the more delicate surgeries. Once again a brain is needed (or, in Fisher's world, a soul) to animate the latest restored cadaver.

Frankenstein clearly is interested in the brain of Professor Durendel. All too conveniently the professor soon commits suicide, hanging himself

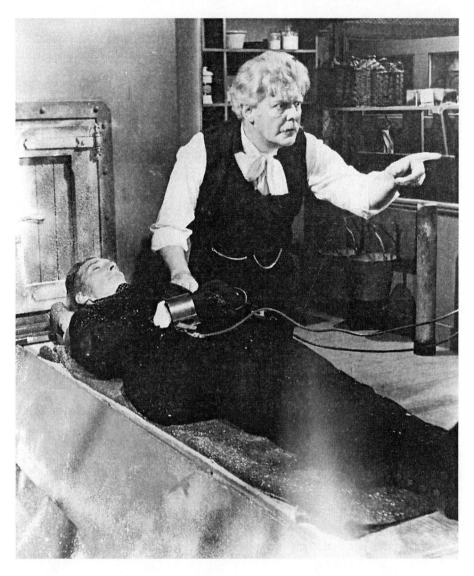

Thorley Walters (standing) and Peter Cushing in *Frankenstein Created Woman* (1967).

by one of his violin strings. Quickly the operation is performed and Simon aids the Baron in placing the professor's brain into the hulking body previously prepared. However Simon becomes suspicious when he finds that a copy of a report declaring the professor incurable had been left in the professor's cell where he couldn't fail to see it. Simon realizes that

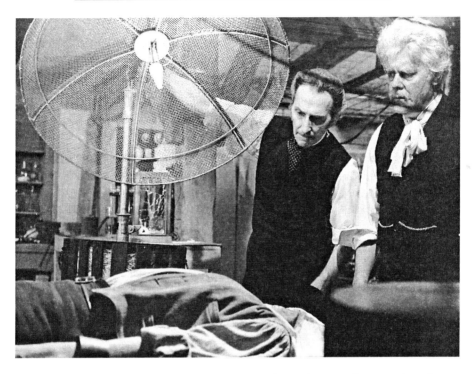

Peter Cushing (left) and Thorley Walters in *Frankenstein Created Woman* (1967).

Frankenstein did this deliberately to drive the professor to suicide so he could use his brain.

The resulting creature nonetheless is one of the most unusual in the long and strange array of Frankenstein films. This "monster from hell" as played by David Prowse has the brain (soul) of the professor in a huge, scarred, almost subhuman body. The creature solves complex mathematical problems on a blackboard. However he can no longer play the violin. The huge stubby fingers that the professor now has can no longer grasp the instrument. In frustration the creature smashes the violin and then weeps at his loss. In this sequence Fisher has created one of his most arresting scenes. Frankenstein soon discovers that his "experiment" once again is not succeeding. The body is rejecting the brain, or rather, overpowering it. The creature will not long survive. Frankenstein has an ingenious idea to keep the experiment alive. He will mate the creature with Angel. She will bear the creature's child and so the experiment will continue. Simon is understandably horrified at this idea and resolves to kill the creature before Frankenstein can implement his plan.

Once again events move beyond Frankenstein's control. He is forced to leave the asylum on a brief trip and warns Simon against interfering with his plans during his absence. After Frankenstein leaves, Simon attempts to destroy the creature while he sleeps. The creature however awakens and turns on Simon. Angel enters the room and screams as she sees the creature menacing Simon. The effect of this trauma reverses the earlier one where she lost her voice. The creature learns that Angel's inability to speak was the result of her having been raped by her father who is in fact the asylum director. Now loose, the creature makes his way outside to the asylum cemetery. Against a dark sky with flashes of lightning he unearths the newest grave and cries out in despair at finding his own (i.e., the professor's) body. Leaving the cemetery, the creature smashes through a glass window and enters the director's office. Enraged at what the man has done to his own daughter, Angel, the creature smashes a bottle and kills him with the sharp glass. The man's screams bring out the guards and the other inmates. As Frankenstein returns, the creature is shot. In an act of desperate longing, the professor/creature reaches out to Angel, touching her hair gently. The inmates mistakenly think he intends to attack her and set upon him, tearing him limb from limb. Frankenstein with the help of the guards manages to restore a semblance of order. Alone with Simon and Angel, Frankenstein reflects on what went wrong with his "experiment." "Next time," he muses, "I'll have to spend more time on the question of biochemistry." Simon and Angel stand motionless watching him as he continues talking about "next time." The camera pulls away to a long shot of the medieval looking asylum as the film ends.

There are no references in the *Reader's Guide to Periodical Literature* to any review of *Frankenstein and the Monster from Hell* at the time of its initial release. Four years later the title performers of this picture, Peter Cushing and David Prowse, would have major roles in another fantasy film which unlike *Monster from Hell* would be immensely popular. That later film was *Star Wars*. It is an odd commentary that religious as well as secular journals fell all over themselves attempting to analyze an essentially escapist film like *Star Wars* but paid no attention to Fisher's last cinematic effort. Fisher died seven years after the release of *Frankenstein and the Monster from Hell*. In a 1975 interview Fisher expressed repulsion at the current state of the horror film epitomized by *The Exorcist*.

Frankenstein and the Monster from Hell portrays a very different world than that found in Fisher's first Frankenstein film, made 16 years earlier. *Monster from Hell* portrays a world in which all authority has become corrupt. The asylum director is clearly that, but so is the pompous and indifferent judge at the film's opening who sentences Simon to the asylum for "witchcraft." The abdication of real authority creates a world in which Frankenstein operates unopposed. In *Curse of Frankenstein* the external social order—symbolized first by Paul Krempe, later by Elizabeth and finally the courts and the church—conspires to stop Frankenstein. In this last film no one is able to stop him. Where Paul and Elizabeth decide not to come to Frankenstein's aid in the first film and so are instrumental in his being sent to the guillotine, Simon and Angel stare in bewildered silence at the conclusion of this last film, unable even to protest, much less oppose the Baron.

In speaking of his films, Fisher always emphasized his conviction that good would ultimately triumph over evil. When asked about this conviction in the light of *Frankenstein and the Monster from Hell*, Fisher emphasizes that the power of good (or God) is seen in the inevitable failure of Frankenstein's efforts. One of the ironies of this film is that no one speaks for God except the madmen who, Frankenstein claims, thinks he is God. At the onset of the film's climax however this "mad" figure quotes a Bible verse which paints a clear picture of Frankenstein:

> All the days wherein the
> plague is in him he shall
> be unclean; he is unclean:
> he shall dwell alone; without
> the camp shall his dwelling be.
> —Leviticus 13:46

A plague is in Frankenstein. It is his obsession to deify himself by becoming the "creator" and disregarding the true creator. The "camp" in this sense is human society. Frankenstein could leave the asylum but he doesn't choose to do so. He has created his own personal hell where he chooses to rule. In Milton's terms he prefers to reign in hell rather than serve in heaven.

Frankenstein and the Monster from Hell portrays a world in moral and spiritual chaos. It does not show a world without moral absolutes but rather a world in which moral absolutes are disregarded. It is a world in the prophet Isaiah's words where "truth stumbles in the street" (Isaiah 59:14). Simon has an interest in the truth but he is frustrated first by a rigid external authority (the judge who sentences him) and second by the asylum's internal authority (Frankenstein). He realizes what Frankenstein is doing is wrong but he is unable to oppose him. The asylum's director ought to oppose Frankenstein but is compromised by his corrupt lifestyle which enables Frankenstein in effect to blackmail him.

The genteel world glimpsed in *Curse of Frankenstein* is here replaced by an insane asylum shot in cold, grey colors as opposed to the lushness

Madeline Smith as Sarah ("The Angel") calms the infuriated Monster (Dave Prowse) inside Dr. Frankenstein's laboratory in Hammer Productions' *Frankenstein and the Monster from Hell* (1972), a Paramount Pictures release. Peter Cushing and Shane Briant star in the film drama produced by Roy Skeggs. Terence Fisher directed from a screenplay by John Elder.

of the earlier film. In the world of *Monster from Hell* there are breakdowns at every level of society. There is the breakdown of the individual symbolized by the monster whose body is completely divorced from his mind. The purposeless science of Frankenstein destroys the art of the professor who can no longer play the violin. There is the breakdown of the family symbolized by Angel who has been abused by her own father. Further there is the breakdown of society symbolized by autocratic laws and an insane population (the two are by no means exclusive of each other). There is the breakdown of science seen in Frankenstein's experiments which now lead to subhuman results and the sexual experimentation which Frankenstein proposes for his monster and Angel. Finally there is the breakdown of morality. By the time Simon realizes how corrupt Frankenstein is he can do little to stop him. In fact he too is implicated in the Baron's corrupt system. Whereas Paul in the first film was able to maintain a measure of independence over against Frankenstein, Simon is in a more precarious position. Paul tries to stop Frankenstein from using a stolen brain. Simon aids him, learning too late how Frankenstein actually obtained the brain. At the end of this last film Simon can only stare at the Baron, whose obsessions continue. This film contains a final conclusion. No one in Frankenstein's world can oppose him any more. Yet it is clear he will never succeed. Like the ancient myth of Sisyphus, he rolls a stone up a hill only to watch it inevitably roll back down. Frankenstein's goal is to take God's place. That goal will never be realized. Yet it is Frankenstein's damnation to continue trying. Not only is Frankenstein's monster *from* hell, Frankenstein is *in* hell. It is a hell he has willed for himself and one from which he can never escape.

Fisher's last film touches on a host of issues which have become major concerns of the past 30 years. These include the breakdown of authority, the amoral character of science and technology, sexual abuse, the lack of moral leadership and the rise of societal violence. The film's final scene gives a sense of desperation and despair. There is a hollow, empty feeling to Frankenstein's nonchalance as he talks about "next time." This is ultimately a film which shows divine judgment. Frankenstein is "unclean" and he dwells alone. Even though Simon and Angel are present he really is talking only to himself. Having become his own god he is totally alone and all his efforts are futile. This is Fisher's depiction of Rousseau's goal to believe finally only in oneself. It is a picture which describes Western culture at the end of the twentieth century with great accuracy. *Frankenstein and the Monster from Hell* is a film which should be neither forgotten nor ignored.

Notes

1. For discussions of Fisher's work prior to *The Curse of Frankenstein*, see Dixon, Wheeler Winston, *The Charm of Evil: The Life and Films of Terence Fisher*; Pirie, David, *A Heritage of Horror*; and Landy, Marcia, *British Genres: Cinema and Society, 1930–1960*.

2. There are numerous discussions available on *The Curse of Frankenstein*'s original impact. There are relevant articles in Phil Hardy's *The Overlook Film Encyclopedia: Horror*; John McCarty's *The Modern Horror Film* and, again, David Pirie in *A Heritage of Horror*.

3. Cf. Phil Hardy. *The Overlook Film Encyclopedia*, p. 98. The American film Hardy mentions, *I Was a Teenage Werewolf*, hardly constitutes a rebirth of gothic horror.

4. Ringel, Harry. "Terrence Fisher: The Human Side."

5. Pirie, David, pp. 73ff.

6. The Epistle to the Romans, chapter 5, verses 12–21.

7. Rousseau, p. 296.

8. Hardy, p. 180.

9. Pirie, pp. 78–80.

10. *Ibid.*, p. 79.

11. *Epic of Gilgamesh*, p. 117.

Chapter Two

THE LUST OF DRACULA

The enormous commercial success of *The Curse of Frankenstein* in 1957 led Hammer Studios to think, not in terms of a sequel, but rather a logical counterpart. The choice, of course, was Bram Stoker's 1897 novel *Dracula*. A generation earlier Hollywood had found these two properties so successful that they offered the 1931 film versions of *Frankenstein* and *Dracula* as a highly successful double feature and eventually placed the Frankenstein monster and Count Dracula alongside each other in several films until, eventually, both were upstaged by Abbott and Costello.

The Curse of Frankenstein showed that a new approach to such classic material could create a worldwide sensation. Michael Carreras, executive head of Hammer, quickly ordered the same team that had done *Frankenstein* to film *Dracula*. The result would be Terence Fisher's most commercially and critically successful film. *Dracula*, or as it was titled in the U.S.A., *Horror of Dracula*, was even more popular than *Curse of Frankenstein*. It is the film which has earned Fisher a lasting place in cinema history, frequently listed among the great British films of all time.[1] Although *Frankenstein* and *Dracula* are frequently linked in the popular (and even critical) mind, they are very different stories coming from quite divergent roots. As interesting as Fisher's Frankenstein series is, his Dracula films are perhaps closer to his own personal views both as an artist and a Christian. To explore this claim we must begin by analyzing his first film masterpiece, *Dracula* (1958).

The opening credits of *Dracula* alert us immediately to the fact that we are in a mythical, nonrational setting. Fisher's camera focuses on the figure of a stone eagle which is seen from several sides as the camera keeps moving. The title credits appear as James Bernard's pulsating music score pounds forth from the screen. The camera continues to roam and eventually descends a stair leading past a locked door into a crypt coming to rest on a coffin marked "Dracula." As the music ends, splotches of blood

The Curse of Frankenstein, Warner Bros. (1957).

appear on the coffin. The opening scene, after the credits, seems pastoral by comparison. A red book titled "Diary of Jonathan Harker" appears. Harker proceeds to narrate his story.

We see Harker (John Van Eyssen) arrive at Castle Dracula which appears, far more accurately, as an Eastern European, almost Oriental looking structure, instead of the decayed, crumbling castle of earlier Hollywood films. Harker describes his arrival at the castle as uneventful except that no birds are singing and the air suddenly feels colder, the result, he assumes, of the cold mountain stream he crosses as he enters. Dracula's castle is quite elegant. It is in fact the same set used in *Curse of Frankenstein*, ingeniously redesigned by Art Director Bernard Robinson, and will reappear in a host of other Fisher films for Hammer. Dracula leaves a note for Harker saying he is unable to welcome him personally but hopes he enjoys the dinner prepared for him. Harker proceeds to eat and then relaxes by the fire. As he adds another entry to his journal, he accidentally knocks over a tray on the table. In bending down to pick it up, the edge of a woman's white skirt appears in the frame. A dark haired sensual woman (Valerie Gaunt) appears suddenly, asking for his help in escaping from the castle. She stares momentarily at his throat and then leaves suddenly. Harker notices a dark figure at the top of the stairs. The figure descends and comes straight into the camera. We have a close up of Count Dracula, handsome, polite and congenial. Dracula (Christopher Lee) shows Harker to his room. Ostensibly Harker has come to index the books in Dracula's laboratory. Actually, he has really come to destroy Dracula. Before leaving Harker's room, Dracula admires a photo of Harker's fiancée, Lucy. After Dracula goes, Harker hears the lock turn at his door. In trying it he realizes he has been locked in.

Sometime later Harker is awakened by a sound at his door. He finds the door now open and goes into the hallway to investigate. Seeing nothing he goes downstairs. The candles in the castle are all lit and yet everything seems empty and still. As Harker surveys the scene the strange dark haired woman reappears. Again she implores him to help her escape from Dracula. "You have no idea what an evil man he is," she tells him. Harker confidently replies, "I'll help you. Don't worry." Seemingly relieved, the woman rests her head on his shoulder. Harker pats her gently. Quickly the camera angle shifts from facing Harker to viewing him from his back. We see the woman raise her head from his shoulder, eyes wide, and quickly, cat-like, she opens her mouth, revealing large white fangs, and bites his neck. Stunned, Harker pulls away, holding his bloodstained throat. Immediately, Dracula himself reappears. Rather than the polite demeanor shown earlier, he is now red eyed with fangs dripping blood. In rapid succession we see Dracula pull the woman away from Harker, hurl him unconscious to the floor, and carry the woman off.

This is a brilliant sequence. Fisher uses a rapid series of different shots to capture the ferocity and intensity of the scene which is augmented by James Bernard's pounding music. Dracula and the woman are revealed for what they are, blood drinking embodiments of evil, hissing and snapping at each other like wild animals. Before them Harker is utterly helpless. There is a sense that he is doomed. Harker awakens in his room later the next afternoon. He knows that he must find Dracula and the woman's coffin while they sleep by day because after nightfall they will walk again. Harker takes the precaution of hiding his journal at a roadside shrine to the Virgin Mary before returning to the castle to search for the vampires. He manages to find the crypt which was shown during the opening credits. Both Dracula and the woman lie separately in open coffins. Harker has already found his task more arduous than he expected. Prepared only for

Dracula, he was enticed by the woman's plea for help and so fell victim to her. Harker intends to pound wooden stakes through the vampires' hearts since this will restore them to their natural state of corpses and keep them from rising to drink the blood of the living.

He pounds the stake into the woman's heart and she screams. A close up is shown of Dracula's face as he lies in an adjacent coffin. His eyes open as he hears the screams. Since the sun has not yet set he is unable to rise. However he turns his head toward the window and sees that darkness is rapidly descending. He smiles with an evil expression, revealing his sharp teeth. The camera switches back to Harker. He is staring into the coffin of the woman. Fisher cuts to a shot looking over the back of Harker's head. The audience sees what he sees. The voluptuous young woman's body has turned into that of an old hag. We realize this was her natural age. The blood of her victims not only kept her alive, it restored her youth.

Harker, nearly exhausted, turns toward Dracula. We are not surprised to see that his coffin now is empty. Hearing a noise behind him, Harker looks toward the entrance to the crypt. He sees a shadow on the wall descending the stairs toward the half opened door. Dracula emerges into the doorway. Harker backs away in sheer terror. Dracula enters and closes the door behind him, obviously relishing his moment of triumph. The screen goes blank. Fisher leaves Harker's fate to our imagination.

This opening prologue has been described in detail because it defines Fisher's early approach to what others have called, "the modern horror film." Nothing in *Curse of Frankenstein* or Fisher's earlier career, or for that matter, earlier supernatural films, prepares one for this opening sequence in *Dracula*. Even today, after more than four decades of far more excessive blood and violence in film and television, it still exerts considerable power. This celebrated opening introduces Fisher's approach to the conflict between good and evil. The first point to note is the emphasis on the attractiveness and seductive power of evil. This theme surfaced in the discussion of *Frankenstein Created Woman* in the previous chapter. In *Dracula* Fisher gives his initial treatment of the theme. Both Dracula and the woman vampire are attractive. Secondly, Fisher here presents another variation on the biblical story of the Fall. Harker's fatal flaw is that he trusts the woman's story. She deceives him and thereby leads to his death. As Eve believed the lies of the serpent, so Harker believes the vampire woman. On this analogy the woman is a serpent figure. This is readily apparent since her fangs and her lunge at him suggest a serpent's attack. Symbolically she suggests the ancient serpent goddess of Middle Eastern belief, a figure referred to both in ancient mythology and the Bible.[2] Fisher will come back to this figure again in later films, most explicitly in *The Gorgon*.

Brides of Dracula, **Universal Pictures (1960).**

Thirdly, Fisher introduces a narrative device here that he will also use again and again. He begins with a prologue in which the leading character of the story is not present. This prologue, again following the model of the biblical account of the Fall of humanity, shows the origin of a particular kind of evil. In Fisher's films, evil, like sin, is a repeating cycle. Unlike the Frankenstein series, however, the films dealing with supernatural evil present a true hero as the leading character. At the conclusion of the prologue this hero is presented as a friend of Harker's who comes investigating his disappearance. His name is Dr. Van Helsing, played by Peter Cushing. The original novel, *Dracula*, describes Van Helsing this way:

> he is a philosopher and a metaphysician, and one of the most advanced scientists of his day; and he has, I believe, an absolutely open mind. This, with an iron nerve, a temper of the ice-brook, an indomitable resolution, self-command, and toleration exalted from virtues to blessings, and the kindliest and truest heart that beats.[3]

Where Peter Cushing's Baron Frankenstein is a modern atheist, his Professor Van Helsing is a modern Christian. Van Helsing is far from being anti-scientific. He is both a medical doctor and a scientist but also a believer in the literal reality of demons and the Christian faith. In fact it is because Van Helsing is open-minded that he accepts the reality of demonic evil. He has seen it too clearly. Cushing captures the essence of Van Helsing very well, including the gesture of a raised index finger to emphasize a critical point referred to several times in the novel. There is one important difference in the Van Helsing character as developed by Fisher and Cushing. Where Dr. Van Helsing in the original novel is an elderly but still active man, Cushing plays him as comparatively young and full of intense energy. As such he is a perfect antagonist to Christopher Lee's Count Dracula.

Dr. Van Helsing is introduced at an inn near Castle Dracula. He is asking for information about Harker. The innkeeper as well as the guests feign ignorance. However a servant girl privately gives Van Helsing a copy of Harker's diary which has been found. Van Helsing goes to Castle Dracula and arrives just as a hearse drawn by galloping horses is leaving. Van

One of Fisher's most controversial films, *Dracula, Prince of Darkness*, Hammer (1965).

Helsing finds Harker's body in the crypt. Harker is obviously a vampire now himself. Van Helsing drives a stake into his body, freeing him from the curse. This is a major change from the original novel in which Harker escapes from the castle having had no prior knowledge that Dracula was a vampire before his coming there. Also in the original novel Dracula comes to London in search of new victims. In Fisher's film the action all takes place in Eastern Europe within a day's carriage ride from Dracula's castle.

There are several possible reasons for these changes. To begin with, the original novel is overlong and made unduly complex by the Victorian convention of telling the story through a succession of journal entries of the various characters. Secondly, there are so many different characters and incidents in the novel that all dramatizations have had to simplify the story. Fisher's version, scripted by Jimmy Sangster, who also wrote the screenplay for *Curse of Frankenstein*, is far closer to the overall spirit and substance of the original novel than any of the Hollywood versions. Finally, Fisher's version streamlines the story as one of spiritual conflict between good and evil, personified by Van Helsing and Dracula. Fisher elevates the character of Van Helsing to the clear position of central protagonist, reducing all other characters, save Dracula, to a secondary status. Following the opening prologue, the film then unravels as a continuous chase with Van Helsing hunting Dracula throughout the rest of the picture.

In approaching the story primarily as a spiritual conflict, Fisher and Sangster demonstrated an understanding of Bram Stoker's original novel that has escaped virtually all other dramatizations of *Dracula*. Stoker's story is essentially a Christian parable linked in English literary history to the allegories of John Bunyan in the seventeenth century and later to the work of George Mac Donald, C.S. Lewis and Charles Williams. The novel is somewhat hampered by Van Helsing's frequent sermonizing. The point nonetheless is driven home throughout the book that the struggle with Dracula symbolizes the ongoing conflict between God and Satan. It is however a conflict in which Good invariably will be the victor. As Van Helsing says in his accented English, "Thus are we ministers of God's own wish: that the world and men for whom His Son died, will not be given over to monsters, whose very existence would defame Him."[4] Van Helsing laments that in the secular, so-called enlightened age of the late nineteenth century, "the doubting of wise men" is Dracula's greatest strength.

Fisher seizes on this material with obvious relish. His later interviews confirm that Stoker's outlook as expressed in *Dracula* is very much his own.[5] That the focus (and success) of Hammer's *Dracula* rightly comes from Fisher can be seen in the fact that these themes recur throughout his films. Fisher's collaborators, Jimmy Sangster among them, do not show the same concern for this spiritual conflict theme in their work apart from Fisher.[6] Fisher's *Dracula* contains far more of the content and specific details of the original novel than any other version, down to Van Helsing's use of a phonograph to record memos and the aforementioned dramatic warning finger. In making Van Helsing younger and more energetic Fisher (and actor Peter Cushing) only make him more vital and heroic. John McCarty, in his otherwise excellent book, *The Modern Horror Film*, misunderstands the character of Van Helsing in Fisher's films. He sees him as an obsessed, almost inhuman figure bent totally on Dracula's destruction.[7] This misses two important points. First, Dracula, whatever tragic dimension he may have (and Lee's performance captures his loneliness), is nonetheless a symbol of total evil, truly satanic. Van Helsing, on the other hand, is motivated by compassion and the need to rescue Dracula's victims from the grip of death. Van Helsing's single-minded dedication is that of a doctor seeking to overcome the threat of a deadly plague.

As the film proceeds, Van Helsing determines that Harker's fiancée, Lucy Holmwood (Carol Marsh) is being attacked by Dracula. Van Helsing is hampered by the fact that Arthur, Lucy's brother (Michael Gough), refuses to heed any of Van Helsing's warnings. The result of course is Lucy's death through loss of blood. Much has been made of the obvious anticipation and delight of Dracula's female victims in Fisher's films. The theme of sexuality, though hardly central, is certainly emphasized more than in the old Hollywood films (although it is certainly present in the German silent film version, *Nosferatu*). Dracula's female victims enjoy being attacked. Lucy prepares herself almost as a ritual sacrifice, laying herself out on the bed, arms extended, looking longingly at the door through which Dracula will enter. Meanwhile, Lucy's brother and her physician, Dr. Seward, talk scientific nonsense about her "anemic" condition. Van Helsing is understandably frustrated by these twin obstacles.

Lucy's death results in her becoming a vampire, and soon the evidence is too clear for even her skeptical brother to discount. As a vampire she passes from being a demure Victorian woman to becoming a raging lustful creature pursuing children. The unstated sexual component of this is clear enough here as in the original novel. It also derives from the Greek myth of the Lamia who sucked children's blood. It bears noting that Fisher, following his Victorian sources, frequently portrays women as either virginal or lustful. While this long-standing stereotype is rightly condemned today, it is worth noting that this dichotomy is ancient and pre–Christian, applying to the goddess Ishtar among others.[8] David Pirie correctly notes that Fisher's handling of this stereotype is somewhat more sophisticated in that he often shows repressed, puritanical women metamorphosing

The Brides of Dracula, Hammer (1960).

into lustful females.[9] This suggests that the lust is already there buried under the repressive exterior. In that sense, repression or sexual denial is not the alternative to wantonness but only its precursor. The sexual nature of Dracula's attack is obvious enough as we shall discuss presently.

Van Helsing and Arthur track Lucy to her crypt. Lucy's incestuous attempt to entice her brother with a kiss is thwarted when Van Helsing holds a cross before her eyes. She is clearly both terrified and transfixed by it. The two men return after daylight. Van Helsing explains to Arthur that this "thing" in the coffin is not really his sister-in-law but only a shell for "the evil of Dracula." Van Helsing proceeds to drive a stake into her heart, and her vampire features disappear, leaving her in the peace of death. As he does so the singing of birds is heard in the early morning hour, the same birds' singing whose absence was noted by Jonathan Harker as he entered Castle Dracula at the film's beginning.[10] The birds' singing, like the dawn itself, symbolizes life in its purity in contrast with the orgiastic, undead existence of the vampires. Van Helsing with Arthur's help now tries to locate Dracula's resting place. He rightly concludes that the hearse he saw leaving Dracula's castle earlier contained Dracula's body in a coffin which included fragments of his native earth. Unless the vampire can return to his coffin by day he will perish in the sunlight. Attempts to find the coffin are fruitless. The two men broaden the area of their search. Following a new lead and wary of Dracula, Arthur gives a small cross to his wife Mina for her protection. To their horror, she passes out when the cross is placed in her hand. It leaves a burn mark in her palm, indicating that she has now become one of Dracula's victims.

Van Helsing and Arthur change their strategy. They decide to watch the house by night, intercept Dracula when he comes to attack Mina next, and track him back to his coffin. All night they wait outside watching the doors and windows to the house. Inside however we see Dracula ascending the stair to Mina's room. She greets him in her nightgown, showing no fear. She lays across the bed as Dracula caresses her face and then proceeds to bite her neck. Such obvious imagery of seduction and rape was quite strong by 1958 standards when the film was released. The fact that Fisher shows no more than this allows one to focus on the symbolism of the act. An important aspect of the scene is that Mina is shown as a passive but willing participant. Dracula's desire for blood represents not only nourishment ("For the blood is the life"— Leviticus 17:14) but sex as well. Some critics have contended that Dracula is not ultimately villainous. Rather he is acting out a biological need over which he has no control. He is therefore not responsible for the harm caused in others. Others have seen him as a force for sexual liberation in the context of strict Victorian repression.[11] This however is far from both Stoker and Fisher's conception. True, Dracula is compelled to search for blood. However his particular choice of victim as well as his even being a vampire is a result of conscious evil choices. As one expert on vampirism puts it, "The Vampire is one who has led a life of more than ordinary immorality and unbridled wickedness."[12] Once again this hearkens back to the Pauline definition of sin as a power, a power however that is the result of the decision to worship "the creature rather than the Creator" (Romans 1:25).

In showing Dracula's attack on Mina, Fisher draws out the implications of Stoker's novel. Dracula's bite symbolizes an attack that is both sexual and violent in nature. The fact that the victim participates and, at some level, even enjoys the experience in no way lessens the horror of what is happening. The image of the woman-vampire-victim conjures up a complex array of symbols which point to the reality of chronically abused women who nonetheless shield their attackers. It also applies to women, as well as men, who choose sexuality the way others choose drugs. Any momentary pleasure is more than offset by the long-term consequences.

These issues were scarcely discussed in the Victorian era in which the novel was written and hardly touched on even when Fisher's film was made in 1958. The fact that society is far more open to discuss these matters today has not eliminated the problem. The advantage of symbolic literature and film is that they allow us to conceptualize issues which often defy any reasonable analysis. To say that women are abused by men who were themselves abused at some point may be true but is hardly an explanation. Nor does such a scenario account for all cases of sexual abuse. The power of films like *Horror of Dracula* or the more contemporary *The Silence of the Lambs* lies in their ability to force us to confront evils that can neither be explained nor controlled rationally.

At daybreak Van Helsing and Arthur are shocked to find Mina's bloody body lying on her bed. She is weak but not dead. Van Helsing spends most of the day administering a blood transfusion from Arthur to Mina in order to revive her. This accomplished, the two men retire to the living room trying to understand how Dracula entered the house without being seen by either of them. Arthur offhandedly asks the maid to bring up another bottle of wine from the cellar. The maid hesitates, adding that Mina had given her strict orders not to go into the basement. Van Helsing suddenly grasps the truth. He races into the basement to find Dracula's coffin, empty. It is now nightfall. Dracula himself appears and locks Van Helsing in before escaping. In response to Van Helsing's pounding at the door Arthur lets him out. Van Helsing barely has time to explain the situation before a scream is heard from upstairs. Dracula kidnaps Mina and heads back to his castle with her. Once there, Van Helsing intones, she will be lost to them forever.

What follows is one of the most famous climaxes of any so-called "horror film." Fisher intercuts scenes of the carriage driven by Dracula with that of Van Helsing and Arthur in pursuit. It is an all-night ride. Dracula just has time to return to his castle with Mina before daybreak. Fisher wisely intersperses this with a humorous touch of an exasperated toll keeper whose gate is alternately broken by Dracula and then again by Van Helsing. Arriving at his castle, Dracula tries to bury Mina alive in an open grave! He is interrupted by Van Helsing and Arthur's arrival. Arthur goes to his wife's aid while Van Helsing pursues Dracula into the castle. Unfortunately Van Helsing left his cross in Dracula's coffin at the Holmwood house so he is, in a sense, spiritually disarmed. Van Helsing and Dracula confront each other in the banquet hall of the castle. Dracula moves toward Van Helsing, certain that he has his nemesis trapped. Van Helsing backs away until he stands against the wall of the room. A sidelong glance at the fold of the heavy curtains covering the room's massive

Original British poster for *Dracula*, Hammer (1958).

window shows him that the sun has begun to rise. Quickly Van Helsing jumps on to the long banquet table, runs down the length of it, leaps into the air and pulls down the curtains. Immediately sunlight floods the room. Dracula dives under the table for cover but not before his foot turns to dust from the sun's rays. Van Helsing seizes two candlesticks and places them together to form a cross. Holding the cross before Dracula's face he forces the vampire out into the sunlight where he decomposes into dust. The floor of the room contains a giant painted circle of the zodiac.[13] Dracula literally decomposes on this floor design. In effect Dracula dies as a symbol of all the mystic, dark arts associated with the images of the zodiac. The burn mark in the palm of Mina's hand disappears. She is free of the vampire curse. In the film's final shot a wind blows through the window and scatters Dracula's ashes. All that remains is his cape and ring. Dracula is completely destroyed. The film ends.

To call Fisher's *Dracula* an unqualified success is to put it mildly. Fisher's control of the material is stamped on every scene. The fact that blood and sexuality are shown at all is what made the film daring in 1958. Fisher knows when to appeal to the audience's imagination with scenes of a dead leaf falling to the ground or moonlight symbolizing Dracula's presence. The climax shows Fisher's directorial skill in pacing his actors through rapid action, pausing at the right moments to heighten tension. The film is a landmark effort ultimately for two reasons. First, Dracula is portrayed as both attractive and sensual. This is contrasted with appearances of him as completely demonic. By comparison, Bela Lugosi's portrayal, memorable in its own way, functions on essentially one level, that of the sinister foreign aristocrat. None of the later portrayers of Dracula — Jack Palance, Louis Jourdan, Frank Langella, Gary Oldham —capture the demonic intensity of Christopher Lee in the role. Secondly, Fisher's approach evokes not only the original novel but a host of mythical archetypes which lie behind the vampire legend. The image of Dracula with its overtones of cannibalism and sexual power goes back to the dawn of human culture. Yet Fisher interprets this image in the context of biblical themes of Lucifer, temptation, fall and the redemptive power of the Cross. It is this interplay of classic myth and biblical symbols which makes Fisher's work, at its most successful, so impressive. Fisher's film, like Stoker's novel, avoids the attempt to make Christianity somehow reasonable in modern terms. In the novel skeptical observers are appalled at what they regard as the primitive nature of Van Helsing's faith. What convinces them is the power of this faith, evidenced in Christian symbols, to defeat the irrational but very genuine reality of evil.

The success of *Dracula* made a sequel inevitable. The sequel did not go into production immediately however. One reason apparently was that Christopher Lee was reluctant to portray the character again for fear of being stereotyped. Fisher directed no fewer than five features for Hammer during 1958–59. Lee appeared in four of them but in only one, *The Mummy*, did he play a "monster." Clearly he was hoping to broaden his acting image after playing Frankenstein's monster and Count Dracula. Hammer finally decided to forgo the matinee appeal of Christopher Lee and assigned Fisher to direct *The Brides of Dracula* but without Dracula!

Brides of Dracula is unfortunately a silly commercial title for one of Fisher's most expressive films, a film which in some ways improves on his *Dracula*. The opening scene shows a dark, misty forest as a narrator explains that Dracula, King of the Vampires, is dead (making the title immediately inappropriate). Yet the curse of vampirism, it is explained, lives on. A racing carriage comes into view. The driver, obviously frightened, whips his horses feverishly. The occupant of the coach who cannot understand his haste is a young French woman (Yvonne Monlaur). The coachman reigns in the horses suddenly when he sees an object lying in the path. Coming down from the coach, he discovers it is only a log and

French poster for *Horror of Dracula* (*Le Cauchemar de Dracula*), Hammer (1958).

tosses it aside. As he does so a strange man comes out of the forest and climbs onto the back of the carriage. A few moments later the carriage stops at an inn. Before the young woman understands what is happening, the coach drives off, leaving her stranded at the inn. The innkeeper is reluctant to let her stay or even to help her. Suddenly another carriage is heard arriving. A Baroness Meinster (Martita Hunt) enters and invites the young

Spanish poster for *Dracula* (1958).

woman, Marianne, to spend the night with her in the castle Meinster. As Marianne leaves with the Baroness, the innkeeper exchanges a look with his wife which strongly suggests that Marianne's stay in the castle will not be a pleasant one.

At the castle Marianne is introduced to the servant Greta (Freda Jackson) supposedly the only other occupant. During dinner (on the same set as the opening scene of *Dracula*), the Baroness tells Marianne of an evil son who has apparently died and whose infernal activities have forced her into essentially the life of a recluse. Marianne, however, glimpses a view of a young man from the balcony of her room. Curious, she secretly makes her way into the wing of the castle where she saw him. The man is indeed the Baroness' son (David Peel). He is chained on the ankle and so is unable to leave his room. Marianne is horrified to learn this. The young Baron claims that his mother has chained him so she could steal his rightful inheritance, the castle and its lands. Marianne finds his story completely reasonable so she sets him free by getting the key which he tells her is hidden in his mother's room. She manages to get the key undetected and throws it to him from her balcony.

Almost immediately she is confronted by the Baroness. The Baroness realizes the key has been stolen. "You don't know what you've done!" she screams. In fact the young Baron, handsome and charming, is a vampire. The Baroness had restrained him on a silver chain (an echo of the legend of silver having power over vampires as well as werewolves). She has brought young girls to him so he could satisfy himself with their blood. Once free, the young Baron turns on his mother and attacks her, killing her and drinking her blood so that she too will become a vampire. Overwhelmed with the horror of all this, Marianne flees from the castle into the night and collapses in the forest.

This opening sequence, similar in a number of respects to the beginning of *Dracula*, is enormously rich in symbolism and mythic content. It is a credit to Fisher that his restrained narrative approach keeps the material from becoming offensive. The concept of a son drinking his mother's blood could easily become disgusting, to say the least.[14] The more sinister dimensions of the situation at Castle Meinster are briefly referred to and much is left to the imagination. The Baron's actual attack on his mother for example takes place off screen. Yet Fisher builds the tension of the scene by showing the freed son giving the ominous command, "Mother … come here."

It is remarkable that a sequence so full of allusions has not received more attention even from critics who regard this film as one of Fisher's best. Intentionally or not, the relation of the young Baron to his mother conjures up both Oedipus and Orestes in Greek myth. Oedipus commits incest with his mother. Since the vampire's bite (especially in Fisher's *Dracula*) has sexual connotations, the idea of a vampire drinking his mother's blood suggests a form of incest. Orestes murders his mother to avenge his father's death. The Baron intentionally murders his mother in an act that is also motivated by revenge. However, while Oedipus and Orestes are both consumed with remorse for their actions, Baron Meinster has no such regrets. He, like Dracula, is a symbol of demonic evil.

The main outline of this opening sequence again recalls the fall of Adam and Eve in the biblical account found in Genesis chapter three. Marianne is a type of Eve — innocent and, as yet, unaware of the power of evil. While she has been warned about the Baroness' son, she succumbs to his charm when she finally meets him and believes his lies ("Now the serpent was more subtle than any other animal"— Genesis 3:1). The result is that the evil Baron, restrained by a chain like Satan in the Book of Revelation, is now set free. Marianne's curiosity in searching out the chained Baron is reminiscent of the myth of Pandora. Like the opening of Pandora's box, the unchaining of the Baron unleashes terrible evil into the world. Finally, the idea that the Baroness had made a practice of bringing young women as victims for her son's bloodlust conjures up ancient images of the sacrifice of young virgins. This was a practice in the worship of some ancient deities and appears both in Homer (Agamemnon's sacrifice of his daughter Iphigenia in the *Iliad*) and the Bible (Jephthah's sacrifice of his daughter in Judges chapter eleven).

As in *Dracula*, the protagonist, Dr. Van Helsing, again played by Peter Cushing, does not appear until after the prologue. Van Helsing finds Marianne passed out in the forest. He revives her and takes her to the finishing school for young ladies where she is to be a teacher. Van Helsing has come to the area at the request of the local priest (Fred Johnson). In the village Van Helsing also encounters a pompous doctor (Miles Malleson in one of several comic roles for Fisher). Fisher here sets up an interesting triad. The priest is a man of faith who, while devout, lacks the practical skills for combating evil. The doctor is a man of science who dismisses the supernatural out of hand as "superstitious nonsense." Van Helsing could be called a man of wisdom since he combines faith with science and practical skill. Van Helsing rejects the Enlightenment confidence in reason as the sole guide to truth. Yet he uses reason as an ally to faith. Fisher has the greatest contempt for the man of science. Such characters in his films are shown to be closeminded and prejudiced in denying any truth that cannot be demonstrated rationally or scientifically. For modern viewers who are used to seeing religious figures portrayed as little better than fools or

Italian poster for *The Brides of Dracula* (*Le Spose di Dracula*).

corrupt hypocrites, it is a striking change to see Fisher's films in which those committed to science are shown as blind and foolish. Van Helsing combines the best of both worlds by holding doctorates in both theology and medicine. In addition to this, he holds the chair of metaphysics at the University of Leyden in Holland and is, of course, an expert on vampires. A formidable figure indeed!

Van Helsing explains to the priest that vampirism is the result of the conquest of Christianity over the pagan cults of the ancient world. These cults went underground and maintained themselves by the twin rites of devil worship and the drinking of human blood. This simple explanation may lack validity but it certainly points up Fisher's orientation to classical Christianity. Along this line the cross is even more in evidence in this film than in *Dracula*. It is Van Helsing's chief weapon against Baron Meinster. Fisher adds another interesting theological touch in showing Van Helsing's meeting with Baroness Meinster who is, of course, now a vampire. However she is a vampire who wants to be released from the curse. Van Helsing tells her that there is a release and she willingly submits to his driving a stake through her heart. No such sequence exists in any previous vampire film. This underscores that for Fisher the vampire curse is a symbol of the bondage of sin. This bondage may be pleasurable but it is also a condition from which one may seek release.

Baron Meinster proceeds to attack two young girls, one from the village (Marie Devereux) and the other a friend at Marianne's school (Andree Melly). Not surprisingly the girls are transformed from demure virgins into lustful predators. In a striking sequence, Gerda, the servant woman from Castle Meinster, coaxes one of the young women out of her coffin. In response to her encouragement we see a hand emerge from the dirt of the shallow grave to be followed by the pale figure of the vampire woman. Peter Cushing's success led to the prominent casting of a number of other Shakespearean trained actors in Hammer Films. Freda Jackson, who had earlier worked with Fisher on *The Last Man to Hang* (1956), is here given full leave to demonstrate her classical acting skills in the role of Gerda. Her combination of evil cackling laughter and occasional shrieks augment the film notably.

The script of *Brides of Dracula* is not its strong point due perhaps to the fact that three different writers worked on the screenplay. For instance, Marianne inconceivably becomes engaged to Baron Meinster (due perhaps to his hypnotic charm?). Also the Baron has abandoned his castle and keeps his victims in a nearby windmill. These plot elements aside, and some weak moments showing a mechanical bat, Fisher's visual power provides a stunning climax. Armed with both holy water and a crucifix Van Helsing comes

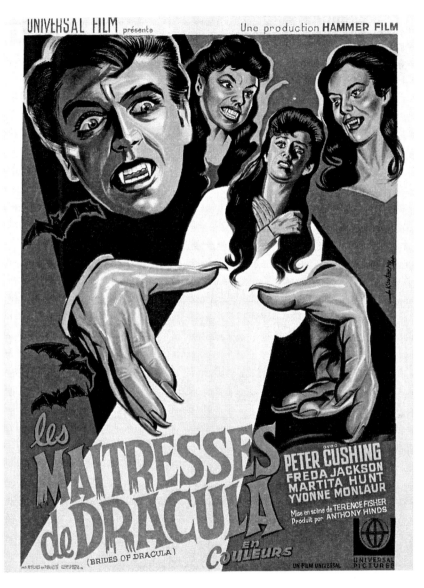

French poster for *The Brides of Dracula* (*Les Maîtresses de Dracula*).

to the windmill where the Baron is hiding. Unfortunately he is surprised by both Gerda and the Baron. The crucifix drops through the floor of the old mill and the Baron strangles him with a chain. He does not kill Van Helsing, however, since he has a worse fate in store for him. While Van Helsing remains unconscious the Baron bites his neck, thereby placing the vampire curse on

him. The Baron leaves Van Helsing unconscious on the floor of the windmill and goes out to fetch his future bride, Marianne. Van Helsing regains
consciousness and realizes to his horror that he has been bitten. Rather than
despair of his fate, he takes a red hot poker from a brazier of burning coals
and places it on his neck. He writhes in pain as he does so and his neck is
burned black. In an effort of extreme self-determination he then takes the
container of holy water and sprinkles it on his neck. His head reclines to one
side, briefly evoking Christ on the cross, and he is completely healed.

The Baron returns with Marianne who now is finally afraid of him.
Confident of his victory, the Baron taunts Van Helsing. Van Helsing throws
the remaining holy water in his face. It acts like acid and the Baron shrieks.
In desperation he kicks over the brazier of hot coals and the windmill
erupts in flames. The Baron staggers out the front into an open yard. Van
Helsing and Marianne must escape through a window because they are
cut off by the fire. Outside the moon is full behind the windmill. Leaving
Marianne for a moment, Van Helsing leaps and grasps one of the arms of
the windmill. His weight brings it down perpendicular to the ground. As
all the arms rotate in succession the moonlight behind the windmill casts
the gigantic shadow of a cross on the open yard. The Baron is caught in
the shadow. He twists, turns and collapses dead. Marianne and Van Helsing make their way down from the windmill to the yard. The final shot
of the film shows another cross in silhouette this time as the raging fire in
the mill sets off the four arms, making them appear as a giant celtic cross.
The credits roll as the pseudo–Bach music score swells.

The Brides of Dracula is one of Fisher's most detailed films. It abounds
in symbolic imagery but the dominant image, by far, is the cross. Once
again evil is presented as attractive and appealing. The sexual element,
first introduced in *Dracula*, is here augmented with the Baron's implied
need of a number of young women (this perhaps also suggests that his
attack on Van Helsing may have a homosexual dimension). Van Helsing's
role as a Christian warrior is likewise enhanced. This battle is clearly
between Christianity and Satan. Yet it is a battle in which the cross is a
dominant symbol of victory. The apostle Paul speaks of the cross having
cosmic dimensions reconciling all things in heaven and earth to God
(Colossians 1:20). For Fisher the cross can be found virtually anywhere.
The cross emerges out of otherwise ordinary elements such as candlesticks
and windmills. This ubiquitous character of the ultimate symbol of God's
victory in the Christian faith gives Fisher's work a prevailing optimism in
the face of evil. Fisher has insisted that if there is any general theme to his
films, it is his emphasis on the ultimate final victory of good over evil.[15]
In Fisher's final Dracula film the power of spiritual good is even stronger.

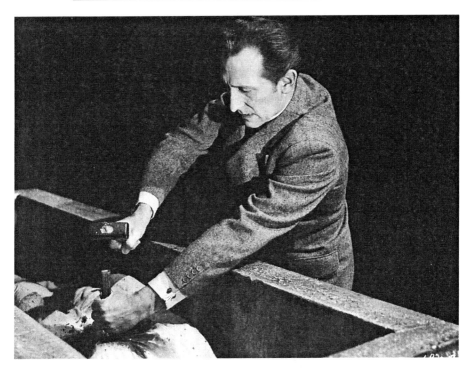

Dr. Van Helsing (Peter Cushing) stakes the vampire Lucy (Carol Marsh) in *Horror of Dracula* (1958).

It would be more than five years before Hammer and Fisher would attempt another Dracula film. In the 1960s the influence of Hitchcock's *Psycho* was felt at Hammer as well as other studios. Another influential film was Robert Aldrich's *Whatever Happened to Baby Jane?* (1962) starring Bette Davis and Joan Crawford. The success of these films, dealing more with psychotic killers than supernatural figures like vampires, combined with the commercial failure of Fisher's *Phantom of the Opera*, led Hammer to turn away from classic Gothic themes. The studio made a succession of *Psycho* imitations with obvious titles like *Maniac* (1962), *Paranoiac* (1962), and *Nightmare* (1963). They cast Bette Davis in *The Nanny* (1965) and Tallulah Bankhead in *Fanatic* (*Die! Die! My Darling* in U.S.A.) [1964]). They also produced a number of costume adventures such as *Devil Ship Pirates* (1963). More disturbingly, Hammer began moving more in the direction of exploitative sexual themes, highlighting Ursula Andress (with Cushing and Lee) in *She* (1965) and Raquel Welch in *One Million Years B.C.* (1966). Fisher was no longer the dominant figure he had been at the studio. Whereas in the years 1958–60, Fisher had directed eight films for

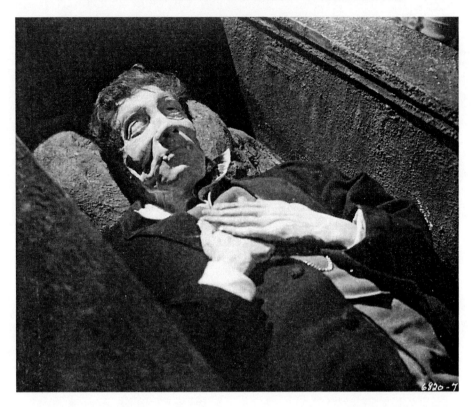

Jonathan Harker (John Van Eyssen) transformed into a vampire in *Horror of Dracula* (1958).

Hammer; in the comparable period, 1963–65, he did only two films. The irony is that these later films represent a more seasoned and perhaps mature approach on his part.

Fisher's last vampire film, *Dracula, Prince of Darkness* (1965), is widely regarded as a disappointment. Although Christopher Lee appears as Dracula, his nemesis in this film is a priest (Andrew Keir) rather than Dr. Van Helsing. The film has its weaknesses and is certainly dependent on the earlier *Dracula*. Nonetheless one would argue that this film, while more derivative than Fisher's previous two vampire films, is not really a disappointment but a further study of themes raised in the earlier films, including episodes and characters from the novel *Dracula* that were not included in the first film.

In *Dracula, Prince of Darkness* the prologue is a repeat of the now famous ending of Fisher's original *Dracula* (or *Horror of Dracula*). We see the final sequence of Van Helsing and Count Dracula from the former film in reduced frame in the screen. Some have felt that opening the sequel

Count Dracula (Christopher Lee) emerges in all his fury in *Horror of Dracula*.

with such a powerful and certainly familiar scene to Hammer film fans was an acknowledgment of a lack of inspiration. This film, like so many sequels, would be just a rehash of the original. Actually, what may have confused critics and audiences alike is that *Dracula, Prince of Darkness*, far from being a copy, is in some ways quite innovative. Rather than repeating earlier films, Fisher is asking his audience to reflect further on the Dracula myth. In so doing he created one of his most controversial films. It is important to remember that *Prince of Darkness* was filmed seven years after Fisher's first *Dracula*. This passage of time provided an opportunity to give greater and perhaps more disturbing consideration to the subject.

In this film the opening prologue plays a different role than in previous films. The opening sequence does not introduce the origin of evil but rather its destruction. It begins with the complete disintegration of Dracula as shown in the first film. The context of this film then is very different from its predecessors. Evil is not released into the world in a new or expanded way. Rather, it has already been eliminated. The issue in this film is not the reality of evil but the fear of evil. Following the prologue, as is typical in Fisher, the film's protagonist is introduced. He is a monk, Father Sandor, no intellectual like Van Helsing, but a rustic and down to earth faith hero. We first see him preventing a group of villagers from attempting to bury the body of a young girl in the middle of a crossroads. This was a common superstition to ward off vampires or evil of any kind. Father Sandor criticizes their behavior as superstition. The girl should be buried in the churchyard. Father Sandor lives in a more confident world in which Dracula has been destroyed.

The priest then goes to an inn (a favorite setting for Fisher) where he meets two English couples on a vacation. The group is composed of two brothers and their wives. They are fairly typical upper-middle-class Victorians (the time is again late nineteenth century). One of the wives, Helen (Barbara Shelley), seems especially uncomfortable in the country inn. She is distressed by Father Sandor entering, going over to the fire and raising his clerical robe slightly to warm his backside. Noting her discomfort, Father Sandor refers to the soothing joy of the fire after riding horseback in the cold. It is clear that Helen finds such a physical demonstration, especially from a priest, to be little short of shocking. In this brief sequence Fisher has established these two characters in a relationship that will be critical to the film's story.

Father Sandor, while clearly a man of faith and the leader of a monastery, is a person who lives apart from illusions. The opening of the film has already shown him rejecting the superstitions of the villagers as well as the prim sense of decorum exemplified in Helen. Father Sandor is a man comfortable with himself. His faith clearly is not a retreat from the world but rather a way of accepting himself and his surroundings. Helen, on the other hand, is condescending, narrow-minded and judgmental. Her whole attitude and demeanor suggests someone who is held in and repressed.

Helen's brother-in-law, Charles Kent (Francis Matthews), asks for directions. As the group is some distance from their intended destination, Father Sandor invites them to come and spend the night at his monastery. After their exchange, he leaves. By the time the two couples have eaten and left, it is after nightfall. They become lost and find themselves, unknowingly, at Castle Dracula. They had been warned at the inn about the "dark castle on the hill" but Charles and his brother, Allan (Charles Ringwell), dismiss this as only another peasant superstition. Lost in the dark and the cold, the two men suggest spending the night in the castle. Charles' wife, Diana (Suzan Farmer), is mildly apprehensive but Helen is downright fearful.[16] The rest, however, persuade her to go in.

Inside they find that the castle is not uninhabited. A servant named Klove (Philip Latham) welcomes them in the name of his deceased master. He explains that his master had left instructions that any visitors were to be made welcome. He therefore invites them to dinner and to spend the night. The two brothers especially are delighted with the idea. A pleasant dinner is served by Klove (reminiscent of the opening of *Dracula*). The others are in good spirits but Helen is positively panic stricken. She does not want to stay under any conditions but, when pressed by the rest of the group for an explanation, can give no clear reason. Charles offhandedly asks Klove what was the name of his deceased master. "Count Dracula," Klove replies. The name apparently doesn't mean anything to the travelers.

After dinner each couple retires to a comfortable bedroom. However, Helen's sense of dread has in no way abated. She still pleads with her husband, Alan, that at least they should go. He dismisses her anxiety and tells her simply to go to sleep. But she can't sleep. In the middle of the night she hears someone walking outside. Suspicious of Klove, she awakens her husband. He assures her there is nothing to fear and he will go investigate. This also makes her apprehensive, but he promises her that he'll be right back.

Fisher handles this whole sequence with considerable skill. The audience knows there is danger in Dracula's castle so can identify with Helen and find the rest of the group, the two brothers especially, maddeningly complacent. Yet one doesn't know what there is to fear. Klove is indeed a suspicious, though very gracious, character. Fisher emphasizes the atmosphere of the castle, even having the candles flutter at the mention of Dracula's name. Yet the prologue of the film indicated that Dracula was destroyed years earlier. So what is there to fear? Fisher answers this question in one of his most unforgettable sequences.

Alan Kent is a shallow figure. He exudes a Victorian confidence which suggests not the slightest trace of belief in the supernatural. However, he

**Terence Fisher and Christopher Lee on the set of *Dracula, Prince of Darkness*
(1965). Courtesy of Ronald V. Borst/Hollywood Movie Posters.**

does not go far in the castle before he is stabbed to death by Klove. Klove,
walking with a limp, painstakingly carries Alan's body down to the crypt.
Slowly and methodically, he ties the dead Alan's ankles to a chain and then
hoists him into the air so he hangs headfirst over an open vault. All of this
is done in a slow, matter of fact manner. In the crypt the ashes are presumably the remains of Dracula. In a brief medium shot the silhouetted
Klove strikes the hanging body of Alan in the throat. Fisher cuts to a shot
of blood dripping on the ashes. Smoke begins to ascend from the bottom
of the crypt. Out of the smoke appears the revived figure of Count Dracula (Christopher Lee).

This scene elicited a storm of outrage when the film was first
released.[17] Those who wish to blame 35 years of graphic media violence
on Fisher have found ammunition in this film more than any other in his
work. A number of observations must be made, however. Klove's knife is
never shown actually striking Alan's body. Fisher handles the scene much
like Alfred Hitchcock when he "shows" Anthony Perkins striking Janet

Leigh with a knife in the famous shower scene in *Psycho*. In both cases the director plays on our imagination. Second, Fisher defended this scene, arguing that he meant to invoke a ritual sacrifice, the sacrifice of a human being. Again Fisher is drawing here on ancient myth and ritual which lie deep in human history and are certainly germane to the Dracula story.[18] Third, Fisher wants the audience to understand that he is presenting demonic forces which cannot be explained away. The title of the film after all is *Dracula, Prince of Darkness*. It is Alan's cavalier dismissal of the supernatural, against the warning of his wife, which prepares him for his fate. Alan represents another example of secular, "enlightened" humanity which has ignored both God and the devil and so has no understanding of the real nature of good and evil. Hence he is totally unprepared for supernatural forces. It is perhaps interesting to reflect that *Dracula, Prince of Darkness* played in the U.S.A. when the so-called "death of god" movement was receiving a great deal of media coverage.[19]

Following Dracula's revival, Helen in desperation begins to search for her husband. Instead she encounters Dracula and becomes his victim. The subsequent transformation of Helen is notable. She becomes, like her predecessors in *Brides of Dracula*, a lustful, destructive figure. Helen's character has received more attention than any other woman in the Dracula series. So while her transformation in itself is not novel, there is greater emphasis on it than in the previous films. Helen's prim repressed former self is changed into a demonic sexuality. Fisher is not really presenting the classic virgin/whore dichotomy here. The virginal implies innocence and purity or at least naiveté. Helen has instead appeared neurotic and repressed. Barbara Shelley, who by this time was a veteran of British horror films, gives a fine performance, capturing both poles of the character. One now understands her fear. It was a fear of herself more than any external threat, a fear of losing control. Yet this is precisely now her fate as she becomes truly a bride of Dracula. In religious terms Helen is the legalist holding to external form while inwardly sin rages, waiting to express itself. "I find that in my flesh there dwells no good thing," the apostle Paul wrote in his epistle to the Romans.[20] In this sense Dracula has not made Helen lustful. Rather he is the agent that has unlocked the buried forces already inside her as Fisher's focus on her throughout the first part of the film has demonstrated.

The remainder of the film pits the surviving couple, Charles and Diana, in the center of a battle between Dracula and the vampiric Helen on one side, and Father Sandor on the other. In a confrontation later in the castle, Diana's cross necklace accidentally burns Helen.[21] Charles and Diana suddenly discover the genuine power of the cross. The cross for

Peter Cushing in *The Horror of Dracula* (1958).

Fisher has objective power. Charles and Diana are able to hold Dracula and Helen at bay using the cross even though they don't really seem to understand *why* it has this power. Later directors would miss this point. For example, Freddie Francis in *Dracula Has Risen from the Grave* (1968) shows the faith of those in combat with Dracula being crucial to success in the spiritual battle. At this stage it is no longer *Christ* against Satan (Dracula), but the *Christian* against the "prince of darkness." The problem in Francis' film is the priest has a lapsed faith so the battle against Dracula goes poorly. It was only a small step from this to *The Exorcist* (1973) which presents an old, infirm priest teamed with a doubting assistant. Neither is effective in their confrontation with the demonic.

Fisher hated *The Exorcist* and didn't care much for Hammer's later Dracula films either.[22] He shared the Pauline view of Christ as the cosmic Lord of Creation. The evil powers of the universe had been led captive in the triumphal procession of Christ's cross (Colossians 2:15) That didn't mean these forces had been eliminated yet but their ultimate power has been broken. A crucial point that has been missed by all critics on this film deals with the nature of the revived Dracula. He is more animal-like, more sub-human in this film than in the first *Dracula*. Our first view of him is his hand crawling like a spider as he is revived in his coffin. He hisses and flashes his fangs like a cobra (a symbol of evil in Fisher's earlier *Stranglers of Bombay*). He has been brought back to life but not at full strength. For example he can no longer speak. (Christopher Lee has commented that there were speaking lines for Dracula in the original script but they were so bad that he declined to use them. However if the issue had only been the quality of the lines surely they would have been rewritten. The fact that Dracula has no dialogue in the final film can hardly be accidental.[23]) This Dracula is not the independent Vampire King of the earlier film. He relies heavily on the assistance of both Klove and Helen. This is a now somewhat emasculated Count. In Fisher's view Dracula cannot completely undo the effects of his earlier defeat. He is present and active but, nonetheless, for all the demonic ritual in restoring him, he is a weakened figure. Hammer would ignore this important point and, after Fisher, try to reinvest Dracula with his full power in subsequent films. The series quickly declined to such travesties as the sadistic *Scars of Dracula* (1970) with its pointless scenes of nudity and whipping, and *Dracula A.D. 1972* which paved the way for later "teenage victim" movies like *Halloween* and *Friday the 13th*.

Charles and Diana eventually take refuge in Father Sandor's monastery. At this point Fisher apparently wants to show the spiritual battle in the clearest possible terms. Helen entices Diana to let her (and Dracula) into the monastery. Dracula already has an agent in the monastery in the character of Ludwig (Thorley Walters) who is quite clearly Renfield, the fly eating madman form the original novel. Another striking scene from Bram Stoker's book has Dracula cut his chest to force Diana to drink *his* blood. Before she can do so they are interrupted. In the book Mina Harker actually does drink Dracula's blood. This is a powerful, symbolic scene containing suggestions of ritual sacrifice, cannibalism and oral sex among others. Again Fisher's treatment is quite restrained considering all the implications (the same themes are much more crudely presented in Brian DePalma's *Carrie* [1977]). The point is that Dracula symbolizes lustful and violent practices as old as human history itself. In the Dracula story, correctly interpreted by Fisher, these practices have a demonic, destructive origin. The same idea is found again and again in the Bible.[24]

The most striking scene in *Dracula, Prince of Darkness* occurs when a group of priests capture Helen. (Fisher and his screenwriter Jimmy Sangster apparently return here to their original view in *Dracula* that vampires cannot change shape, thereby avoiding the somewhat embarrassing bats in *Brides of Dracula*.) At Father Sandor's order she is held down on a table. Helen snaps, hisses and writhes like a cornered animal or a giant serpent. She is wearing an ancient Grecian dress which, literally, is absurd in late nineteenth century central Europe. However Fisher is casting her symbolically like one of the Greek furies. Father Sandor explains to Charles that this wild figure is not the sister-in-law he loved but only a shell for "the evil of Dracula" (again echoing a similar scene in *Dracula* between Van Helsing and Arthur Holmwood). As Helen shrieks and wrestles, Father Sandor takes a stake and drives it into her heart. Charles turns away in horror (which is also the viewer's reaction). Father Sandor goes over to him and gently leads him to the table when he sees the peaceful face of Helen in death, devoid of its lustful grimace. Father Sandor makes the sign of the cross on her forehead. A bell tolls her entering final rest.

Much has been written about this scene, calling it a symbolic rape or an extreme case of violence against women.[25] Fisher's treatment of women is discussed in a later chapter but suffice to say here that such charges seem to ignore everything Fisher is exploring in this scene. It is not Helen ultimately who is evil. Nor is it Helen really who is staked. Whatever lustful origin may have existed in Helen's repressed nature has by now been totally dominated by Dracula's demonic influence. The writhing, screeching figure at the end bears no resemblance to the original Helen. In theological terms, sin has totally defaced Helen's humanity so that she has now become more a beast than a person like the Gerasene Demoniac in the Bible (Gospel of Mark 5:1–13). Her staking is, for Fisher, her purification, her release. Fisher here again is stressing ritual but in this case it is the symbolic ritual of exorcism.

Dracula, Prince of Darkness ends with a chase in which Dracula's coffin slides out of a carriage onto the frozen moat of Castle Dracula just before dark. Once night has descended Dracula leaps from his coffin and attacks Charles, who was trying to rescue his wife. Dracula begins to choke him. Trying now to aid her husband, Diana on the bank of the moat grabs Father Sandor's rifle and shoots at Dracula. Father Sandor is about to tell her that bullets cannot harm Dracula when he realizes the shots have punctured holes in the ice and water is running at Dracula's feet. Father Sador sees that Dracula has a terrified look and remembers that running water can destroy him. He proceeds to fire a number of shots into the ice until Dracula is stranded on a small block of ice. Running water is all around him. Helplessly he falls into the water, his face contorted in pain. His inert body rises to the surface some distance away and his face can be glimpsed under the ice. The film ends.

Dracula, Prince of Darkness completes Fisher's Dracula trilogy, the most creative and faithful approach to the Dracula story to date. Dracula's final demise in running water is unique in film treatments. Here Fisher has gone back to ancient symbols behind Stoker's novel. Running water is ultimately, in Western culture, a Christian symbol found in the gospel of St. John. Jesus speaks of the need of being born "of water and the Spirit" (John 3:5). Here the reference is probably also to baptism. Jesus later says, "The water that I will give will become in them a spring of water gushing up to eternal life" (John 4:14). The end of the Book of Revelation speaks of "the river of the water of life ... flowing from the throne of God" (Revelation 22:1). Father Sandor briefly states that running water symbolizes life. Ultimately it symbolizes the source of life for Christian belief, Jesus Christ himself. Fisher once again uses a biblical image to illustrate the universal triumph of God over the power of Satan. Fisher shows a remarkable grasp of Bram Stoker's novel in this trilogy to the extent that he is able to expand on Stoker's own material in depicting the central theme of the supernatural triumph of good over evil.

Notes

1. Cf. Vermilye, Jerry, *The Great British Films*, pp. 172–174.
2. Campbell, Joseph, *The Masks of God: Occidental Mythology*, pp. 9ff. Biblical references to Asherah (I Kings 15:13; II Kings 23:7) and the Queen of Heaven (Jeremiah 44:17–19) refer to this goddess figure.
3. Wolf, Leonard, ed. *The Essential Dracula*, p. 147.
4. *Ibid.*, p. 379.
5. Eyles, Adkinson, Fry. *The House of Horror*, p. 15.

6. One has only to compare Fisher's vampire films with an example like Sangster's *Lust for a Vampire.*

7. McCarty, John. *The Modern Horror Film*, p. 29.

8. Campbell, Joseph. *The Masks of God: Primitive Mythology*, p. 412.

9. Pirie, David, pp. 89–92.

10. I am indebted to my associate, the Rev. Brandi Wolf Drake, for this observation.

11. Rigby, Jonathan, pp. 52–53.

12. Summers, Montague. *The Vampire: His Kith and Kin*, p. 77.

13. Here I am indebted to my associate's husband, Dr. Evan Drake, for calling my attention to this important point.

14. The drinking of blood as a sacred or initiating rite has been well documented, cf. Campbell, Joseph, *The Masks of God: Primitive Mythology*, pp. 222–224; Young, Dudley, *Origins of the Sacred: The Ecstasies of Love and War*, p. 133. Its symbolism underlies the celebration of Holy Communion in Christian worship. For an extensive discussion of this topic, see Tom Driver's discussion of "Ritual, Theater and Sacrifice," in *The Magic of Ritual*, pp. 79–106.

15. Eyles, Allen; Adkinson, Robert; Fry, Nicholas, p. 15.

16. Pirie, David, p. 89.

17. Butler, Ivan. *Horror in the Cinema*, p. 49.

18. For a summary, see Driver, Tom, *The Magic of Ritual.*

19. *Time* magazine's April 8, 1966, issue carried a famous cover with the question, "Is God Dead?"

20. Romans 7:18.

21. There is an editing mistake in this sequence. Immediately after Helen is burned we see Diana holding her cross. After a cut we *then* see Diana look at the cross around her neck and lift it up.

22. Eyles, Adkinson, Frye, op. cit., p. 15.

23. Different reasons for this have been given, including the claim that Christopher Lee did not like his dialogue as written. I find none of these to be convincing.

24. There are many examples but one of the most explicit is found in Numbers 25:1–9.

25. Prawer, S.S. *Caligari's Children*, pp. 255ff.

Chapter Three

THE DEVIL'S CURSE

By the late summer of 1958 it was clearly apparent that Hammer Studios had achieved an unprecedented worldwide success with Fisher's work on the first two Frankenstein films and *Horror of Dracula*. Responding in good commercial fashion Hammer kept Fisher and his team working on other film sources of gothic horror. Universal International Studios were so impressed with Fisher's films that they gave Hammer the rights to their own copyrighted horror films.[1] Plans were drawn up for Fisher to do remakes of *The Mummy*, *The Wolf Man* and *The Phantom of the Opera*. However before any of these projects were undertaken, Fisher and the same essential team that had done *Curse of Frankenstein* and *Horror of Dracula* began work on the most famous of all Sherlock Holmes stories, *The Hound of the Baskervilles*.

At first glance Sherlock Holmes might seem an odd choice to follow Frankenstein and Dracula. Yet *The Hound of the Baskervilles* is as much a tale of gothic horror as it is a detective story. This novel, like some of Sir Arthur Conan Doyle's later Holmes stories, deals with the theme of the supernatural.[2] Holmes has the memorable line, "In a modest way I have combated evil, but to take on the Father of Evil himself would, perhaps, be too ambitious a task." Although the hound in the novel is actually a real dog made up to look supernatural, its appearance is horrific enough so that Dr. Watson can say of it, "Never in the delirious dream of a disordered brain could anything more savage, more appalling, more hellish be conceived." Further, Holmes himself in this particular story takes almost a back seat to the ominous, dark atmosphere of the moor with its quicksand-like Grimpen Mire and strange howls in the night.

Not surprisingly, Fisher relished this material, and thematically the film becomes an extension of *Dracula* in its description of an evil power which places a curse on an unwitting victim. *The Hound of the Baskervilles* was the first of three Fisher films dealing with the theme of a devilish curse.

U.S. publicity poster for *The Hound of the Baskervilles*, United Artists (1959).

Many today regard it as one of Fisher's finest films.[3] Like its predecessors it initially provoked extreme reactions in both the American and British press. After complaining that the Frankenstein and Dracula films had too much blood, some complained that *Hound of the Baskervilles* was too tame.[4]

Several critics, especially in America, showed their literary short-comings, as they had in reviewing Fisher's previous films, by evaluating the film in comparison with the Basil Rathbone version of twenty years earlier rather than the original novel. Fisher's *Hound* has stood the test of time, however, and a number of critics today regard it as the best of the many film versions of *The Hound of the Baskervilles*.[5] To evaluate the film in terms of Fisher's overall perspective of the conflict between good and evil the picture itself must be examined.

The opening prologue of *Hound* is perhaps the most intense of any of Fisher's films. The credits open on a scene of the moor with another forceful music score by James Bernard. As the credits roll the camera moves closer to a large manor house finally to rest on a stained glass window of the house. A voice intones, "Know then the legend of the Hound of the

Baskervilles..." Suddenly a human figure is hurled crashing through the window and lands in the moat which surrounds the house. Smashing glass is a favorite image of Fisher's, suggesting the breaking in of some ominous or frightening reality (as when Karl breaks through a pair of glass doors to identify "Dr. Stein" as Frankenstein in *The Revenge of Frankenstein*). From the outset it appears that something frightening is about to break into the manor house known as Baskerville Hall. The figure thrown through the window is dragged from the moat back into the house. The evil Sir Hugo Baskerville (David Oxley) and his seventeenth century companions are in the midst of one of their nightly revels. The man thrown through the window is the father of a farm girl whom Sir Hugo has kidnapped and locked upstairs for some unsavory pleasures later in the evening. Sir Hugo takes the poor man and holds him over a large open fireplace until he screams in pain. Hugo then casts the man aside like a doll and is confronted by his cronies with demands to pay a wager. Hugo agrees to pay "not in gold, but in kind, with a plaything I was saving for myself."

All of this constitutes a breathless opening. We have here another example of Fisher's beginning prologue presenting the origin of evil (or

British poster for *The Hound of the Baskervilles*, Hammer (1959).

"Fall") which will be dealt with later in the film. In this case once again Fisher, like his contemporary New Wave directors in France, begins his scene in the middle of the action.[6] Sir Hugo's party is in progress, a girl has been kidnapped and her father has come to plead for her release. All this has happened before the opening shot of the father being thrown through the window. Once again this is the same set that served as Frankenstein's house and Castle Dracula. Sir Hugo Baskerville, however, bursts on the screen as a full blown sadist unlike the more restrained first appearances of Baron Frankenstein and Count Dracula. Fisher here is not simply repeating past narrative approaches. He is stepping up the pace. Evil is in full fury as this film begins. Some critics at the time, as well as later writers, have suggested that Fisher and Hammer are overdoing it here, turning Sir Hugo into a sadistic, malevolent figure to create more of an atmosphere of horror.[7] Certainly Hammer was going for a horror approach (Sherlock Holmes is not even mentioned, much less pictured, in any of their U.S. advertising posters for the picture). Yet Fisher and his staff knew their material. Conan Doyle himself describes Sir Hugo as "a most wild, profane and godless man" having "a certain wanton and cruel humor." Sir Hugo in Hammer's film fits this description to perfection.

Having established Sir Hugo's "cruel humor" the captive farm girl (Judi Moyers) is then shown locked in an upper chamber. She hears the commotion from down below. Sir Hugo ascends the stair and heads for her room as claps of thunder sound. Fisher's camera is extremely mobile throughout this sequence, seemingly walking alongside and then behind Hugo as he comes down the hall to the girl's room. He finds that the girl has escaped out her window and apparently climbed down the ivy which covers the outside wall. Hugo confronts his guests in mad frenzy ("The bitch has got away! Damn her! Damn her!"). Fisher alternates between close-ups of Hugo in his rage and long and medium shots of his friends. This gives heightened intensity to the frantic character of Hugo. Hugo, holding a part of the girl's dress torn on the ivy, orders his hunting dogs to follow the scent of the dress and hunt her down on the moor. Even Hugo's friends, no Boy Scouts themselves, think this is too cruel. Hugo responds with the critical plot line, "May the hounds of hell take me if I cannot hunt her down!" Lightning flashes and thunder roars as Hugo speaks this line. He rides off across the moor, following the hunting dogs.

The scenes on the moor in this sequence have been criticized because they are day shots filmed through a filter to give a night effect.[8] I think this choice was intentional. Years ago this writer visited the scene of the novel in Dartmoor and was struck by the silvery light which is found on the moor at night. The author was informed that this was due to certain properties in the soil of the region. In any event it creates a strange shadowy effect in which you feel you can see more than you actually do. While Hammer's version was not shot on location (it was actually filmed in Surrey) the depiction of this sequence captures well the strange night appearance of Dartmoor.

The frightened girl tries to hide in an abandoned ruin on the moor. Hugo however sees her enter the structure. A terrible howl is heard. The hunting dogs retreat — whimpering. Hugo's horse balks at going forward. Hugo then enters the old ruin on foot. The girl watches him from a hiding place. After she sees him enter a door she begins to move. While she wanders through the ruins looking for a way out Sir Hugo's arm suddenly grasps her from behind. As the music mounts in intensity Hugo forces her down on a stone slab which suggests one of the Druid sacrificial altars common to Dartmoor. Fisher frames the action from behind Hugo at a slight angle. Hugo holds the girl with one hand and with the other reaches into his belt. The sexual suggestion is clear. He pulls out a knife and stabs the screaming girl to death. We see only his face as this is happening. The thunder is heard again and also the strange howl. Hugo stands and backs away from the body uncertain of where the sound originates. The camera focuses on him. Lightning flashes cast a menacing ray of light across his face. A deep growl is heard. Hugo looks straight into the camera. He is now terrified. The camera takes the point of view of the thing that is pursuing him (a device used effectively in Steven Spielberg's *Jaws*). It comes on top of him. He shrieks and drops out of the frame as the savage sounds increase. The bloodstained dagger falls from his hand and comes to rest alongside the edge of the dress of the murdered farm girl.

The narrator's voice resumes, telling of the curse that has come upon the Baskerville family since the time of Sir Hugo, a curse that has taken the form of a hound of hell bringing death to the Baskervilles who rashly cross the moor at night "when the powers of evil are exalted." The scene changes to 221B Baker Street, the home of Sherlock Holmes. The change could not be more striking. The shift is from a dark ruin on the moor with crashing thunder and lightning, terrible howls and dark murderous passion to a light, comfortable Victorian room. The narrator, a large bearded man (Francis De Wolff) with the document he has just read in front of him, turns and asks someone off camera, "Well, Mr. Holmes, what do you think of that?" Fisher cuts to a close-up of Sherlock Holmes (Peter Cushing) eyes closed, deep in thought. "Ah!" says Holmes as he turns to a chessboard beside him and makes a move. Answering the question, Holmes dismisses the harrowing prologue we have just witnessed as a fairy tale.

The large bearded man, a Dr. Mortimer, is about to leave angered at this dismissal. Holmes stops him, observing that the doctor carries a copy of a recent Devonshire newspaper suggesting that something "more recent" has brought the physician from Dartmoor to London. Dr. Mortimer (Francis de Wolff) proceeds to tell Holmes and Dr. Watson (Andre Morrell) of the recent strange death of Sir Charles Baskerville found dead on the moor in the same spot where Sir Hugo was killed. The body was untouched, Mortimer informs, but his face was contorted by fear and horror. He adds that the last of the Baskervilles, Sir Henry, is about to arrive in London from South Africa. Dr. Mortimer, a man of science, indicates that he cannot explain the strange events surrounding the Baskerville family rationally. At this point Holmes indicates, to Watson's surprise, that he will at least agree to meet Sir Henry, the new heir to the fortune and curse of the Baskervilles.

So much happens in the first quarter hour of *Hound* that the rest of the film runs the risk of being anticlimactic. Fisher's control of setting and theme is the highest he had achieved up to this point. The opening of this film makes the Frankenstein and Dracula films seem almost stately by comparison. As this prologue makes clear the primary emphasis in the film is going to be neither on science nor the supernatural (though both are present) but on evil itself. Holmes' line from the original novel that he has "combated evil" is used several times. Fisher gives Sherlock Holmes a decidedly metaphysical slant. This is not surprising since Peter Cushing's portrayal of the great detective has more than a hint of Dr. Van Helsing to it. Holmes is not investigating crime. He is "fighting evil." When Watson asks later, "What is the meaning of it all?" Cushing's Holmes does not answer in the classic words of the Conan Doyle text, "It is murder, Watson — refined, cold-blooded, deliberate murder." Instead he replies, "There is more evil around us here than I have ever encountered before."

One of the reasons this film has been the subject of debate for over forty years is that Fisher and his Hammer collaborators follow the original novel very closely at times and at other times they take definite liberties. When Watson accompanies Sir Henry and Dr. Mortimer down to Baskerville Hall (because Holmes supposedly cannot leave London) the film follows the novel very closely. Holmes is revealed later as hiding on the moor in order to observe events and remain undetected. Watson first spots Holmes unknowingly as a distant "man on the Tor" when he and Sir Henry go out on the moor in search of a figure signaling the house at night. This figure is later identified as Seldon, an escaped convict who is the brother of Mrs. Barrymore, the housekeeper at Baskerville Hall. All of this follows the novel closely, more closely actually than did the Basil Rathbone version of 1939. Fisher introduces significant innovations also. When Holmes and Watson go to meet Sir Henry (Christopher Lee finally in a nonhorror role) in a London hotel, Holmes has to save him from a tarantula in a sequence unknown to Conan Doyle. Seldon the convict is killed by the hound because he is wearing Sir Henry's stolen clothes (as in the novel). Following his death, a "revolting sacrificial rite" is performed on the body using the same knife with which Sir Hugo killed the farm girl (none of which is in the original story). In the novel Frankland is an eccentric who sues people and spies on the populace with a telescope. In Fisher's film Frankland is an eccentric bishop who keeps a rare collection of spiders (including tarantulas) and also spies with a telescope.

In reality Fisher and Hammer hadn't done anything different in adapting *The Hound of the Baskervilles* than they had done with Mary Shelley's *Frankenstein* or Bram Stoker's *Dracula*. In the case of the Shelley and Stoker novels they took basic characters and plot structure and then adapted them to fit a new pattern. The difference this time was that more people had probably read *The Hound of the Baskervilles* than had read the overlong *Frankenstein* and *Dracula* novels. Hence the criticism of "changing the story" was raised more frequently.[9]

Examining *Hound* in the light of the previous Fisher films is more revealing than comparing it with the Conan Doyle source novel. Frankland as played by Miles Malleson is a comic relief character as he would be in the first two Dracula films. He is made a bishop so that he can symbolize Fisher's "man of faith." The companion "man of science" is obviously Dr. Mortimer who prides himself on being "something of an archaeologist." Both figures are ineffective in the conflict with evil. Holmes obviously is the "man of wisdom" in this film. The Enlightenment confidence in reason could not account for evil or, better yet, sin. The Bishop here becomes an unwitting accomplice of evil. It is his tarantula which is stolen in order to frighten Sir Henry, who has a weak heart. It is he who asks Sir Henry for some cast-off clothes which Seldon eventually takes and wears to his death. At one point Holmes ironically asks for the Bishop's help, adding, "I am fighting evil, fighting it as surely as you are." But the Bishop is not fighting evil. He is both literally and symbolically in a fog regarding the tragic events taking place around him. He seems more concerned about the "wormwood in the belfry" than in the diabolical mystery that Holmes is trying to unravel. The Bishop's purely institutional religion is no more effective than Mortimer's scientific posturings (Mortimer, supposedly taking a scientific approach, inclines toward a supernatural explanation when in fact that is *not* the case).

Sherlock Holmes (Peter Cushing) shows Sir Henry (Christopher Lee, center) his missing boot as Dr. Watson (Andre Morrell) looks on in *The Hound of the Baskervilles* (1959).

Evil in this film ultimately takes the form of lust. That point is made clear in the opening prologue which plays the same role structurally as in Fisher's other films. The view of the Fall in the *Hound* is not so much a succumbing to temptation as it is a depiction of the consequences of sin once conceived. It is not known how Sir Hugo has become as evil as he has. He is not a seductive figure as were Baron Frankenstein and Count Dracula (or Baron Meinster). Rather he is a picture of unbridled desire. He kidnaps a girl, tortures her father, plans to have her raped, and finally kills her. He operates with a demonic intensity, making every effort to act out his desires. He is destroyed by a "hound of hell" and thereby initiates a curse on the Baskervilles.

But what is the "curse of the Baskervilles?" It is too simple to say that it is a threat of attack by a demon hound if one crosses the moor alone at night. The curse, according to Fisher, is found in Sir Hugo's lust for the farm girl. As has been noted there is a definite class theme in Fisher's work.[10] Sir Hugo is one of many degenerate aristocrats in Fisher's work. The curse of the Baskervilles is not that the Baskerville *men* (women descendants are not mentioned) simply go out alone at night. Rather they go out, as Sir Hugo did, in lustful pursuit of "farm girls." This leads to the villain in Fisher's film, a dark peasant girl who more than a little resembles the girl in the opening prologue.

In Conan Doyle's original novel a brother and sister, Jack and Beryl Stapleton, are actually revealed to be a distant Baskerville relative and his Latin American wife posing as brother and sister. The villain really is Jack Stapleton who forces his beautiful wife to masquerade as his sister so that she can be the bait which will lure Sir Henry out onto the moor at night. Stapleton hopes to gain the Baskerville inheritance. He had used his mistress, Frankland's daughter, to be the excuse to entice Sir Charles Baskerville out onto the moor which ultimately led to his death. In the novel, when Beryl learns of the existence of her husband's mistress she turns on him. Stapleton then ties her up and tries to carry out the plot on his own. Sir Henry is attacked by a monstrous glowing hound who is killed by Holmes and Watson. Stapleton attempts to escape into the Grimpen Mire but is presumably sucked down into its depths. Holmes and Watson free Beryl but the saddest part of the ordeal for Sir Henry is that he realizes he was betrayed by the woman he loved. Beryl, however, did not intend to do wrong to Sir Henry directly. She was acting under the power of her husband whom she both loved and feared.

So much for the original novel. Most adaptations of the story both before and after Hammer's 1959 version have taken great liberties in the portrayal of the Stapletons. The closest to the novel actually is the BBC TV production from the late 1970s starring *Dr. Who*'s Tom Baker as Holmes. Mark A. Miller has rightly observed that changing the character of Beryl Stapleton is a valid move because Conan Doyle's description of her character is so complex and convoluted as to strain credulity.[11] In fact most film versions have changed the Stapletons somewhat. Fisher is no different in that respect but his approach is unique. First, Fisher presents the Stapletons as father and daughter instead of a husband and wife pretending to be brother and sister. The state of film censorship in Britain in 1959 actually might have precluded a literal portrayal of such a marital masquerade.

Secondly, the Stapletons are presented as poor peasants. Their desire for the Baskerville fortune then is all the more understandable. However, by establishing such a class difference between the aristocratic Sir Henry and the peasant Stapleton daughter (here named Cecile and for once correctly portrayed as Spanish), Fisher removes any prospect of a legitimate relationship. There is no way that someone of Sir Henry's class in Victorian

England could acceptably marry such a peasant girl. His interest in her is therefore tainted from the first. His desire to walk with her across the moor at night suggests a less than honorable intention. What is unfortunately never clear is the film's attempt to introduce some quasi–Druid references to "revolting sacrifices." It almost seems that the Stapletons are somehow trafficking in the occult. Yet this is never explained or adequately developed. One wonders if this were an attempt at an obscure reference to Conan Doyle's own interest in spiritualism. In any event these pagan references are unnecessary since the reality of evil in the film is clear enough without them. Cecile quite simply is acting the role of the Romantic Fatal Woman in luring Sir Henry to his death.[12]

In the original novel Holmes and Watson decline an invitation to dinner at the Stapleton home because they supposedly must return to London. Here Holmes has injured his leg so he and Watson supposedly remain at Baskerville Hall. However, unlike the original novel in which Beryl refuses to carry out the deception, Cecile (Marla Landi) in the film is asked by Sir Henry to meet him and walk across the moor together to her house. She leads him to the ancient ruins where Sir Hugo met his fate. Sir Henry's own intentions are made clear when he attempts to kiss Cecile passionately in the deserted ruins. She lets him kiss her at first and then slaps him. She proceeds to indict him for the *real* curse of the Baskervilles, their lust for "peasant girls." She reminds him that they are in the place where Sir Hugo died. She reveals that his uncle Sir Charles had met his fate there as well "because he wanted me." She adds, "He died screaming. I know. I watched him." Cecile then informs Sir Henry that "the curse of the hound is on you!" She speaks almost as the avenging ghost of the first peasant girl who was the object of Sir Hugo's lust. Neither Sir Henry, nor presumably his uncle, have been guilty of the murderous designs of Sir Hugo. They have however been guilty of the same lust which motivated him: "then when lust has conceived, it gives birth to sin, and that sin, when it is fully grown, gives birth to death" (Epistle of James 1:15). Fisher's treatment makes it plain that Sir Henry is not a pure victim. His own desires and actions have contributed to his fate.

Fortunately for Sir Henry, Holmes and Watson have been following all this. As Cecile's father (Ewen Solen) unleashes the giant hound it springs at Sir Henry. Holmes and Watson fire at the beast. Stapleton, having unleashed the hound, madly tries to stop Holmes and Watson. He attacks Watson using Sir Hugo's dagger in spite of the fact that Watson clearly holds a gun. Watson shoots him and he is then attacked by the wounded hound who now turns on him and kills him. Cecile attempts to escape and sinks into the Grimpen Mire. Sir Henry, though badly shaken, has been saved from the twin threats of the hound and Cecile. The film ends with Holmes and Watson sharing tea back at Baker Street.

The Hound of the Baskervilles is one of the most perfectly realized of Fisher' films. In this picture Fisher further advances themes he had presented in the Frankenstein and Dracula pictures. Once again evil is attractive but deadly. Even Sir Hugo is an attractive figure physically in spite of his overt cruelty. Also the Baskerville victims are attracted to the evil which destroys them, as in the Dracula films especially. Rationality by itself offers no help against evil. The hero, Sherlock Holmes in this case, uses reason but understands ultimately that he is dealing with the irrational, evil itself.

Fisher's use of the hound itself is noteworthy. Nothing of the beast is seen at first, which in some ways enhances the film. The audience is very much aware of its presence through its howl and through the various characters' comments on it. Much, perhaps too much, has been written on the hound itself.[13] Its initial appearance unfortunately is a disappointment. A savage, spectral beast should have been shown, but what is given is a stationary shot of a great dane standing on a shadowy cliff. Many critics have scorned the actual beast of the title for this reason.[14] However once the hound springs into action there is a genuine, if rather melodramatic, excitement. One problem of present day critics is that so much is now known from books and interviews, published over the years, about the problems Fisher and his co-workers faced in bringing the hound itself to life, that all that background information now apparently colors their impression of what actually takes place on the screen. While Christopher Lee in his autobiography, *Tall, Dark and Grusome*, discusses the difficulties of motivating what had become a friendly great dane on the set to look frightening (and his account is really quite funny), the truth is the hound finally did perform to the extent that Lee was bitten on the arm by the beast and had to be taken briefly to the hospital.[15] So much for the hound being placid. The truth is that more of the hound is seen in Hammer's version than in most of the many versions made since. In some adaptations the hound looks like little more than a bear rug placed on top of Sir Henry while the actor screams for the camera's benefit.

For Fisher the hound is a symbol. It symbolizes the lust of the Baskervilles. Like original sin, especially in the view of St. Augustine, this lust is passed on from father to son.[16] In every case it is self-destructive. Neither Bishop Frankland, the man of faith, nor Dr. Mortimer, the man of science, perceive the lustful nature of the Baskervilles. Holmes, Fisher's man of wisdom, realizes that the real issue is "evil," which here could be seen as a code name for lust and its consequences. Fisher's *Hound of the*

Baskervilles then is a symbolic parable on the reality of lust, which, for Fisher (and the classic Christian tradition) is one of the most deadly forms which evil can take.

Three years after filming *Hound of the Baskervilles* Fisher returned to the theme of a curse that is passed on from one generation to the next. The film, *Curse of the Werewolf*, bears a number of structural parallels to *The Hound of the Baskervilles*. Where *Hound* shows the effect of a curse on a family, *The Curse of the Werewolf* shows its impact on an entire village.

The Curse of the Werewolf, like *Hound of the Baskervilles,* opens with a narrator and a prologue. This opening however is more ominous than forceful. A beggar (Richard Wordsworth) arrives at a village in Spain. The time is late eighteenth century. The beggar is puzzled because, although it is not Sunday, the streets are deserted and the church bell is tolling. Following a familiar Fisher pattern he enters a tavern. There he is informed that the town is observing the wedding of the Marquess and the villagers have been ordered to celebrate. The town spokesman (played by Francis De Wolff, the Dr. Mortimer of *Hound* in an uncredited appearance) also informs the beggar that no one in the inn can help him since the Marquess

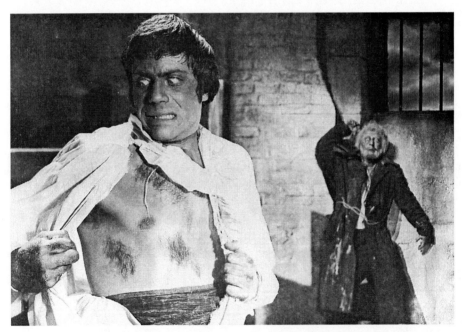

Leon (Oliver Reed) begins to change into a werewolf as a terrified fellow prisoner (Michael Ripper) looks on in *The Curse of the Werewolf,* Universal-International (1961).

has taken all their money. The parallel with *Hound of the Baskervilles* is strengthened by having the same actor warn of a corrupt nobleman. Fisher shows the wedding party in progress at the castle. The Marquess is played by British veteran character actor Anthony Dawson and he is clearly a kindred spirit to Sir Hugo Baskerville. While not as intense he is just as cruel. Unhappy with his chef, he throws a tray of food to the floor and then forces the poor man to pick it up. The bride (Josephine Llewellyn) is considerably younger than her husband and, while not a kidnapped victim as in *Hound,* she is certainly under the domination of her new husband.

The beggar makes the mistake of coming to the castle looking for alms. A servant at the door tries to warn him to leave before the Marquess sees him. The warning is not heeded. The Marquess demands to know who is there. The beggar is brought in and forced to become a humiliating spectacle for the Marquess and his guests. This group is less rowdy than Sir Hugo and his companions but their more aristocratic demeanor makes their cruelty sharper. The young bride tries to intercede for the poor beggar. In spite of this the poor man is thrown into the castle dungeon and left to rot. The only people who show him any kindness are the jailer and his little daughter who is mute.

The narrator continues the story, telling of the passing of years. The Marquess has driven his young bride to an early death by his cruelty. Debauchery and cruelty have taken a fearful toll on him and his face shows its ravages. In one of Fisher's most truly horrific scenes the old Marquess is shown picking dead skin from his white and scarred face. The beggar still languishes in the dungeon. The jailer has died but his mute daughter has grown into a voluptuous beauty (Yvonne Romain). Discovering this beauty within his household the still lecherous Marquess accosts her in his room. Repulsed, she flees from him. In anger the Marquess orders that she be thrown into the dungeon until she agrees to be "more friendly."

In the dungeon cell the young woman is confronted by the old beggar, now wild and hairy. He rapes her and then dies. She in turn signals to the jailers that she is ready to be released and returned to the Marquess. Brought again into the aristocrat's chamber she now hides a knife behind her. She kills the old man and escapes into the forest. The narrator continues the story, adding that she now was forced to live like an animal. In an effective sequence using a moving camera Fisher shows her running through the forest at night and then tracks to a daylight scene of a lake showing her collapsed body in the water. The narrator adds, "This is where I found her."

The narrator is then introduced in one of Fisher's scenes which combines physical beauty with the effects of human cruelty. Against the pastoral lake scene the body of the exhausted young woman is carried to the shore by the man who has narrated the prologue. The man is the town doctor, Don Alfredo Carido (Clifford Evans). He brings the woman to his home where he and his servant Teresa (Hira Talfred) care for her. They learn that the girl is pregnant, the result of her being raped by the beggar. Teresa expresses her concern that the young woman will give birth in December and fears the child could be born on Christmas Day. Don Alfredo remarks that surely such a possibility should be a cause for rejoicing rather than fear. Teresa responds that in the village of her youth there was a widespread fear that an unwanted child born on Christmas was an affront to heaven and could result in evil.

While *Curse of the Werewolf*, like Fisher's other horror films, has a literary source (this time Guy Endore's *Werewolf of Paris*), the film again draws on mythic sources which predate any literary version. In this case the fear of an unwanted birth on Christmas Day harks back to a medieval European belief. Of course the baby is in fact born on Christmas and the unfortunate mother dies following the birth. Fisher shows Teresa and a midwife using various herbs and scents to offset any evil presence, again showing the director's interest in ritual. In a notable shot the newborn infant is shown against the backdrop of a painting on the wall of the Madonna and child.

Fisher cuts to a scene of the child's baptism. In a long shot Don Alfredo and Teresa stand before a large baptismal font and a priest stands in the front of a gothic church. The priest recites the Lord's Prayer in Latin. He then prepares to baptize the infant. As he does so the sky outside the window turns dark and the water in the font churns. Don Alfredo and the priest peer into the font and see a demonic face. They realize it is "only" the reflection of a gargoyle on one of the stone columns overhead. In this one sequence Fisher has alerted the audience to the central issue of this film as well as furnished a powerful image of his own cinematic vision. The conflict of good and evil, or more particularly of Christ and Satan, is evoked in this memorable scene. The power of evil is seen in the darkening sky, the churning baptismal water and the gargoyle figure inside the church. However the disturbance is momentary. The holy sacrament (or sacred ritual) is completed finally in peace. This in effect summarizes Fisher's entire outlook. Evil is a genuine force which can even be felt in the center of religious faith. However evil cannot ultimately prevail. Its power is not overcome by the believers' own strength but by the power of God's Spirit manifested in sacred symbol and ritual.

Unfortunately, Teresa's worst fears are realized. The child as a young boy, christened Leon (Justin Walters), gives evidence of evil influences.

He is terrified at the sight of blood. While on a hunting trip he is forced to touch a dead squirrel and as a result finds blood on his fingers. Licking the fingers he finds the taste sweet. The child is also obsessed with bad dreams especially during the time of the full moon when evil spirits are rumored to be active. In addition to this, the bodies of goats and cats have been found in the village, apparently the victims of an attack by a wolf.

This movie still retains the triad, the "man-of-science-faith-wisdom," of other films of Fisher. Don Alfredo as a doctor is the inevitable figure of wisdom who gives the essential spiritual interpretation of surrounding events. The ineffectual man of faith figure is the priest who baptized Leon as a baby (John Gabriel). The pure "man of science" is the town's mayor, Don Enrique (Peter Sallis) who refuses to believe that Leon can be a werewolf. Don Alfredo, in a crucial sequence, goes to consult the priest regarding Leon's strange dreams. The priest explains that there are elemental spirits in the world which seek entrance into human beings to capture and destroy them. A child such as Leon is susceptible to the influence of such spirits because of the tragic circumstances surrounding his birth. "Can nothing be done?" Don Alfredo asks. The priest replies that the influence of these evil spirits cannot determine the outcome of a person's life. If a person is exposed to goodness and love the power of the spirits will be negated. However if evil is present their power is enhanced.

Such an explanation, needless to say, places this film in a whole different category from Hollywood's werewolf films. Hollywood's various "wolfman" and werewolf films were both more secular and more mechanically structured than *Curse of the Werewolf*. In those films the protagonist turned into a werewolf solely under the influence of the full moon.[17] Little more substantial is found in such 1980s demonstrations of special effects as *The Howling* and *An American Werewolf in London* and in the 1990s' more mainstream *Wolf* with Jack Nicholson and Michelle Pfeiffer. In none of these examples was there any discussion of "elemental spirits" on the power of goodness to offset the werewolf curse. Fisher's version, like so many of his films, explores the sources behind the legends being portrayed as well as adding his own Christian perspective.

Don Alfredo and Teresa set about trying to negate the impact of the evil spirits on young Leon. They are successful as Leon grows into adulthood without further incidents of bad dreams or local wolf attacks. As a young man, Leon (played now by Oliver Reed in one of his early roles) takes a job working in the wine company of a Don Fernando (Ewen Solen, who played Stapleton in *Hound*). Leon falls in love with Don Fernando's daughter Cristina (Catherine Fuller), who reciprocates his love. However

Cristina is betrothed by her father to a young nobleman named Dominique (George Woodbridge). Hence Leon and Cristina are forced to hide their love. A comment is in order on the character of Cristina. Fisher's films, as well as Hammer's output in general, were often criticized for stereotypical heroines with inevitably large, heaving bosoms. This is certainly true of the two young women who have appeared in the film up to this point, the Marquessa and the servant girl who is Leon's mother. Fisher admittedly is succumbing here to a female stereotype which Hammer Studios was all too eager to exploit (and would do so even more in subsequent films with such stars as Raquel Welch and Ursula Andress). Conversely, Cristina, while somewhat pretty, is far from being either beautiful or voluptuous. One notes here a Victorian tendency on Fisher's part to assume that the more virtuous a woman is, the less overtly sexual she will be. In Fisher's world, like St. Augustine's, sexuality is very close to sinfulness.

This view is apparent in a scene when Leon is separated from Cristina because she is required to be with her fiancé, Dominique. A friend entices Leon to go to a local tavern. It is the night of the full moon. Leon appears ill as he is surrounded by excesses of drinking and thinly veiled prostitution. A young woman invites him to her room "to make him feel better." Once Leon is on her bed a transformation begins to take place. When the woman goes to kiss him he bites her. She gets off the bed in disgust, thinking him perverted. Leon now is off camera. Fisher cuts to a shot of the tavern which clearly has become a center of vice. The next scene shows the young woman being strangled by a furry hand. Throughout this sequence Fisher never shows Leon's face. He is seen as a shadowy figure moving along the tops of buildings and attacking his victims as they emerge from the tavern. One of these victims is the "friend" who brought him to the tavern.

Here again lust is the gateway to sin. The curse, following the earlier warning of the priest, has come to fruition. As in *Hound* the effects of the curse are not automatic. The tendency toward sin is there, "lurking at the door" (Genesis 4:7). Yet it only springs into reality as the result of a certain kind of behavior. Fisher is affirming in good Augustinian fashion both original sin and human responsibility.

Leon awakens the next morning at the home of his stepfather and is horrified to learn the truth about himself. This truth however is not an implacable destiny. In a remarkable sequence Leon spends the next night of the full moon with Cristina. Unaware of his true dilemma she tries to comfort his anxiety. Fisher shows Leon lying down, resting his head in Cristina's lap while she strokes his hair. He falls asleep peacefully. There is no suggestion of sexual activity. He awakens the next morning in the same position. Cristina verifies that he slept throughout the night. In spite of the full moon he did not become a werewolf. Cristina's love prevented the transformation. Once again Fisher's conception of the "curse of the werewolf" is far more nuanced and insightful than the scores of films, both before and after this one, in which the effect of the full moon functions as mechanically as turning on a light switch.

Unfortunately the redemptive power of Cristina's love for Leon is not allowed to continue. Leon is accused of the murder of the girl whom he did indeed kill as the werewolf. Cristina's father also has become aware of his daughter's love for Leon and wants him removed so as not to upset his plans for Cristina to marry Dominique. Leon is imprisoned in the town jail. The priest and the mayor foolishly prevent Cristina from staying with Leon as the night of the full moon approaches. All warnings as to what may happen during the night of the full moon are ignored by them. As the light of the moon shines through his cell window the transformation begins. There is nothing this time to stop it. Now Fisher shows Leon's face as he metamorphosizes into a werewolf. A fellow prisoner is his first victim after which he escapes to terrorize the town.

Learning that Leon has become a werewolf, Don Alfredo loads his gun with a bullet fashioned from a silver crucifix. Appropriately Don Alfredo confronts his stepson in the belfry of the village church. Cristina looks on helplessly from below in the town square, surrounded by a mob of villagers who watch in fascination. Don Alfredo shoots and Leon collapses, grasping the bell rope of the church. Don Alfredo covers his son's werewolf face in death with his cloak. The crowd below rushes into the church presumably to view the body, leaving Cristina, seen from the long shot perspective of the church belfry, alone in the square. The film ends as it began with the tolling of a church bell.

The Curse of the Werewolf is arguably the film which introduces Fisher's period of greatest maturity as a director. It is a period which includes *Phantom of the Opera*; *Dracula, Prince of Darkness*; *The Gorgon*; *Frankenstein Created Woman* and, supremely, *The Devil Rides Out*. It is appropriate to consider this film in comparison with *The Hound of the Baskervilles* since both films share a number of structural similarities. Both deal with a curse which originates in the action of a cruel and lustful aristocrat. In both films the curse is activated by male lustful desire which leads to a number of murders. And of course in both the personification of the curse is a supernatural nocturnal beast who howls before attacking its victims. However the focus of the curse broadens in the two films. In *Hound* the curse only affects the Baskervilles and those who come close to them like the convict Seldon. In the *Werewolf* film an entire community feels

British publicity poster for *The Curse of the Werewolf*, Hammer (1961).

the impact of the curse. If the curse in the *Hound* represents original sin in the genitive sense (passed on from generation to generation), the curse in the *Werewolf* is seen in its extensive sense with its impact penetrating an entire village.

There are also important differences in the two films. The curse in the Werewolf film is genuinely supernatural while the Baskerville curse is only apparently so. There is no dominant Van Helsing–type hero in *Werewolf*. More significantly, while the focus of the *Hound* is evil in some general primordial sense, the evil of the *Werewolf* is more specific in its description of "elemental spirits." Christian imagery is also very specific in *Werewolf* as it was in the Dracula films. Love kills as well as protects in *Curse of the Werewolf*. The love of Cristina is a temporary antidote to the influences of evil. The real conquest of evil must come from the cross. Again, as in *Dracula*, the power of the cross lies in itself, not in the one who holds the cross. Leon is killed but he dies within the confines of the church. Fisher's final shot of Cristina left alone in the town square is a bittersweet one. Where the tolling of the bell at the opening of the film set the stage for cruel lust, its tolling at the end underscores the image of a figure who represents tender love. For Fisher, such love is the final goal of the conquest of evil. The tragedy of Leon's death shows that the victory over evil in this film is real but incomplete.

Such is not the case in *The Devil Rides Out*, a film which justifiably lays claim to being Fisher's finest work, a masterpiece of the supernatural on film. *The Devil Rides Out*, based on a novel by Dennis Wheatley, was released in Britain in 1967 and the following year in the U.S.A. with the title *The Devil's Bride*. Nowhere else in Fisher's corpus, nor in any other film of the past half century, can a more powerful example be found of the total conquest of Christianity over the forces of evil. This was one of Fisher's last films and was indeed the last he would make with Christopher Lee. In this perhaps supreme achievement of his career he had the benefit of an excellent cast including Charles Gray as the satanist Mocata as well as a fine script by the outstanding fantasy screenwriter Richard Matheson.[18] In this film, The "Devil's Curse" does its worst but it is more than matched by the power of the cross.

The Devil Rides Out does not begin with the usual prologue but plunges right into the central story. The period setting is not Victorian but early twentieth century Britain in the 1920s. The film's hero, the Duc De Richleau (Christopher Lee), represents the ultimate evolution of the mystical-rational spiritual warrior first seen in Dr. Van Helsing. As the film opens, De Richleau confides to a friend, Rex Van Ryn (Leon Greene), that he is concerned about a mutual friend of theirs, a young man named Simon Aron (Patrick Mower). De Richleau fears that Simon is becoming reclusive and distant. De Richleau persuades Rex to accompany him to Simon's house to see how their young friend is doing. Upon their arrival it appears that a formal social gathering is taking place. Among the guests is a distinguished gentleman known as Mocata (Charles Gray). The unexpected arrival of the two friends at Simon's house seems to have upset the other guests for some reason. The main concern appears to be that there are now more than 13 people present. De Richleau and Rex discover this concern in speaking to an ethereal young woman named Tanith (Nike Arrighi). "There can't *possibly* be more than 13 guests," she insists.

Their friend Simon has been talking with Mr. Mocata. Simon proceeds to explain to the two of them that this is a closed meeting of an astronomical society and he unfortunately must ask them to leave. Before going De Richleau insists on seeing Simon's upstairs observatory. The goat's head design on the floor and a basket containing a rooster and a hen confirms his worst fears. Simon has become involved with a witchcraft cult. The evening's "meeting" will involve black magic. Hence the requirement of only 13 in attendance. De Richleau implores Simon to leave the house immediately with him and Rex. Simon says that is not possible. De Richleau suddenly punches him, knocking him unconscious. The two men manage to escape the house with its insensible host and find safety in their car. Simon is then hypnotized by De Richleau and laid to rest in a bedroom of De Richleau's house with a crucifix around his neck for protection (as in the Dracula films). Unfortunately some other influence counters De Richleau's hypnotic trance and Simon begins choking himself to death with the chain of the crucifix. A servant, hearing him gagging, comes to his aid and of course removes the crucifix. Moments later Simon is gone.

Rex is puzzled by De Richleau's distress at all this. De Richleau asks him if he believes in evil. Rex answers that he does as an idea. "That's where you're wrong!" snaps De Richleau. For him evil is a supernatural power. The man Mocata is a master of the black arts, and Simon's soul is imperiled. Once Simon is baptized into the devil cult he will be lost to them forever, warns De Richleau. The two men return to Simon's house looking for clues regarding the cult and Simon's whereabouts. Visiting the observatory again, they encounter an evil spirit who gains control over Rex. The spirit departs when De Richleau throws a cross at it. Rex is now convinced that De Richleau is right about the forces of evil. Together the two men make plans to rescue Simon before it is too late.

The Devil Rides Out summarizes all of Fisher's previous work on vampires, curses and the reality of evil. A number of motifs from earlier films are present. The evil figure, Mocata, is charming, well dressed and pleasant. His antagonist, the Duc De Richleau, is a combination of Van Helsing, Father Sandor and Sherlock Holmes. The supernatural battle focuses on young attractive victims who are being enticed into a web of evil. The ultimate source of power is God, symbolized by the cross. However this film adds considerably to Fisher's previous work. Narrative is at a minimum. The film consists of a number of confrontations between De Richleau and his supporters and Mocata's followers. The focus of these confrontations are Simon and the girl Tanith. Both are scheduled to be baptized into the Devil's cult of which Mocata is the high priest.

The fascination and power of this film lie in its visual confrontations between good and evil, God and Satan, symbolized by De Richleau and Mocata. Fisher is at his strongest as a director in this film, breaking away from what was becoming a formula at Hammer. The emphasis on blood and sex (symbolized by incredibly endowed heroines) of earlier films is minimized. One could argue that Fisher was able to use or offset those emphases in previous films. Fortunately, in this work, such distractions are absent. Nike Arrighi is an appropriate actress for the somewhat mystical Tanith. She has none of the overt sexuality of the French actresses, all of whom interestingly were named Yvonne (Yvonne Furneaux [*The Mummy*], Yvonne Monlaur [*Brides of Dracula*], Yvonne Romain [*Curse of the Werewolf*], whom Hammer Studios had been promoting to enhance the commercial appeal of their films.

Fisher creates a dreamlike atmosphere in this film reminiscent of Charles Williams' novels. The picture structurally is built around four specific confrontations. In the first, Rex follows the devil worshippers to a forest where Simon and Tanith are to be baptized into the cult. He sneaks back to the main road and telephones De Richleau. They return to the forest scene to find the black sabbath in progress. Goat's blood is spilled on Tanith's dress and a woman cavorts seductively around Simon. Fisher is showing the essence of the cult. In response to the incantation of Mocata, a figure in a goat's head suddenly appears. "It's the goat of Mendes," De Richleau whispers to Rex, "the devil himself!" In a remarkable sequence De Richleau drives his car with its headlights beaming into the middle of the frenzied group. As he recites the 91st Psalm ("He that dwelleth in the secret place of the most High shall abide under the shadow of the Almighty..."), Rex throws a crucifix at the goat. It vanishes and in the confusion Simon and Tanith are rescued.

In the second confrontation Mocata visits the home of De Richleau's niece Marie and her husband Richard (Sarah Lawson and Paul Eddington), where Simon and Tanith are resting after their escape. De Richleau has left, Holmes-like, to do some further investigation. Afraid that something might happen, De Richleau assigns Richard to watch Simon and Rex to watch Tanith. Rex is beginning to fall in love with Tanith. Mocata arrives after De Richleau leaves and sits down to talk with Marie. In an extraordinary sequence which has been much discussed, Mocata begins to hypnotize Marie with his soothing voice, telling her that magic has been stereotyped and misunderstood.[19] Her uncle, De Richleau, has filled her head with a lot of "nonsense." Fisher matches Mocata's hypnotic voice with his carefully controlled shooting of the sequence which maintains a precise rhythm between shots of Mocata speaking and Marie listening. The key to the scene is, as David Pirie rightly notes, Marie's absent-minded handling of her little daughter's doll throughout the sequence.[20] While this is going on downstairs, Simon and Tanith are responding to hypnotic spells upstairs and are about to murder their respective bodyguards. Fisher flawlessly intercuts all this action to create a tremendously suspenseful episode. The spell is broken abruptly when Marie's daughter, Peggy (Rosalyn Landor), enters the room apparently looking for her doll. Suddenly, Simon and Tanith awaken from their spells, sparing the lives of Richard and Rex, and Marie, likewise recovered, orders Mocata out of her house.

The third confrontation finds De Richleau, Simon, Marie and Richard in a giant circle which De Richleau has drawn on the floor of the home's library. The circle is surrounded with biblical phrases in Greek, Hebrew and Latin. De Richleau insists they must pass the night inside the circle for safety since he now fears a direct demonic assault. Rex is outside in a wood hut with Tanith who has fled the group after realizing that she has become Mocata's medium and he is endangering the rest through her. Marie and Richard's daughter, Peggy, is upstairs in her room with one of the servants. As the nightly vigil inside the circle begins, Richard expresses his thought that this is all "foolishness." His skepticism (as another "man of science") is the first assault of evil, De Richleau warns. In this comment Fisher's warnings against Enlightenment rationalism are clearly summarized.

Throughout the night the four spiritual warriors are assailed with a host of false images designed to lure them out of the protective circle. The most frightening of which is little Peggy being threatened by a giant tarantula. "It's not Peggy!" screams De Richleau as he forcibly tries to keep the distraught parents inside the circle. When a pitcher of water is thrown at the image it disappears. Finally, in perhaps the most startling scene in Fisher's career, the Angel of Death enters on horseback like a knight out of medieval lore. The horse and rider are slightly in slow motion and their movements are repeated by the simple device of moving the film backwards and forwards. The net effect creates a dreamlike sensation with the force of a nightmare. The Angel of Death is no illusion. It is real and it has come for those inside the circle. De Richleau speaks a powerful exorcism in Latin which he only dares to speak at the precise moment of greatest peril. The angel departs just as its dread skull face is revealed.

Immediately following this the group learns that Tanith is dead, taken by the Angel of Death. Furthermore Peggy has been kidnapped by Mocata's followers. This sets up the fourth and last confrontation. In order to learn where Peggy has been taken, De Richleau hypnotizes Marie and through her contacts the spirit of Tanith. He begins by asking the spirit, "Do you acknowledge our Lord Jesus Christ?" The spirit of Tanith answers "yes" through Marie's mouth. Even with this protection, the spirit is wary of following the spirits associated with Mocata. Enough information is given however to ascertain Peggy's location.

As De Richleau and his friends arrive at Mocata's headquarters Fisher's ultimate demonic ritual is revealed: the intended sacrifice of a little girl. Peggy is strapped to a sacrificial table and Mocata prepares to slit her throat. The rest of the worshippers are gathered around to witness the sacrifice. De Richleau, Rex, Simon and the frantic parents are prevented by the Satanists from getting close to Peggy. Mocata intends to sacrifice Peggy in the name of the Egyptian god of evil, Set, so that he can exchange her soul for that of Tanith. Marie pleads with De Richleau to pronounce again the ritual words which delivered them from the Angel of Death. De Richleau says that it is too risky. They could all be destroyed. There seems to be no hope.

Then, in a sequence that almost defies analysis, the voice of Tanith speaks again through Marie: "Only those who love without desire will be granted power in the darkest hour." In a remarkable scene in which acting, directing and music are all carefully integrated, Marie, possessed again of the spirit of Tanith, moves down a stairway to the platform where Peggy is about to be executed. Everyone stands aside restrained in the grip of some unseen power. Marie helps Peggy off the sacrificial altar and in the voice of Tanith instructs her to speak the words of the same ritual which exorcised the Angel of Death. The child repeats the words which invoke the archangel Uriel. Suddenly lighting strikes the altar. Fire breaks out on the platform. A curtain backdrop goes up in flame as a large gold cross appears on the back wall. Mocata and the devil worshippers writhe in torment. The next moment they are gone without a trace. De Richleau and his friends stand now alone in the room with no evidence of the devil worshippers, their altar or the flames that consumed them. All that remains is the cross on the wall. Fisher then cuts to De Richleau, Simon, Richard and Marie inside the circle in the library. Time has been reversed. They have reawakened the morning of the same day. Only now Tanith is alive and well. So is Peggy. So are they all. The Angel of Death has taken Mocata. "Thank God," says Simon. "Yes, Simon," adds De Richleau, "He is the One we must thank." With this appropriate comment Fisher's greatest film ends.

The Devil Rides Out incorporates the best of British supernatural fantasy. It draws not only on Dennis Wheatley's original novel (which again has been adapted to Fisher's vision) but also on Charles Williams and C. S. Lewis. This film portrays a universe in which spiritual realities underlie all physical reality. The devil's curse here has a cosmic dimension. The world of time and space is penetrated by it. The curse though is thoroughly overcome by the power of the cross. All of life, however, is caught up in the cosmic struggle. The rationalists who deny the existence of the supernatural only become unwitting allies of the power of evil. There is no scientific explanation of supernatural reality. It simply exists and its power can be felt. All spiritual reality plays into the conflict between Christ and Satan. De Richleau can invoke Osiris, the "good" god of ancient Egypt, just as Mocata invokes Set, Osiris' evil brother. As C.S. Lewis would say, all mythology derives from an ultimate theology.[21] Fisher's vision integrates a sustained interaction between spiritual and physical, evil and good. Yet there can be no doubt about the ultimate focus of this vision. It is the cross of Christ which in the words of the apostle Paul reconciles all things to God "whether on earth or in heaven" (Epistle to the Colossians 1:20) and delivers man from "this present evil world" (Epistle to the Galatians 1:4). The cross is the unshakable hope in the confrontation with a very real spiritual darkness. *The Devil Rides Out* is a masterful statement of this hope.

Nevertheless, the film as an ultimate statement of Fisher's own spiritual outlooks is not beyond criticism. So much in Fisher's spiritual universe depends on the heroic figure of a De Richleau–like character, the so called "man of wisdom." As powerful and universal as the cross is, its influence seems overdependent on a spiritual champion. What happens when such a person is not available, or worse, is untrustworthy? How is the power of the cross mediated then, especially given Fisher's apparent lack of confidence in the institutional church and its clergy? (One thinks of the later Hammer film also based on a Dennis Wheatly novel, *To the Devil a Daughter*, in which Christopher Lee's priest is no Christian warrior but a disguised satanist himself.) Roman Polanski could easily satirize Fisher by making the Van Helsing–De Richleau hero into a dimwitted old fool as he did in *The Fearless Vampire Killers* (1967). *The Exorcist* (1973) made its spiritual hero into a tired old man whose heart gives out in the struggle. Fisher's confidence would no doubt remain, given his faith in the fundamental, external power of the cross. In reality, De Richleau himself does very little at the climax of *The Devil Rides Out*. Still the question persists, does Fisher present Christianity as a religion of unique spiritual heroes? (A complete answer to this question will have to await a later discussion of the whole Redeemer Hero motif in Fisher.)

The Devil Rides Out virtually overwhelms the viewer with spiritual details. Rites, rituals, archangels and even Egyptian deities are all referred to. While this may underscore a mystical orientation, it also runs the risk of becoming spiritual mumbojumbo in which religious life becomes more esoteric than real. Special effects, again, are something of a drawback even allowing for the pre-computer era in which the picture was filmed. Depictions of goat demons and giant tarantulas, like vampire bats and hell hounds, are difficult to film at best. The situation was not helped by Hammer's somewhat limited resources in the area of special effects.

The cross has always been a very concrete symbol for Fisher and this is understandable, given his equally concrete view of evil. However, the frequent use of the cross in *The Devil Rides Out* almost makes it seem like a spiritual hand grenade blowing up evil spirits. Finally the reference to "those who love without desire" reinforces the Augustinian view that sexual desire, even in the context of marriage, is always impure to some extent.

These reservations aside, *The Devil Rides Out* remains a truly remarkable film. As an allegory of the struggle between good and evil it achieves an almost poetic level. It is supremely a film of spiritual hope. Fisher could not have known in 1967 that horror films would soon lose any sense of hope in what would become a depressing celebration of evil. This only makes *The Devil Rides Out* a film to be appreciated more now than when it was first released.

Notes

1. Eyles, Adkinison, Fry, op. cit., pp. 22–33.
2. This is true of several stories such as "The Devil's Foot," "The Sussex Vampire" and "The Creeping Man." Like *Hound* these are only apparently supernatural. Holmes solves each case by finding a rational explanation for the alleged supernatural "event."
3. Rigby, Jonathan. *English Gothic*, p. 58.
4. McCarty, John. *The Modern Horror Film*, p. 42.
5. *Ibid.*, Hardy, Phil, ed., *The Overlook Film Encyclopedia: Horror*, p. 114.
6. Fisher's work actually predates much of the French New Wave which does not actually begin until 1959 with François Truffaut's *The 400 Blows* and Jean-Luc Godard's *Breathless*.
7. Miller, Mark A. *Christopher Lee and Peter Cushing and Horror Cinema*, p. 101.
8. This was a common practice in Hammer Films, cf. Rigby, Jonathan, p. 129.
9. Pohle, Robert W., Jr., and Hart, Douglas C. *Sherlock Holmes on the Screen*, p. 204.
10. Rigby, p. 57.
11. Miller, p. 101.
12. Pirie, p. 57.
13. Mark Miller summarizes most of the objections. See Miller, pp. 108–109.
14. Steinbrunner, Chris, and Michaels, Norman. *The Films of Sherlock Holmes*, p. 200.
15. Interestingly enough these objections regarding animals are not new in Sherlock Holmes adaptations. Conan Doyle's own theatrical adaptation of "The Speckled Band" apparently used a real snake which some critics scorned as a "fake." See Higham, Charles, *The Adventures of Conan Doyle*, p. 192.
16. Augustine's view of original sin is that it is genetically transferred from parent to child.
17. This is the case specifically with Universal's Wolf Man films made in the 1940s with Lon Chaney, Jr.
18. Matheson's screenplay credits include such outstanding films as *The Incredible Shrinking Man* (1957), *House of Usher* (1960), *The Pit and the Pendulum* and *The Omega Man* (1971).
19. Everson, William K. *More Classics of the Horror Film*, p. 175.
20. Pirie, pp. 61–63.
21. Lewis, C.S. "Myth Became Fact," in *God in the Dock*, pp. 63–67.

Chapter Four

THE ANCIENT CURSE

The Mummy (1959) was Fisher's first film that was overtly a remake of one of Universal Studios' original horror movies. While Universal had originally done Frankenstein, Dracula, the Werewolf and Sherlock Holmes, Fisher's versions of these classics bore little, if any, resemblance to their Hollywood antecedents. *The Mummy* was different. Unlike previous films which had clear literary origins, *The Mummy* was a screen original. Actually Universal had made a number of films around the figure of the Mummy (as they had also done with Frankenstein, Dracula and the Wolfman). The original *Mummy* was filmed in 1932 by Karl Freund, one of the veterans of the German horror films of the 1920s. It starred Boris Karloff as a mummified Egyptian high priest who is brought back to life accidentally in the twentieth century and goes in search of the reincarnation of his lost love. Universal continued the theme a decade later in a series of "B" films with Lon Chaney, Jr., playing an overweight shuffling Mummy forever in search of his reincarnated princess Anaka. Jimmy Sangster, who had scripted both *Curse of Frankenstein* and *Horror of Dracula*, drew on elements from all the Universal Mummy films to write the screenplay for Hammer Studios' remake of *The Mummy*.

From the outset a number of changes were introduced. Most significantly, the treatment of the Mummy itself was strikingly different. Rather than a slow moving or shuffling figure, the Mummy as played by Christopher Lee was an aggressive, rapid moving angel of death. Fisher's *The Mummy* contains some of his best Technicolor scenes in contrast to the moody black and white of the Karloff version. Adapting *The Mummy* to Fisher's previous series at Hammer, the film is set in the Victorian period with most of the action taking place in England. Fisher's most distinctive approach to the story, not surprisingly, lay in his juxtaposition of a Christian England with the ancient religion of Egypt. This juxtaposition is epitomized in his treatment of the dual characters of Isobel Banning,

102

The Mummy, Hammer (1959).

wife of the hero John Banning, and Anaka, the ancient Egyptian priestess. Both characters are played by Yvonne Furneaux, the best of the glamorous French actresses which Hammer Studios were using in an attempt to spice up their films. Yvonne Furneaux, in contrast to many of the others Fisher was compelled to use, was an actress of real merit. Following this film she would have leading roles in such notable pictures as Federico Fellini's *La Dolce Vita* (1960) and Roman Polanski's *Repulsion* (1965), among others. Here she plays the first of two women in Fisher films who are apparently the reincarnation of some ancient goddess. To understand the significance of this figure for Fisher one needs to consider his treatment of *The Mummy* and see how it compares and contrasts with the earlier Universal films.

Superficially, the structure of the *Mummy* follows the same plot outline as the Universal Mummy films. In ancient Egypt a beautiful princess dies an untimely death. Her lover, an Egyptian high priest, tries to use magic to bring her back to life. His stealing a forbidden scroll of life is considered blasphemous and he is caught in the act before he is able to resurrect the princess. As punishment he is buried alive as a mummy. Centuries later when archaeologists discover, and thereby desecrate, the tomb of the Princess Anaka the mummified high priest comes to life as one of the archaeologists discovers and reads the ancient Scroll of Thoth.

The Mummy, once revived, goes on a twofold quest. First, he attempts to kill those who dared enter the tomb of Anaka and, second, he searches for the present-day woman who is the reincarnation of Anaka. This essential story, which was used by Universal in several films, draws on some of the same gothic roots Fisher had used in previous films. Mummies and Egyptian princesses could be found in Bram Stoker's *Jewel of the Seven Stars* as well as Arthur Conan Doyle's short stories, "Lot No. 249" and "The Ring of Thoth." These works, at best, however were distant sources of inspiration for the various Universal scriptwriters whose efforts were further adapted by Hammer's Jimmy Sangster, working again with Fisher.

There are several differences between the Universal Mummy films and Fisher's version. Most notable is the introduction of a young hero, John Banning (Peter Cushing). Banning is the son of the archaeologist, Stephen Banning, who finds the tomb of Anaka. It is the senior Banning who enters the ancient tomb, finds the forbidden scroll, reads it and unwittingly brings the Mummy to life. Confronted with the resuscitated Mummy, Stephen Banning (played by the distinguished character actor, Sir Felix Aylmer) goes mad. While this scene is shown directly and powerfully in Universal's *The Mummy* (1932), Fisher treats it indirectly. In Fisher's version the Mummy is not shown coming to life. The audience hears only the screams of Professor Banning from outside the tomb. John Banning in this crucial sequence is not with his father because of a leg injury. Those who rush to Professor Banning's aid find only an empty compartment where the Mummy was kept and no trace of the Mummy itself. Fisher introduces the Mummy dramatically by showing him rise as a black figure from a greenish-purple bog in England. This sequence is greatly enhanced by Jack Asher's Technicolor camera and is totally unlike anything in the Universal films. Once revived, the Mummy proceeds to track down those who defaced the tomb of Anaka. As in the Universal originals, he is guided by a present-day Egyptian high priest named in this case Mehemet (George Pastell).

The leading character of John Banning shifts the focus completely in Fisher's treatment. Like his father he is an archaeologist. He is also knowledgeable in the field of Egyptian religion. He has studied the "cult" of Karnak, the Egyptian god whom the Mummy serves. Anaka is a high priestess of Karnak. Her feathered costume suggests the great goddess, Isis (Karnak in actuality is the name of an Egyptian temple not a god). There is nothing overtly Christian about John Banning but his character clearly suggests the Van Helsing–Sherlock Holmes figure of other Peter Cushing portrayals.

The Mummy is an interesting picture in Fisher's development. In this film, theme is more important than narrative. Fisher's first "gothic films" for Hammer were based on famous literary works which, as noted, were adapted to fit Fisher's outlook. *The Mummy*, unlike *Curse of Frankenstein*, *Dracula* and *Hound of the Baskervilles*, is clearly a remake of an earlier film (or films in this case). The narrative of the film is not as central as it was in his more literary based Hammer productions. Fisher appears more interested in subject and treatment than in plot development. This is why the introduction of the character of John Banning is so significant. Banning is both hero and chorus. He narrates crucial parts of the story. He tells the audience the origin of the mummy as well as deciphering what happened to his father in Anaka's tomb. More importantly, he relates what he thinks of the religion of ancient Egypt. It is the perspective on Egyptian beliefs that is central to Fisher's film.

The earlier Universal films had assumed the reality of Egyptian gods and curses as a matter of course. This was consonant with their naive acceptance of vampires and werewolves. In reality, however, Universal's films did not emphasize the supernatural. More accustomed to the scientific orientation of the 1930s and 1940s, their "horror" films had emphasized science fiction and human cruelty rather than the supernatural. Outside of Dracula, the majority of their considerable horror output focused on science gone amuck (e.g., Frankenstein and an assortment of mad scientists) and crazed figures bent on revenge (e.g., Bela Lugosi as an Edgar Allan Poe–obsessed surgeon in *The Raven* [1935]). Even the treatment of the Wolfman focuses more on the psychological and in *House of Dracula*, Lawrence Talbot, the Wolfman, is psychologically cured. It is striking to note that Boris Karloff and Bela Lugosi in their many films together never once appeared in a film dealing directly with the supernatural.[1] This is very different from their successors, Peter Cushing and Christopher Lee.

In reality, Universal Studios never seemed very interested in the supernatural. This is why its treatment in their films has a perfunctory quality as noted earlier in their mechanical approach to the full moon in the Wolfman series. Their Mummy pictures are equally perfunctory. The curse on Anaka's tomb and the resurrection of the Mummy are handled with the sort of fantasy approach one expects from *Peter Pan*. The problem of evil or religious belief is never really explored (as it was in Rouben Mamoulian's *Dr. Jekyll and Mr. Hyde* made at Paramount after Universal's *Dracula* and *Frankenstein*). So the heroine in Universal's *The Mummy* can appeal to a statue of Isis in order to be saved from Boris Karloff's revived high priest. In succeeding films in the series, the spirit of Anaka is inevitably reincarnated in a variety of modern-day heroines, one of whom even turns into a mummy herself when carried into a swamp.

The tone of Universal's films is essentially agnostic, again reflecting the more sophisticated attitude of their period. European directors working at Universal — such as James Whale, Edgar G. Ulmer, Karl Freund and Robert Siodmak — seem indifferent at best to the issue of religion. Occasionally their approach is cynical (as in Whale's *Bride of Frankenstein*). From this perspective there is no contradiction in Universal's presenting the cross as a symbol against evil in *Dracula* and then a year later using symbols of Isis to the same effect in *The Mummy*. All supernatural images operate on an essentially equal level of myth and fantasy.

A debate has been going on for over forty years in film circles regarding the relative merits of Universal vs. Hammer Studios in their approach to gothic horror films. To this writer's knowledge no one has mentioned the essential thematic difference between Universal and the Hammer approach exemplified by Fisher. Whereas Universal's approach to the supernatural is essentially irreligious and agnostic, Hammer's is decidedly religious and specifically Christian. In Fisher's films non–Christian religions are either demonic or illusory. This is very evident in *The Mummy* since it is the one clear example of Fisher remaking a Universal film.

Universal's *The Mummy* accepts the reality of the goddess Isis as a spiritual force for good. The image of Isis protects hero and heroine against the malevolent Im-ho-tep (Boris Karloff). The statue of Isis rescues the heroine at the film's climax. The film also accepts the idea of reincarnation. The heroine, Helen Grosvenor (Zita Johann), really is the reincarnation of the ancient priestess Anaka. Any reference to Christianity, direct or indirect, in the Universal Mummy series is simply out of place. These films operate within the context of Egyptian beliefs which, as far as Universal is concerned, is no more or less mythological than the Christian cross or Tibetan plants that cure werewolves. Ironically, the whole notion of Egyptian goddesses has taken on a much more contemporary note in today's world with the revival of interest in the ancient goddess figure in contemporary feminism. Gloria Steinem in her book *Revolution from Within* speaks of having a spiritual experience visiting an ancient temple of the Egyptian goddess Nut.[2]

Fisher's approach to Egyptian deities is, not surprisingly, quite different. While Christianity is not specifically mentioned in *The Mummy*, its presence is implied throughout. Firstly, the bulk of the action takes place in a Victorian, and nominally Christian, England rather than in Egypt. Secondly, Fisher's film takes a decidedly critical view of Egyptian gods and goddesses. In a remarkable scene, not found in any of the Universal Mummy pictures, John Banning goes to visit the Egyptian priest, Mehemet. At this point in the story, Banning knows the mummy is real and has been revived. He strongly suspects Mehemet is involved and is deliberately trying to provoke him. Peter Cushing as Banning is at his best in this scene. He casually dismisses the whole religion of "the great god Karnak" as something no intelligent person could believe. In response to Mehemet's question, "Does it not occur to you, Mr. Banning, that this 'religion' could inspire a profound and deep devotion?" Banning offhandedly replies, "It occurred to me but I dismissed it."

The scene works on two levels. Banning is being intentionally caustic trying to goad Mehemet into action that will betray him as the link to the Mummy. On another level, however, the sequence gives Hammer's (and Fisher's) most distinguished actor a ripe series of lines in which he dismisses, in effect, ancient Egyptian religion as false and insubstantial. This is consistent with the handling of the prologue which details the death of the Princess Anaka and the origin of the Mummy's curse. This sequence in Fisher's version is far more elaborate than in the Universal film. Fisher is at pains to emphasize that the religion of the "great god Karnak" (essentially a pseudonym for Osiris) is little more than a bloodthirsty cult, not unlike the cult of the Indian goddess Kali which Fisher portrayed in the film which followed this one, *The Stranglers of Bombay*. The untimely death of Anaka is presented by Fisher as the occasion for an orgy of sacrifice and murder. The cruelty culminates with the high priest Kharis having his tongue ripped out before being buried alive. Fisher's negative treatment of Egyptian religion is vulnerable to charges of caricature and colonialism.[3] In today's allegedly more "tolerant" and "diverse" context, Fisher's central focus on Christian faith can be dismissed as simply intolerant. Certainly such post-modern concerns never occurred to Fisher in 1959 but, nonetheless, if they had, he would emphasize that a religion, paraphrasing Jesus, is known by its fruits.[4] For Fisher Christianity is the religion of forgiveness and redemption and it alone has the power to overcome evil and lead to goodness. Pagan religions, Egyptian or otherwise, ultimately celebrate bloodshed and power. They too often become evil themselves. Fisher in the 1950s could point to the recent memory of Nazi Germany and the Cold War Soviet Union as examples of modern "pagan" religion. Nor was Fisher unaware that Christianity itself could become corrupt or ineffectual as can be seen from his less than flattering portrayals of institutional religious figures. Yet for him this was not Christianity's essence. Fisher's rational mystic heroes—celibate and obsessive as they invariably are — are nonetheless expressions of Christian love and commitment, rescuing and indeed saving those in the deadly grip of evil. Fisher never articulated such a stance explicitly in any of his interviews but it is implicit in the "world view" expressed in his films. Before Fisher's views are too easily dismissed, it is well to remember that his basic Christian outlook was shared by a number of his more sophisticated contemporaries including T.S. Eliot, Dorothy L. Sayers and C.S. Lewis. Even those today who champion diversity must still wrestle with such historic "religious" practices as human sacrifice and the mistreatment of women and children.[5] Fisher clearly believed that not all religious expressions are equally true or beneficial. This is consistent with his overall Christian outlook. Granting his rather naive view of British colonialism (seen here and also in *Stranglers of Bombay*), he nonetheless took religion seriously and saw it either as an expression of God's grace or the Devil's malevolence.

Fisher's treatment of Princess Anaka is a prime example. Universal had no reservation in presenting the heroines of their various Mummy films as genuine reincarnations of the ancient princess Anaka, priestess of "Karnak" and ultimately the great goddess Isis. The figure of Isis is an imposing one found throughout the ancient world. Isis is one form among many of a female deity as old as civilization itself. One of her most famous descriptions occurs in *The Golden Ass* written by Lucius Apuleius in the second century:

> I am she that is the mother of all things, mistress and governess of all the elements, the initial progeny of worlds, chief of the powers divine, queen of all that are in hell, the principal of them that dwell in heaven, manifested alone and under one form of all the gods and goddesses. At my will the planets of the sky, the wholesome winds of the seas, and the lamentable silences of hell are disposed; my name, my divinity is adored throughout the world, in divers manners, in variable customs, and by many names.[6]

For Fisher this character represents a dangerous illusion. She justifies immorality and blood sacrifice. Yet being an illusion, repudiated by the truth of Christian faith, she has no ultimate spiritual reality. To the extent her cult has any power it is demonic.

Given all this it is consistent that Fisher reduces the status of the goddess and her various reincarnations to nothing more than a superficial image. Banning's wife Isobel is identical to Princess Anaka (both are played by Yvonne Furneaux). However the resemblance is coincidental, nothing more. As a narrative point this is a far-fetched contrivance but at a thematic level it is extremely revealing. In Fisher's version there is no reincarnation. Isobel Banning may look like Princess Anaka but she is *not* Anaka. This point is made very clear in two parallel scenes. The first time the Mummy tries to kill Banning his wife appears in a nightgown with her long hair draped over her shoulders. In shock, she screams, "No! Stop!"

The Mummy believes her to be Princess Anaka and so follows her orders. A second time she is dressed for an evening out with her hair pulled back. This time the Mummy does not see her resemblance to Anaka and therefore ignores her protestations. Her husband tells her to let down her hair (a classic fairy tale device as in "Rapunzel"). She does so and again orders the Mummy to stop. This time he responds because the resemblance to Anaka becomes evident with her hair down. Mehemet tries to kill her because he realizes that the Mummy is being confused by a superficial resemblance. The Mummy, thinking the priest is attacking Anaka, kills him and carries her off. The Mummy brings Isobel into a bog. In response to her husband's instruction, she commands him to set her down. He does so and she escapes. The Mummy is then shot repeatedly by the police and sinks into the mire.

Isobel Banning only looks like Princess Anaka. There the resemblance ends. Fisher here dismisses one of the core themes of the Universal Mummy series, that of the wandering spirit of Anaka inhabiting present-day women.[7] In this respect Fisher had demythologized the story. (To say this is not to minimize the role of screenwriter Jimmy Sangster. Fisher's hand in the story development of his films is supported by the continuity of certain themes despite working with different screenwriters. As noted, in earlier films such as *Four Sided Triangle* Fisher had received screenplay credit. There is no reason to doubt his role was any less in later films.) The supernatural is present in *The Mummy* but it is both demonic and limited. Fisher, as a Christian, could not embrace reincarnation so it is not surprising that it is deleted from the film. Isis herself is also absent.

A final word on *The Mummy* concerns the role of women in this and other Fisher films. Here the female character is central to the story. In the twin characters of Princess Anaka and Isobel Banning Fisher establishes a traditional Christian dichotomy. Anaka as a goddess figure is a ruling princess. Like Kali, she rules over a bloody cult strongly based on human sacrifice. In this respect Fisher is essentially correct historically. The goddess, contrary to contemporary attempts to see her as a feminist champion, was a dark, fearful character, capricious and associated with ritual prostitution as well as human sacrifice.[8] She appears in the Hebrew scriptures as Astarte and Ashtoreth, destructive deities in Israel's history. Isobel Banning, on the other hand, is the devoted, obedient wife. Fisher in 1959 could scarcely conceive of the feminist issues of the past 30 years. Clearly for him the ideal woman was a devoted wife and mother obediently supporting her husband. Fisher, not surprisingly, is very traditional in this respect. The more flamboyant (and interesting) females in his world are the evil women, female vampires and seductresses like Cecile Stapleton.

Having said this, it must also be noted that women of virtue in Fisher's film are not completely bland (as they certainly are in Universal's horror films). Isobel Banning does after all save her husband. Marie and Tanith in *The Devil Rides Out* both demonstrate strength and resolve in the conflict with the forces of evil. The strangest and most fascinating woman in all of Fisher's cinema is the subject of one of his most original films in which the ancient goddess is truly present.

The Gorgon (1964) was Fisher's first film for Hammer following the dry period after the commercial failure of *Phantom of the Opera* (to be discussed in the next chapter). In the interim Fisher had directed only two films: a Sherlock Holmes picture in Germany with Christopher Lee as the great detective and a science fiction film for the small Lippert Studio entitled *The Horror of It All*. In *The Gorgon* Fisher returned to strength working again with Peter Cushing and Christopher Lee. The script of *The Gorgon* was done by John Gilling who would direct a film on the goddess theme himself two years later titled *The Reptile*.

The Gorgon opens like many of Fisher's previous films with a prologue. The story begins in the small German village of Vartoff at the turn of the century. A young man named Bruno Heitz is an artist living in a cottage in the woods. In the opening scene he is at home painting his lover, Sascha (Tori Gilpin). She asks him when he plans to marry her. Bruno (Jeremy Longhurst) is not ready for marriage and an argument ensues. She tells him she is pregnant. Bruno insists on telling her father so that he can fulfill "his obligations in the matter." He walks out of the cottage into the dark woods. Sascha chases after him. Already the symbol of the cross has been introduced. During the argument in Bruno's cottage a cross is seen hanging on the wall. It is never referred to but it is visually prominent throughout the film. Now outside in the dark woods Sascha runs past a shrine with a crucifix, again shown clearly by Fisher's camera. In the dark Sascha sees something. She screams in horror (at something of-camera). The prologue ends.

In what has now become a familiar structure Fisher follows the prologue with the main characters of his film. Dr. Namaroff (Peter Cushing), who is both a doctor and scientist, is introduced. However this time Cushing's character is not the hero. Namaroff presides over a sanitarium. His assistant is a beautiful young woman named Carla (Barbara Shelley). Sascha's dead body is brought to Namaroff to confirm the cause of death. Her body completely covered by a sheet is wheeled in on a stretcher by Carla. Carla accidentally brushes against a table with the stretcher. Something snaps and falls to the floor. It is a stone finger. Carla pulls back the sheet. The dead Sascha has been turned to stone. The police find the body

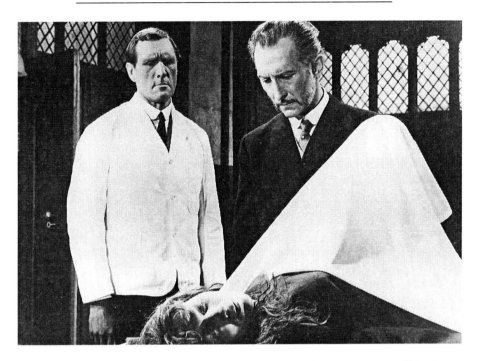

Dr. Namaroff (Peter Cushing) examines a dead body as his assistant Ratoff (Jack Watson) looks on in *The Gorgon*, Columbia Pictures (1964).

of Bruno hanging from a tree by the neck. In a following scene Dr. Namaroff discusses the "death" of Sascha with the police inspector (Patrick Troughton). They speak of her as being a murder victim. A number of unexplained "murders" have apparently occurred in the village over the past several years. The inspector volunteers that Bruno probably murdered Sascha in a lovers' quarrel and then in remorse killed himself. Namaroff concurs with the inspector's theory. Carla is aware that Namaroff and the inspector are uniting in a conspiracy to cover up the real truth. The implication is obvious that the previous "murder" victims have also been turned to stone but the facts about their death have not been revealed.

An inquest is scheduled in which Dr. Namaroff is clearly going to obscure the truth in his testimony. The inquest is obviously a charade in which no one in the village will challenge the cover-up. The problem with this however is that Bruno's father, a prominent university professor (Michael Goodliffe), comes to the village. Professor Heitz refuses to believe that his son could be guilty of murder. He sees through the artificial proceedings of the inquest and strongly suspects some kind of cover-up is taking place. He has no way, of course, of guessing the truth.

Following the inquest Professor Heitz intends to remain in the village to find out the actual circumstances of his son's death (which the inquest listed as suicide). He goes to visit Dr. Namaroff to get some more information on the death of his son and the young woman. Namaroff offers him none and advises the professor to leave the village and forgo any further investigation. Professor Heitz resolutely refuses to do so until he has learned the "truth" of his son's death. He takes up residence in his son's cottage. The townspeople resent his presence and even hurl rocks through his windows. The police inspector offers little protection and also suggests he leaves. All of this only deepens the Professor's suspicions.

The following night Professor Heitz hears a strange sound, a kind of song or chant. He leaves the cottage to investigate and finds his way into the deserted castle nearby. He sees the shadowy figure of a woman. There is a full moon. The strange singing becomes louder. He sees something that causes him to shriek in terror. He finds his way back to the cottage as the autumn winds begin to blow more forcefully. Inside the cottage he holds his head down as his servant asks him what is wrong. He raises his head into the full light. It is completely white. He is turning to stone — gradually. He asks that pen and paper be brought to him while he still has time. He writes to his second son, Paul (Richard Pasco), and concludes the letter by saying he is turning to stone. Fisher shows Paul, a student at the University of Leipzig. Paul's teacher is also seen for the first time, a Professor Meister. Meister is the sort of Fisher hero seen before as Dr. Van Helsing, Sherlock Holmes or the Duc de Richleau. Meister is played by Peter Cushing's counterpart, Christopher Lee.

Paul comes to investigate the second family death to have occurred in the village. He encounters the same cover-up by Dr. Namaroff which his father confronted regarding his brother's demise. Paul has the benefit of his father's letter, however, and proceeds to exhume his father's body. He finds the corpse completely turned to stone. The one ally Paul encounters in the village is Namaroff's assistant, Carla. She seems prepared to aid him in his investigation. Yet we also see her giving information back to Namaroff. Carla apparently has strange abilities which include, among other things, a photographic memory. She had seen some of Professor Heitz's letter to Paul before it had been sent. What she read she also memorized. It seems that Professor Heitz had been warning his son about the spirit of Megara, one of the serpent-headed gorgons whose face turned those who looked upon it to stone.

Before Paul can continue his investigations further he has a harrowing experience. One night in his brother's cottage he hears the strange singing which lured his father to his doom. Like his father before him he follows the sound as though hypnotized by it. He also encounters the same dark figure in the adjacent castle. Knowing what happened to his father he is aware of the danger. He sees the figure reflected in a pool of water as autumnal leaves swirl around him. He collapses and reawakens in the village hospital where Carla cares for him. His hair and complexion have turned a chalk white pallor. Carla informs him that he has been unconscious for a number of days.

After returning to the cottage, Paul hears a knock on the door. As he goes to open it Fisher's camera again shows the crucifix on the wall in the center of the frame. Paul opens the door to find Professor Meister who has come looking for him. Meister is shocked at the change in Paul. Paul tells him that he believes Carla will aid him in finding out the truth of the gorgon and the mysteries surrounding the deaths of his father and brother as well as the other unexplained "murders" in Vartoff. Meister begins to suspect that Paul is falling in love with Carla. He also becomes suspicious of Carla herself.

Meister begins his own investigation with Paul's help and ascertains that Carla's arrival in the village coincides with the first report of the strange deaths in Vartoff. Paul reacts against any suggestion of Carla's possible involvement. Meister becomes conscious that Paul, like Dr. Namaroff, has become increasingly obsessed with the young woman. In fact Carla and Paul have been meeting secretly. At first Carla implores Paul to take her away from the village. Paul answers that he cannot leave until he has finished his investigation into his father and brother's deaths. Later as Paul begins to believe that there may be something to Meister's suspicions he offers to take her away. She responds that it is too late. The cycle of the full moon is about to begin.

The climax of *The Gorgon* occurs during the first night of the full moon. Against Meister's wishes Paul goes to the abandoned castle after dark. There he encounters Namaroff. Both men are looking for Carla. Namaroff oddly carries a sword, and he and Paul engage in a sort of duel in the moonlit decayed castle. Paul is knocked unconscious. The siren sound of the gorgon is heard. Namaroff turns from Paul's inert body and proceeds up the castle stairs to confront the gorgon holding his sword. He tries to avoid looking at the creature's face but he is unable to resist. Seeing her, he shrieks, drops the sword and falls backward down the stairs. At this point Meister arrives at the castle having traced Paul there. The gorgon moves toward Paul as he regains consciousness lying on the castle floor. The gorgon is unaware that Meister is behind her and has picked up Namaroff's fallen sword. Meister warns Paul not to look at the creature. Paul however can no more resist than Namaroff could. He gazes at her face and screams. As he does so Meister has come close enough to the monster to decapitate her from behind. The hideous serpent-haired head rolls down the castle steps and proceeds to metamorphosize into the head of Carla. Paul crawls over to be near her as he realizes he is being transformed into stone. "I tried to warn you," laments Meister. Paul collapses beside the head of Carla. Fisher's camera pulls back to a long shot of the castle. The film ends.

The Gorgon is probably the most richly symbolic film Fisher ever directed. It is also one of the most grim in tone and outlook. Every major character in the film, with the exception of Professor Meister, is destroyed by the gorgon's spirit. Of all of Fisher's pictures this one is the most completely mythical. As mentioned above, this particular film was not based on a major, well known literary source as most of Fisher's films for Hammer were. To appreciate this enigmatic and, at times, brilliant film it must be seen in terms of its mythic origins.

The central mythical figure in this picture is the goddess. Interest in this figure is widespread today although that was hardly the case in 1964 when this film was produced. The gorgon in the film is actually a composite of four figures from Greek mythology. The first obviously is the gorgon figure itself. Initially there were three gorgons of whom the queen was Medusa. They lived beneath the sea and were more monstrous than human with scales, tusks and serpents in place of hair. They were so horrifying in appearance that those who gazed on them were turned to stone. Medusa was destroyed by the hero Perseus who, guided by her reflection in his shield, was able to behead her.

The element of the sea introduces a second mythological figure, the siren. The sirens appeared as beautiful women down to the waist with an eagle's talons for feet and the tail of a fish. They lured sailors to their doom with their bewitching songs. Ulysses protected his men by putting wax in their ears and had himself tied to a ship's mast to resist their hypnotic allure. Throughout Fisher's film a siren-like song is heard which lures the victims into the presence of the gorgon. A third figure is Megaera. Actually in Greek myth Megaera is not a gorgon but one of the furies or eumenides who were avenging goddesses of the underworld. The link here is that the furies also had snakes for hair. They were the spirits who pursued Orestes after he had murdered his mother Clytemnestra.

The final figure, a familiar one for Fisher, is the beautiful vampire seductress. This is the Lamiae, daughters of the ancient Lilith who was supposedly the first wife of Adam. There is an oblique reference to these figures in the biblical book of Isaiah (34:14). These beautiful women attacked young men and drained their life blood as they slept. They also preyed upon children as Lucy did in *Dracula*. Vampire women had of course featured prominently in Fisher's earlier Dracula films and would do so again in *Dracula, Price of Darkness* and *Frankenstein Created Woman*. Barbara Shelley, title star of *The Gorgon*, would give her finest role as a vampire in *Dracula, Prince of Darkness* the following year.

The most striking feature of *The Gorgon* is its subtlety. This may in part be due to John Gilling's screenplay. However, his own directorial effort in a related film, *The Reptile* (1966), is not as sophisticated. *The Gorgon* skillfully weaves together a number of mythical themes into a single character. Given the restrained approach one almost wishes we didn't have to actually see the face of the gorgon with its patently artificial snakes (Hammer's special effects again being their weak point). Nonetheless the gorgon in its twin incarnation of Carla and Megaera is both erotic and terrifying. This is the essence of the goddess figure in ancient mythology. Camille Paglia has rightly criticized the romanticized goddess figure of modern feminism.[9] The ancient goddess, whether in the biblical accounts of the Canaanite figure Astarte, the Babylonian Ishtar, or countless other forms of the "mother goddess" was a bloodthirsty and overtly sexual figure whose worship could include mutilation and human sacrifice as well as ritual prostitution.[10] This figure, known as Megaera in the film, is a far more accurate representation of the ancient goddess myth than the sanitized figure imagined by writers like Gloria Steinem. Fisher's character captures something of the fearful grandeur of the "Great Whore" described in the Book of Revelation, chapter 17.

For Fisher this figure represents unrelenting evil. Evil, however, is beautiful and seductive. This is nowhere emphasized more clearly in Fisher's career than in this work. In one way or another the primary characters are fascinated by the gorgon. This includes Carla herself who has been possessed by Megaera's spirit. She demands to know from Namaroff why she is being followed by one of his assistants, why *he* has such a fascination in her. Yet when Paul gives her the opportunity to escape from Vanderhof she doesn't take it . The appeal of Megaera is too strong. Professor Heitz, his son Paul and Namaroff all insist on pursuing the elusive figure of the gorgon, and in the end she is too much for them. They are all destroyed. Each one has the opportunity to escape the spell, to flee or look for help. None takes it.

The personification of spiritual help is Professor Meister, Fisher's spiritual celibate hero. He alone regards the gorgon as totally evil. He seeks no knowledge or answers from her. Her allure has no effect on him. Hence he alone can destroy her. Professor Meister is another stage in the development of Fisher's hero who began as Dr. Van Helsing and would reach his final development as the Duc De Richleau. He uniquely among all the characters is focused on spiritual goodness. In a Platonic sense, the beauty of spiritual goodness is far stronger than the allure of the goddess vampire figure. In a variety of ways Fisher's hero tries to turn the other characters away from the physical attraction of evil to the spiritual attraction of goodness (or God). This is symbolized noticeably in this film by the unmentioned but very visual presence of the cross. In the opening sequence as Bruno goes off into the woods he passes by a shrine with a crucifix. It's as though he leaves the domain of Good for the dark domain of Evil. In the cottage a cross is clearly visible on the center wall. It stands in the center of the frame in several scenes. The characters' own obsession with the goddess-gorgon figure moves them away from the symbol of God's power to the symbol of evil. Meister who symbolizes the strength of this power is unable to persuade both Paul and Namaroff of the dangers they face. And so the two men die the same night under the gorgon's spell. Evil is destroyed in *The Gorgon* but those who persist in following it, even while seeking to overcome it in their own strength, are nonetheless destroyed with it.

The Gorgon is ultimately a film about the obsessive fascination of evil. This fascination is underlined by the decor and design of the film. It can be seen in the rich colored images of the decaying castle in late autumn, the dark forests and even in the costumes worn by Barbara Shelley, including a striking shot of her sitting on a throne-like seat in the castle wearing a cape and cowl. Fisher is commenting here that the old myths are right. The goddess is fascinating and enticing but like the sirens' song she lures those who follow her to destruction. Professor Meister respects her power. He makes no attempt to face her. In effect Fisher is showing that there are times when a face to face encounter with evil is unwise. It is too strong for us. Meister is more cautious than the others. Representing the forces of spiritual goodness, he nonetheless does not attempt a frontal assault. He steals up behind the goddess. In chopping off her head he reveals the truth about her. She had inhabited the body of Carla. Some will see here only the echoes of the patriarchal myth in which the aspiring male hero destroys the ancient mother goddess. Meister's triumph though is a spiritual one in classic biblical terms. He represents light, knowledge, faith, courage and above all a selfless love for Paul, his student, whom he came to save. The gorgon represents darkness, fear, manipulation and control. Meister is an Elijah figure destroying the forces of Jezebel. For Fisher it is ultimately not a question of male good versus female evil (Dracula after all was emphatically a male figure). Rather it is the most ancient of all spiritual issues, the conflict between God and the demonic. For Fisher there is never any doubt about the ultimate outcome.[11]

Notes

1. Only *The Body Snatcher* (1944) comes close but even here Karloff's ghostly appearance at the end is more in the mind of Henry Daniell's villainous doctor than in reality.

2. Steinem, Gloria. *Revolution from Within*, p. 310.

3. It is hard to escape the impression that Peter Cushing's John Banning is expressing views that Fisher also shared. See Miller, Mark A., p. 117. On colonialism in the related film, *The Stranglers of Bombay*, see Hardy, Phil, p. 123.

4. Matthew 7:16.

5. Baring, Anne, and Cashford, Jules. *The Myth of the Goddess*, pp. 160ff.

6. Quoted in Campbell, Joseph, *The Masks of God: Primitive Mythology*, p. 56.

7. This theme is present most strongly in *The Mummy* (1932) and the particularly grim *The Mummy's Ghost* (1944).

8. Baring, Anne, and Cashford, Jules, pp. 197ff.

9. Paglia has interesting comments on the Gorgon figure as part of this critique, Paglia, Camille, pp. 30–32.

10. Baring, Anne, and Cashford, Jules, pp. 175ff, 358; Campbell, Joseph, *The Masks of God: Occidental Mythology*, pp. 17ff. For an opposing view, see Tikva Frymer-Kensky, pp. 199–202, but even she acknowledges the deadly sexuality of Ishtar (Inanna), p. 78.

11. This conviction is the core belief of what David Pirie calls Fisher's "world view" (*Weltanschauung*), Pirie, David, p. 51

Chapter Five

THE DIVIDED SELF

The theme of the divided self actually runs throughout Fisher's film career. It appears in various forms in many of the films already discussed, e.g., *Stolen Face, Four Sided Triangle, The Mummy, The Curse of the Werewolf* and *The Gorgon*. Fisher's world is essentially one of polar opposites: God and Satan, good and evil, rich and poor, knowledge and ignorance, truth and falsehood, flesh and spirit. It is not strange then that many of Fisher's characters have a dualistic nature. Their identity is not totally their own. They either share their self with an identical replica (*Four Sided Triangle, The Mummy*) or struggle against indwelling demonic spirits (*Curse of the Werewolf, The Gorgon*). The alternative to this is the Fisher hero. He (and *he* is invariably masculine) is not without weaknesses and quirks. However, for Fisher, he is the ultimate unified self. He evidences the purity of heart which wills one thing. Like Galahad of old, he seeks only the good and true whatever the cost. As an Augustinian ideal he is able to resist the tremendous power of the flesh. In his various guises of Van Helsing, Sherlock Holmes or Professor Meister he is the ultimate conqueror of evil. (Interestingly enough, Sherlock Holmes is the only Fisher hero to have been played by both Peter Cushing and Christopher Lee.)

There are however at least three films Fisher made which focus on the struggle of the divided self without the resolution provided by the unified hero. The continuing development of this hero figure is, as explored later, the culminating theme of Fisher's entire cinematic work. He certainly reappears throughout Fisher's major gothic films (i.e., *Dracula, The Hound of the Baskervilles, The Mummy, Brides of Dracula, The Gorgon, Dracula, Prince of Darkness* and *The Devil Rides Out*). He is not present in the Frankenstein films chiefly because Frankenstein himself represents the unified figure in those films. Frankenstein's unity however comes from his obsessive desire to imitate God and he is therefore an Anti-hero. The fact then that in at least three films Fisher presents a dualistic struggle without a central hero is in itself striking. Perhaps for this reason these three films have generally been considered minor or particularly flawed efforts in Fisher's career. That estimate may be challenged in considering three often dismissed pictures: *The Man Who Could Cheat Death* (1959), *The Two Faces of Dr. Jekyll* (1960) and *The Phantom of the Opera* (1962).

The Man Who Could Cheat Death was released in 1959, the same year as *The Hound of the Baskervilles* and *The Mummy*. It was to a great extent overshadowed by those two films which received far greater attention. Indeed most critics with the exception of John McCarty dismiss *Man Who Could Cheat Death* as a very minor work.[1] Posterity has not been helpful since, unlike many of Fisher's other films, *The Man Who Could Cheat Death* is not available on video and is only rarely seen on television.[2] Nonetheless *Man* was filmed by essentially the same team that had done *Curse of Frankenstein*. It reunited Christopher Lee and Hazel Court from that film with veteran character actor Anton Differing in the title role as Dr. Georges Bonnet. In addition it is one of the most beautiful Technicolor films Hammer ever produced. Nothing suggests that this film was ever conceived as a minor production. To the contrary, it comes from Fisher's (and Hammer's) most prolific and successful period. The film is a remake of *The Man in Half Moon Street,* made at Paramount Studios in Hollywood in 1944. That film in turn had been adapted from a stage play. Certainly as a commercial property this film had nowhere near the status or recognizability of Frankenstein, Dracula or Sherlock Holmes. Its story was an intriguing one nonetheless.

Georges Bonnet (Anton Differing) is a Dorian Grey–like character. Years before the time period of the film he and a colleague, Dr. Ludwig Weiss (Arnold Marle), had discovered a glandular extract that could prolong a person's youth. Bonnet was the first recipient of this experiment and so, as the film begins, appears youthful in spite of advanced age. Dr. Weiss is an old man at this point. The problem for Bonnet is that the effects of the glandular extract are temporary. After seven years the treatment must be repeated if the youthful effects are to continue. The film's opening scene shows a murder in a deserted park on a foggy night. All the audience sees of the murderer is a long coat and a gladstone bag.

Dr. Bonnet is a sculptor in Paris in the late nineteenth century. As the film begins he is showing off examples of his sculpture. His favorite subject is beautiful young women. His involvement with them apparently extends beyond using them as models. Dr. Bonnet is especially enamored of a particularly striking model named Janine Dubois (Hazel Court). She is also the object of attention of a young physician named Dr. Pierre Gerrard (Christopher Lee).

The film's story is essentially a simple one. Bonnet must murder victims to obtain the glandular extract which his accomplice Dr. Weiss uses to maintain Bonnet's youth. No one may learn his secret. When one young woman stays too long with Bonnet, the glandular effect begins to wear off and he has to forcibly get rid of her. In a struggle to make her leave the young woman (Delphi Lawrence) is accidentally struck by some acid. Bonnet locks her in a cell in his laboratory to prevent her from giving away his secret. Eventually Dr. Weiss becomes too old to continue the medical treatment. Bonnet can obtain the necessary glands through his murder victims but still needs a physician to perform the required operation.

Bonnet approaches young Dr. Gerrard for assistance but Gerrard suspects (rightfully) that there is more involved than what Bonnet tells him regarding his "experiment." In an effort to force Gerrard's hand Bonnet kidnaps Janine. He promises to release her only on the condition that Bonnet perform the glandular operation for him. Gerrard appears to consent. However he only pretends to do the surgery. Bonnet comes out of the anesthesia believing he has another seven years of youth guaranteed. He attempts to ingratiate himself with Janine before releasing her but before her eyes he ages horribly into a disfigured old man. She flees in terror. At the end the young woman whom he had earlier struck with acid escapes and sets his studio on fire. Bonnet perishes in the flames.

The Man Who Could Cheat Death is Fisher's second gothic thriller for Hammer in which theme is more important than narration (the other was *The Mummy*). In this development the film helps serve as a bridge to later, more complex works such as *Phantom of the Opera* and *The Gorgon*. Yet *Man* in itself is not without interest. Georges Bonnet is a perfect example of the man "who gains the whole world and yet loses his soul."[3] Bonnet is quite obviously a derivative of Fisher's conception of Dr. Frankenstein except that Bonnet uses himself as the object of experimentation. Like Frankenstein he is cultured, handsome, and well-mannered. Bonnet though has a lecherous side which is more pronounced than Baron Frankenstein's offhanded interest in an occasional servant girl. Georges Bonnet actually is a particularly clear example of the villains found in Fisher's early films for Hammer. He is a self-indulgent aristocrat who has not the slightest hesitancy in using people. Women are his special victims. He is a figure devoid of moral principle or scruple. He summarizes traits which can be found in Baron Frankenstein, Count Dracula and Sir Hugo Baskerville.

Bonnet is another example of Gilgamesh in that he is searching for the secret of eternal youth. The Gilgamesh epic is probably the oldest piece of literature in existence. Gilgamesh's various adventures including fighting monsters, befriending a half-human, half-beast companion and warding off

U.S. publicity poster for *The Phantom of the Opera* (1962).

the fearful attentions of an enraged goddess, have inspired much of the content of world literature, particularly that dealing with myth and legend, from the *Iliad* to Harry Potter. The key theme of Gilgamesh, though, which runs throughout philosophy as well as literature is the search for eternal life. Bonnet, like Gilgamesh, pursues this search unilaterally. Even more self-obsessed than Frankenstein, he intends to allow nothing to stand in the way of his own immortality. In the course of this pursuit, his external life masks his true self.[4]

Bonnet's duality exists on several levels. He appears youthful when in fact he is very old. He manifests a creative side as a sculptor when in fact he is destructive. He evidences a polite charm in society when in private he is a ruthless murderer. He feigns an interest in women which is actually only an interest in himself. Finally he gives a poised air of self-confidence when in reality he has an overpowering fear of his own mortality. The word in the title "cheat" summarizes his own character. However it is not only death which he "cheats" but everything and everyone around him. The title is ironic also since he does not ultimately cheat death. In fact his destruction is as multi-faceted as his deceit. Everyone he seeks to manipulate in the film finally turns on him and plays a role in his final demise. Bonnet's self-destructive and murderous pattern illustrates the theme that "the wages of sin are death."[5] Evil for Fisher, like St. Augustine, exists as its own negation. As the absence of good, it is inherently self-destructive.

The issues presented in *The Man Who Could Cheat Death* are dealt with in a far more involved manner in the following year's *Two Faces of Dr. Jekyll*. This is in fact one of Fisher's most complex and fascinating works. As in other adaptations of classic stories Fisher follows the spirit of the original while adapting the work to fit his own world view. This picture incidentally is important in seeing Fisher as the "auteur" or author of his films. The screenplay of *Two Faces of Dr. Jekyll* is not by any of the Hammer "regulars" (i.e., Jimmy Sangster, Peter Bryan) but is rather the work of noted novelist and screenwriter Wolf Mankowitz. Mankowitz had received critical acclaim for adopting his novel *A Kid for Two Farthings* for the screen a few years earlier. His presence on a Hammer film project testifies to the large success of the studio by 1960. Mankowitz adds a decided philosophic and literary slant to the film but nonetheless Fisher's critical themes are also present. Fisher's basic outlook remains constant irrespective of his varied screenwriters, testifying to his role in shaping the themes of his films.

The Two Faces of Dr. Jekyll is a very different reading of Robert Louis Stevenson's "Strange Care of Dr. Jekyll and Mr. Hyde" from previous film versions. The most immediate obvious difference lies in the fact that Fisher sees Mr. Hyde as evil rather than ugly or monstrous. Fisher has maintained, rightly, that Stevenson's emphasis in his novella is more on Hyde's "radiance of a foul soul" and his "displeasing smile" than on any physical deformity. Consequently, Fisher presents Hyde as charming, youthful and handsome in sharp contrast to all previous film versions. On the other hand, Jekyll is seen as pedantic, older and rather dull. While this conception is not literally that of Stevenson's, it is nonetheless far closer to his original idea that the popular view of the story which has emerged especially in dramatic portrayals both in theater and on screen. Hyde, in Stevenson's description, is "wicked-looking" but hardly the hairy monster or dishelved fiend usually found in most dramatizations of the story. Fisher's view of Hyde then as debonair and charming fits his own understanding of the seductive charm of evil and is closer to Stevenson's original conception.

The opening scene of *Two Faces of Dr. Jekyll* introduces a bearded Henry Jekyll discussing his theories of human nature with his mentor Dr.

The Phantom of the Opera, Hammer (1962).

Litauer. Jekyll describes his view of the two selves in every person in terms of the will more than moral character. In speaking of the "will to power" Jekyll sounds like an early exponent of Nietzsche. It is the exercise of the will in breaking away from all constraint and social limitation which grants true freedom, he believes. Jekyll refers to a group of children playing in the courtyard of his home as animals guided essentially by instinct. They lack in his view the fully realized will which creates human maturity. The will for Jekyll lies stifled within because of society's pressures and training. True selves will only be revealed when these shackles are thrown off.

This is more philosophizing than what is usual in Fisher's work, although many of his films after *Stolen Face* have their share of philosophic (not to mention theological) implications. The sort of formal discussion in this picture is probably the result of having a novelist like Wolf Mankowitz write the screenplay. It points up the fact that *Two Faces of Dr. Jekyll* is one of the most ambitious films Fisher or Hammer ever attempted. It is unfortunate that a version this literate and fresh of the oft filmed story of Jekyll and Hyde has seldom received the attention it merits.

Dr. Litauer, playing the role of Greek Chorus in the film, is more than a little shocked at Jekyll's view. Referring to the children, he protests: "These are not animals, Jekyll. They are children." Jekyll is unresponsive. His experiments are designed to lead him to power, a power that can be achieved only by an unfettered will. Fisher's Jekyll is not unlike Baron Frankenstein except that Jekyll is seeking to recreate himself rather than animate some other life form.

Jekyll, as played by Canadian actor Paul Massie, is married rather than engaged as in most stage and film versions. His wife, Kitty (Dawn Addams), is frustrated by his obsessive scientific work. She is also apparently bored by him as a person. Dr. Litauer (played by veteran character actor David Kossoff who had appeared in *A Kid for Two Farthings*) senses this and suggests Jekyll would do well to be more attentive to his wife instead of pursuing his experiment on the human will. The fact is Kitty already has developed another interest in the person of Jekyll's dissolute friend, Paul Allen (Christopher Lee). Paul frequently asks Jekyll for loans to pay off his gambling debts. To add insult to injury he uses the money to take Jekyll's wife out. It is obvious that Jekyll and Kitty have been drifting apart for some time. The culmination of Jekyll's research precipitates two crises in his life. On the verge of experimenting on himself with the drug that he believes will liberate his inner self, Jekyll pleads with Kitty not to go out to her "dinner party" but remain home with him. Kitty rejects his pleas, insisting she could not disappoint her hostess on such short notice. In actuality Kitty is planning a night out with her lover, Paul.

After Kitty leaves Jekyll makes the critical decision to experiment on himself alone. Jekyll proceeds to take the drug and goes through the same contortions as so many of his predecessor actors in the myriad versions of Stevenson's story. Hyde is first shown from the back. He leaves the laboratory and steps into the street. He turns toward the camera, his face now fully revealed by the light of the gas lamp. Instead of any deformed, monstrous or even sinister appearance, this Hyde is handsome and youthful.

In pursuit of London's nightlife Hyde inevitably encounters Kitty and Paul. With an evil delight he cultivates their acquaintance. He asks Paul to introduce him to London's nocturnal pleasures. Hyde's fierce depravity is effectively suggested by Fisher. He bargains for a young girl in a seedy pub. He tramples a beggar (rather than a little girl as in Stevenson's original account) in a striking sequence in which Fisher shows only Hyde's head being elevated as he stands on the man's body. The victim's moans are heard off camera.

Hyde becomes fixated on a cabaret performer named Maria (Norma Marla) who dances with a python in a club called The Sphinx. Paul confesses

Christine (Heather Sears) is reassured by her boyfriend Harry Hunter (Edward De Souza) in *The Phantom of the Opera.*

Harry and Christine eye the falling chandelier in *The Phantom of the Opera.*

that this particular exotic woman is one of the most sought after in London but is unfortunately out of his league. Not so for Hyde who is the embodiment of unfettered will. Hyde takes her as his mistress. The symbolism surrounding this so-called "Exotic Dancer" is all too obvious. Complete with giant snake and scanty costume, she is overtly the seductive mythical serpent-goddess so often seen in Fisher's films. Using her as an unwilling accomplice, Hyde plots an elaborate crime which apparently is intended to unify the conflicting worlds of Jekyll and Hyde.

Hyde seeks to ingratiate himself with Kitty, thereby in one sense reclaiming his (or Jekyll's) wife and, in an act of poetic justice, stealing her away from Paul. Hyde, pretending to be Jekyll, sends word to Paul and Kitty suggesting that they meet at the Sphinx Club to sort out their differences. Once there Hyde lures Paul into Maria's bedroom to be killed by the python. Hyde then confronts Kitty and proceeds to rape her in Maria's apartment while can-can music plays below in the cabaret. The ferocity of the rape, which is only suggested, is heightened by the formal dinner attire both are wearing. Kitty passes out in the attack and awakens wearing only her underclothes in the bed of Hyde's mistress. Disoriented and alone, she stumbles through the apartment only to find her dead lover Paul in the grip of the python. In a state of shock she falls through a glass window and crashes to the dance floor below.

Meanwhile Hyde has taken Maria to Jekyll's house. He makes passionate love to her in Jekyll's bed only to have Jekyll reassert himself. As the transformation occurs with Jekyll overpowering Hyde by an act of Jekyll's will, Jekyll ends up strangling Maria. In effect then Hyde has killed Jekyll's wife and Jekyll has murdered Hyde's mistress. Hyde proceeds to burn Jekyll's house and frame Jekyll for the murders. In a final scene Hyde is present at an inquest which rules that Jekyll went mad, committed the murders and then took his own life. Hyde is now completely free of Jekyll. In leaving the courtroom however Jekyll once again asserts himself and Hyde is transformed back into Jekyll. The police inspector (Francis De Wolff) proceeds to arrest Jekyll for the murders which Hyde committed and for which, ironically, Hyde had attempted to frame Jekyll.

The Two Faces of Dr. Jekyll is very much a mixed work. On the positive side the relationship of Jekyll and Hyde is much closer to Stevenson's novel than in previous films. Jekyll, as in Stevenson's original work, is middle-aged, stolid, respectable and dull. He is appropriately horrified by Hyde's activities while at the same time retaining a vicarious pleasure in them. Hyde, on the other hand, is completely indifferent to Jekyll, viewing him as nothing more than a cover for his evil deeds. As noted, the portrayal of Hyde as handsome and dashing is an intriguing innovation consistent with Fisher's depiction of evil in other films.

The film's retitling of the original story is also appropriate. Stevenson makes clear that Hyde is not a complete opposite to Jekyll but rather a repressed, hidden side of Jekyll's own personality, truly a second "face." The two faces motif is further emphasized by the fact that the other principal characters in the film also have two faces. Kitty and Paul are both two-faced. Kitty on the surface is Jekyll's wife but is having an affair with his friend. Paul is likewise friend in appearance and betrayer in actuality. Even the police inspector who appears at the end of the film apparently has a hidden side since he knows more about the unsavory side of the cabaret than he wants to admit. Maria, the snake woman, represents the classic mythical dualism of sexuality and death. The phallic symbol of the python also testifies to both sex and death. This motif is extended to the social setting of the film itself. Victorian society is "two-faced," prim and respectable on the outside, yet evil and debauched below the surface. The cabaret in which much of the film's action takes place exemplifies this. Its exotic entertainments furnish a safe veneer behind which prostitution takes place.

In spite of these aspects however the film has a number of negative elements. Most fundamentally, its symbolism is simply too complex. The picture never seems to come together. The various themes and relationships never jell. More seriously, none of the characters are appealing. Granted that Fisher's films are essentially allegories with the characters being types, the characters still need to be interesting. Paul Massie's Hyde is surprising bland for all his deviance (as opposed to Cushing's Baron Frankenstein). His Jekyll is uniformly stiff and dull. Kitty can hardly be blamed for wanting to get away from him. Kitty and Paul's amorality makes them neither sympathetic nor appealing. Fisher has more than the usual amount of erotic imagery in this film, including endless shots of can-can dancers. The imagery, however, never seems as focused as in the Dracula films or *The Gorgon*. Maria, the "snake woman" with her python, is so overt as to be downright clumsy.

On a more serious level the motivations of Hyde are never completely clear. He seems to delight in acting out an elaborate revenge for Jekyll. Yet he also says he cares nothing for Jekyll. Why then does he even bother with Kitty and Paul? He claims to want freedom by disposing of Jekyll. In the novel, however, Hyde literally "hides" behind Jekyll's identity to escape from the police. How does disposing of Jekyll guarantee freedom for Hyde since Jekyll represents a means of escape? The theme of the will after first being introduced in the picture is never adequately developed. Ultimately it seems that Jekyll's will is stronger than Hyde's. This, however, runs counter to Stevenson's original story.

In spite of these difficulties, *The Two Faces of Dr. Jekyll* is an interesting film. The unusual portrayal of Hyde is reason alone for this. In many ways this is a transitional work for Fisher. It is certainly a more ambitious film in theme and treatment than its immediate predecessors, *The Mummy* and *The Man Who Could Cheat Death*. The film retains some striking images combining sensuality and death. In the ensuing decades these images would come to predominate a number of films devoid of the moral and philosophic aspects of this picture. Fisher would deal with the divided self motif more successfully in the following year's *Curse of the Werewolf*. But his most adroit handling of the theme would come in 1962 in his remake of *The Phantom of the Opera*.

Hammer's version of *The Phantom of the Opera* was the most elaborate and expensive film they had made up to that time. Unfortunately the film was a commercial and critical failure and led, as previously noted, to

Ian Wilson as the dwarf responsible for the murders in **The Phantom of the Opera.**

a two year hiatus from Hammer Studios during which time Fisher only made two films. The essential problem with Fisher's *Phantom of the Opera* was that it was perceived more as a love story than as a tale of terror. This objection seems hard to grasp following the long running success of the Andrew Lloyd Weber musical which follows the same essential approach to the story. However critics and audiences alike in the early 1960s were far more familiar with previous film versions starring Lon Chaney and Claude Rains than they were with the original Gaston Leroux novel. Their expectation of the story followed the familiar line of a mad killer abducting an innocent heroine. They were totally unprepared for Fisher's lush, romantic version which some contemporary critics regard as one of his finest films.[6] The fact that the role of the Phantom was apparently originally intended for Cary Grant is one reason for the more romantic approach.[7] Yet in retrospect this film can be seen as the culmination of tendencies already present in Fisher's earlier films.

The film's opening is similar to that of other versions of *The Phantom of the Opera*. The action, however, has been transported from Paris to

London for obvious reasons in a British production. The London Opera House has been beset by strange occurrences. Singers, stage hands and management are unnerved by rumors of a "phantom." One box in the Opera House remains empty during each performance because it is said to be haunted. The one person who has no tolerance for all this is the composer, Lord Ambrose D'Arcy (Michael Gough). D'Arcy is a complete personification of the Fisher aristocratic villain. He is vain, arrogant, condescending and ruthless. He resents any intrusion into the performances of his work, especially any talk of an opera ghost.

The fears of the opera company are borne out when a hand is seen tearing through a panel of scenery to reveal the hanged body of one of the stage crew. The leading lady refuses to sing again and so a replacement must be sought. A young woman named Christine Charles (Heather Sears) gives a strong audition. However, when she rebuffs Lord D'Arcy's advances she is dropped from further consideration. This is not the end of the matter though. She hears a voice in her dressing room telling her she will be a great singer one day but that she must work hard to achieve that end. She confides this to a young male friend, Harry Hunter (Edward De Souza). Hunter becomes suspicious of the events taking place in the

Lord Ambrose D'Arcy (Michael Gough) has villainous designs on Christine (Heather Sears) in *The Phantom of the Opera.*

Opera House, including the dominant role of the composer, Lord D'Arcy. It is at this point that Christine is kidnapped by a strange masked figure who brings her to an elaborate lair under the Opera House. The Phantom (Herbert Lom) insists that he means her no harm but he must teach her to sing.

Hunter meanwhile seeks to unravel the mystery of Christine's disappearance. In the course of his investigation he learns that the music attributed to Lord D'Arcy is not really D'Arcy's work. Rather it is the composition of a Professor Petrie who had disappeared mysteriously some years earlier. As shown in flashback, Professor Petrie was a music teacher with modest resources who sought to have his compositions published. He came to see Lord D'Arcy who offered to buy the full bulk of Petrie's work for 50 pounds. Petrie believes his compositions are worth much more but needing money and anxious to have his work published, he agrees to D'Arcy's offer. Later he visits the publishing house where D'Arcy has arranged to have the compositions printed. To his horror he realizes that his name has been replaced by D'Arcy's own as the composer. Furious, he confronts D'Arcy who coldly replies that since Petrie had sold him the rights the compositions are now *his* music and are being published under his name. In desperation Petrie breaks into the publishing house that night and tries to burn the newly printed scores. In this attempt he unwittingly starts a fire. Petrie picks up what he believes to be a basin of water to throw on the flames. The basin actually contains flammable chemicals which burst into fire and scar Petrie's face badly. In pain he rushes into the street and runs blindly until he falls into the river. He is swept along by the current and borne into the sewer system which brings him into the underground lair of the Opera House. Here he is found and cared for by a dwarf who is mute (Ian Keith).

Hunter's investigations lead him to retrace Professor Petrie's trail. Following the river's current he comes to the hidden depths of the Opera House where he discovers Professor Petrie, masked now as the so-called Phantom, Christine and the dwarf. Petrie shares his tragic origin with Christine and Hunter and begs them to help him see that his opera is performed as he envisions in spite of D'Arcy's usurping of it. They agree to help and to keep his secret. Petrie then continues preparing Christine to sing the lead of Joan of Arc in his opera.

On the opening night of the new opera Petrie confronts D'Arcy in his office in the Opera House. D'Arcy pulls off Petrie's mask and turns to run in horror. The professor's face is hidden. He replaces the mask and takes his place in the so-called "haunted box." Christine performs brilliantly and the opera proceeds well. Backstage, however, the dwarf is seen and chased

Christine (Heather Sears) sings the lead role of *Joan of Arc* in *The Phantom of the Opera*.

by some stage hands. Trying to escape, he leaps onto a chandelier which stands over Christine. As the dwarf seeks to climb to safety, the chandelier breaks free and starts to fall. Petrie, seeing the danger, rips off his mask, leaps to the stage, pushes Christine out of the way and is himself crushed by the falling chandelier. The final shot of the film shows the Phantom's mask as the credits roll.

Fisher's *Phantom* is a departure in a number of respects from both the Gaston Leroux novel and Universal Studios' two earlier film versions. Professor Petrie is a genuinely sympathetic figure who truly cares for Christine. The murders in this version are all the work of the dwarf. This strong romantic emphasis prefigures the Andrew Lloyd Weber musical and picks up a key theme from the novel which the previous two versions had neglected. At the close of the novel Christine shows her affection for the Phantom by kissing him. This is essentially the same spirit one finds in Fisher's version and is markedly different from the crazed figure played by Lon Chaney and Claude Rains. It is unfortunate that audiences in 1962 were unable to appreciate Fisher's approach.

Professor Petrie is one of the most tragic of Fisher's protagonists. His crime, or one might say sin, was to break into D'Arcy's publishing house and try to burn the plagiarized copies of his compositions. Even here he is shown in a very sympathetic light. Petrie's unresolved complexity lies in the fact that he is both creator and destroyer. It is in this respect that he is a divided self. As such he is an interesting contrast to Victor Frankenstein, who in another sense is both creator and destroyer. The two figures are linked together as being ultimately self-destructive. Frankenstein's creation is essentially blasphemous since he is seeking to emulate God. Petrie on the other hand creates music which is, more often than not, seen as an act of praising God. The tragedy of Petrie's life is that he attempts to destroy that which he creates. He composes a wealth of music which he loses to D'Arcy. While he is certainly a victim in one sense, he nonetheless also contributes to his own fate. D'Arcy is so obviously a ruthless figure that the audience can't help feeling that Petrie should have done more to protect himself. For example, he asks for nothing in writing acknowledging D'Arcy's receipt of his work. Petrie is presented as frantic, naive and essentially obsessed with his work. This makes him vulnerable, of course, but it also establishes another tie with Baron Frankenstein who was equally obsessed with his work.

Petrie is placed in the contradictory situation of having to destroy what he has created. This in fact is the essential theme of Fisher's film. He attempts to burn the very compositions he worked so hard to write simply to keep D'Arcy from getting the credit for them. Once in the Opera House he seeks to prevent the performance of his own work. The two sides of Petrie's character are personified by Christine and the dwarf. Christine represents his creative side and is appropriately a singer capable of giving voice to his music. The dwarf exemplifies Petrie's negative side and is therefore silent. It is in the interaction of these figures that Petrie's essential conflict lies. The relationship to each of the two is itself ambiguous. Petrie truly cares for Christine but is not above frightening her and abducting her. Once he has brought her to his lair he forces the understandably distressed woman to keep singing until she collapses. On the other hand Petrie appears benignly indifferent to the dwarf who is responsible for several murders in the Opera House. He is grateful for the dwarf's helping him but can scarcely be unaware of his benefactor's violent side. This is all the more striking since many of those in the Opera House blame the mysterious Phantom, i.e., Petrie himself, for the murders. In one respect Petrie identifies with Christine's singing. In another, however, he apparently also identifies with the dwarf's violent character.

These two sides of Petrie intersect at the film's climax. Christine is singing his music brilliantly. He is so moved that a tear runs down his mask. It is at this precise moment that the chaotic side of the dwarf asserts itself. When the dwarf clutches the chandelier hanging above Christine's head, Petrie's destructive side is threatening to kill his creative self. Confronted with this conflict Petrie tears off his mask, the symbol of his hidden self. He rescues Christine at the expense of his own life. In effect he dies in order to save his music. His creation is more important to him than his own existence. This sacrifice becomes necessary because of his unresolved inner conflict between creation and destruction. At the end of the film the conflict is only resolved by his own death.

The contrast between Professor Petrie and Baron Frankenstein is notable because of the parallels between the two. Frankenstein also exhibits both a creative and destructive side. The difference lies in the fact that Frankenstein's creations are inherently destructive. This is amply demonstrated in Fisher's long running Frankenstein series. Frankenstein is fixated on the act of creating yet he never dreams of sacrificing himself for the benefit of his creation. It is always the reverse. The creation exists to benefit or reflect Frankenstein in some sense. The parallel with Professor Petrie is more significant than might appear at first glance. Frankenstein's creations arise from science while Petrie's come from art. In both cases the creations are ultimately personified. Frankenstein relates to his created figures objectively. They exist to be controlled and manipulated by him. This in itself is a self-destructive process since the essence of the original Mary Shelley *Frankenstein* novel is that the creature takes on a life of its own. Not only does it refuse to obey Frankenstein, it finally threatens his life. Frankenstein's very act of creation carries with it the seeds of self-destruction.

Professor Petrie creates Christine the singer in the same mythical sense as Pygmalion creates Galatea. The difference is that Petrie, like Pygmalion, is subjectively and emotionally involved with his creation. It is not Petrie's creative side that is destructive here. Rather it is a contradictory, vengeful, other side of his nature that interferes with his creativity. Petrie the musician, however, is completely positive in his act of creating. Frankenstein though is hardly positive in his creating. Frankenstein's creativity in its very character has a strongly negative aspect.

The final difference between the two lies in their respective roles as creators. Frankenstein as a scientist represents a questionable figure in Fisher's universe. He is fascinating and at times dominant. Yet his fixation on himself and his inherent disregard of God marks him as a dangerous individual. Professor Petrie as a musician might be said to be more on the side of the angels. There is no explicit reference to God or even religion in *The Phantom of the Opera*. Nonetheless Petrie's opera is based on Joan of

Arc and Christine sings the title role. Petrie's self-sacrifice to save Christine and, symbolically, his creation, suggests something of the cross of Christ, a vivid symbol in so many of Fisher's films. Those who have said that Fisher's fantasies are devoid of symbolism have missed the essential allegorical nature of his films. It would perhaps be too much to say that the Phantom is a Christ figure. It would however be equally wrong to deny the possibility that Fisher implied such a reference in this, his most underrated film.[8]

Notes

1. McCarty, John. *The Modern Horror Film*, pp. 45–47.
2. It has occasionally surfaced on the Sci-Fi network in a very attractive print.
3. Matthew 16:26.
4. This is essentially the same point as Oscar Wilde's *The Picture of Dorian Gray* and also Robert Louis Stevenson's *Strange Case of Dr. Jekyll and Mr. Hyde*.
5. Romans 6:23.
6. Hardy, Phil, p. 150.
7. Maxford, Howard. *Hammer, House of Horror*, p. 60.
8. McCarty, John. *The Modern Horror Film*, pp. 77–79

Chapter Six

THE REDEEMER HERO

The subject of Terence Fisher's so-called "world view" has been discussed for many years. It is certainly the case that a "world view" is
implicit in his films. In order to see the full nature of Fisher's philosophy
of life it is necessary to look beyond the Gothic tradition in which he did
his most famous work. A genuine "world view," which in cinematic terms
translates into an "auteur" perspective, would pervade all of a director's
work, not simply that of a particular, or even favorite, genre. In a famous
quote Fisher once said,

> If my films reflect my own personal view of the world in any way, it
> is in their showing of the ultimate victory of good over evil, in which
> I do believe. It may take human beings a long time to achieve this,
> but I do believe this is how events work out in the end.[1]

The full extent of Fisher's "view of the world" is, of course, what is
seen on the screen. The specific focus of this outlook centers on Fisher's
special hero, encountered in various forms as Van Helsing, Sherlock
Holmes, Father Sandor, Professor Meister and the Duc De Richleau. If this
figure is truly the key to Fisher's philosophic and religious outlook, it
should be expected to appear in Fisher's work outside the context of "Hammer horror." To test this thesis four additional films of Fisher's will be discussed, none of which is a Hammer gothic horror film. The films range in
quality and importance. However, all of them were made in the period of
Fisher's major work, from 1959 through the late sixties. The four films in
chronological order are *The Stranglers of Bombay* (1959), *The Sword of
Sherwood Forest* (1960), *Sherlock Holmes and the Deadly Necklace* (1962)
and *Island of Terror* (1966). Each of these pictures represents another
dimension of Fisher's cinematic work and, while other examples could
perhaps be chosen, as a group they show Fisher's range during the period

The Stranglers of Bombay, Hammer (1959).

when some of his most famous films were being made. Together they provide a major insight into the character who is at the heart of Fisher's cinematic artistry, the Redeemer Hero.

The Stranglers of Bombay was made by essentially the same team that had done all Fisher's previous gothic horror classics from *Curse of Frankenstein* through *The Man Who Could Cheat Death.* The only exception is that the photography is done by Arthur Grant rather than Jack Asher. Yet *Stranglers* is a very different looking film both in tone and composition. Whereas the previous films are all shot in color on recognizably the same set at Bray studio and featured either Peter Cushing or Christopher Lee, this is not the case with *Stranglers.* It is shot in black and white at a Bray lot which has been transformed into nineteenth century India. The only familiar Hammer face in the cast is George Pastell who plays a similar role in *The Mummy,* released the same year. In contrast to the other films, *Stranglers* is very rarely seen on television and is not available on video. David Pirie is one of the few critics who recognizes the film's significance in Fisher's work, yet even he devotes only a single paragraph to it in his groundbreaking book, *A Heritage of Horror.*[2] To assess the film's importance it needs to be analyzed in some detail.

Stranglers of Bombay opens with a pre-credit sequence showing a group of Indians worshipping the goddess Kali. Kali is a deity whose worship demands the sacrificial death of those who do not believe in her. However, death cannot involve the shedding of blood so silk scarves are used to strangle their victims. The foundation of this sequence historically is the Thugee cult which terrorized India during the era of British colonialism (the same cult is the focus on the famous 1939 film *Gunga Din*). The leader of the cult is a high priest (George Pastell) who in the opening scene is initiating new devotees into the worship of the goddess. A young man's arm is slit with a knife and then branded with a hot iron as he is made into an official follower of Kali. All this takes place before the credits are shown!

East India company executives, deeply concerned over the strange disappearance of their caravans, hold a meeting that is presided over by the British military commander, Colonel Henderson (Andrew Cruickshank). The former Indian ruler of the territory, Patel Shari (Marne Maitland), is also present and some of the East Indian representatives believe he could do a better job protecting the area. Into this tense meeting walks

Marie Devereaux, the symbolic goddess figure, pours water on the ground in front of a thirsty Captain Lewis (Guy Rolfe) in *The Stranglers of Bombay*, Columbia Pictures (1960).

Fisher's hero, Captain Lewis (Guy Rolfe). Lewis is deeply concerned not only about the material losses but by the large numbers of Indians who have disappeared without a trace in recent years. Colonel Henderson agrees to appoint a special team to investigate the disappearances as the meeting breaks up.

Returning to his home Lewis tells his wife (Jan Holden) that he will be the logical choice to head up the special investigation. His wife reminds him that he has just sent a letter to London applying for a new, and better paying, job. Lewis however says that he can't leave the chance for this important investigation. He is haunted by the "sad-eyed faces" of those whose loved ones have disappeared without a trace. His wife agrees and then urges him to send his house boy, Ram Das, to intercept the letter. Ramdas is immediately dispatched to retrieve the application. However, it turns out that Lewis has presumed too much. Colonel Henderson regards Lewis as too unorthodox to conduct the investigation and turns the assignment over to the son of a friend of his. The son, Captain Connaught-Smith (Allan Cuthbertson), is completely inexperienced and also quite arrogant. Lewis is shocked to learn that he will not be given the assignment to lead the investigation. His offer of help to Connaught-Smith is ignored.

Just as Connaught-Smith is arriving, Lewis captures two Thugees and finds their silk scarves. Before Lewis has the chance to understand the significance of his capture, the two prisoners are rescued by Thugees in the city. Lewis himself is attacked in an alley, and the silk scarf he is carrying is stolen. In addition, his house boy, Ram Das, claims to have seen a caravan with his brother who was abducted as a child. Ram Das asks permission to go in search of the caravan. Lewis grants the request and offers him both a horse and money to help him in his search. In gratitude Ram Das gives Lewis a family medallion for safekeeping and also asks him to watch his pet mongoose during his absence.

While this is taking place Fisher reveals the fate of the two Thugees whom Lewis had captured. After being rescued they are informed by the high priest that they have defied the great goddess Kali. For punishment they will be blinded and their tongues will be torn out. Witness Patel Shari, introduced in the earlier scene with the East India Company representatives, is now revealed as one of the Thugees. In fact, unknown to the British leaders there are many Thugees who have infiltrated themselves into the military and into the East India Company itself. Fisher handles the gouging out of the men's eyes and tongues in a suggestive but very powerful way that has lost little of its impact over more than forty years. The sequence is rounded out by the presence of a dark, voluptuous young woman (Marie Devereaux) who silently smiles at the men's fate as she throws food and water into the cage where they are confined. All of this creates a powerful series of images that surpass any previous depiction of lust and cruelty in Fisher's work.

Lewis begins to learn the reality of what is going on when the hand of Ram Das is tossed through a window into his kitchen to his wife's horror. Lewis goes to Colonel Henderson and proceeds to indict the East India Company and indeed British colonialism itself for their failure to recognize the severity of what is happening in India (this is somewhat striking for an English film made in 1959). Exasperated, Lewis resigns in disgust. Shortly thereafter, while on a hunting trip, he comes upon a mass shallow grave holding many of the bodies of the Thugee victims. He traces the Thugees to their lair and, rather foolishly, gets close enough to be caught. What follows is one of Fisher's most remarkable sequences.

Lewis is tied down spread-eagle under the hot sun in front of the idol of Kali. The high priest is prepared to offer him as a sacrifice. The dark, silent woman taunts him overtly by drinking water while he looks on helplessly and obviously suffering from thirst. On a covert level she exudes sexuality, sitting to one side of the black, naked statue of the goddess. Lewis' spread-eagle posture itself suggests a sexual victim. When the high priest kneels over him with a raised knife we seem to be witnessing an implicit castration. The high priest, however, cuts into his leg and the blood begins to flow. A cobra is loosed and menacingly approaches Lewis. As the cobra is almost on top on him, Ram Das' mongoose, which was in Lewis' saddle bag, jumps out and runs over to the cobra. They fight but soon the mongoose has the cobra's neck in its mouth. The snake is dead. Seeing this as an evil omen, the high priest orders Lewis to be set free.

Lewis returns to the military base with the news that they are dealing with a deadly, religious cult. His efforts are undermined both by the blindness of the British leaders and the deceit of the Thugees who have infiltrated much of the colonial station. An expedition led by Captain Connaugh-Smith ends in disaster and in his own death. At the conclusion of the film Lewis once again spies on the Thugee camp. A funeral pyre is being prepared. One of the bodies to be placed on it is the corpse of Ram Das. Standing in the forefront of the funeral pyre is the dark woman again, her large breasts silhouetted against the burning torches as the high priest demands that Lewis be added to the pyre. Lewis however is wearing Ram Das' medallion. The young initiate first introduced in the prologue wears a matching one. He is Ram Das' long-lost brother. Realizing he has been tricked into taking part in his own brother's murder, he cuts Lewis' bonds. Lewis rushes at the high priest. In the struggle the high priest

Maid Marian waits for Robin Hood in *The Sword of Sherwood Forest* (1960).

falls onto the burning pyre. The worshippers disperse in a panic. Lewis escapes again and finally unmasks the hidden Thugees including the Patel Shari.

The contrivance of the film's plot does not mitigate its power nor its disturbing imagery. *The Stranglers of Bombay* is an essential work in Fisher's career. While not technically a horror film, it contains more grisly detail than any of the Frankenstein or Dracula films Fisher did in this period. Yet violence is never an end to itself and Fisher's scenes of torture and mutilation involve suggestive camerawork that only makes them more effective. It is unfortunate that *Stranglers* is a much less familiar work than Fisher's color gothics. There are several important features of the film that need to be noted.

First, the character of Captain Lewis expresses the full range of Fisher's hero. Lewis is dealing with a much broader, more profound dimension of evil than is faced by other Fisher heroes. Van Helsing, Sherlock Holmes, Father Sandor and Professor Meister all confront evil but invariably in a very focused form. Their opponents are concrete and tied to a specific locale, usually only affecting a single family. Captain Lewis, on the other hand, faces a complex goddess cult which accounts for thousands of victims a year and threatens all of India and indeed British colonialism itself. The sheer body count in *Stranglers* is overwhelming. Second, Lewis is called upon to sacrifice himself extensively. He is rejected by his peers. He loses his job. His whole family is put at risk and he himself runs the risk more than once of becoming an offering to Kali. His personal vulnerability and indeed suffering exceeds that of the other Fisher heroes. Interestingly enough, he is one of the few Fisher heroes that is not celibate. He has an attractive blond wife who symbolically offsets the dark haired sensual woman of the cult. Lewis, not personally at risk initially, is prepared to sacrifice himself for thousands of others who do not even know who he is, and many of those who do know him dismiss his efforts (or work to destroy him).

Referred to several times previously, the ancient Gilgamesh epic suggests Fisher's depiction of Frankenstein and others who seek eternal life by their own pursuits. Lewis stands for another mythical dimension of Fisher's cinema. This is the equally ancient figure of the Redeemer Hero. This figure emerges as the defending hero who is prepared to take on the power of evil at the cost of his own life in order to save the world. The Babylonians called him Marduk. The Canaanites called him Baal; the Egyptians, Osiris. He is the precursor of Hercules and Achilles along with King Arthur, Charlemagne and Robin Hood. In modern culture he is found in many examples from the Harry Potter books to TV science fiction shows like *First Wave*. Some would argue that Jesus Christ is simply another variation on this mythical hero.[3]

The Kali mother cult in this film taps into a deep reservoir of mythology also. Kali is an older form of the ancient goddess already discussed in other Fisher films. Kali, however, is explicitly a mother figure. She is especially complex in that she both gives birth and brings death.[4] Her only personification in this film is the silent dark woman. This is a much more abstract representation than that found in *The Mummy* or *The Gorgon*. Another ancient myth, equally as old or older than the stories of Gilgamesh or Marduk, is the Sumerian account of Inanna's descent into hell. Inanna is the primordial goddess who descends to the underworld in search of her lost love, dies, is resurrected and then executes vengeance on her lover.

These myths have a minimum of narrative but convey a rich assortment of themes and imagery. They evidence the interdependence of death and sex, of love and vengeance, of fear and mystery.[5] The Redeemer Hero, according to some feminist scholars, represents the brutal suppression of the goddess tradition by the emergence of male warriors who usher in the era of patriarchy.[6] However, as noted earlier, it is difficult to see the goddess in these most ancient legends as a nurturing, caring mother figure. The maternal aspect exists alongside a vengeful, destructive and seductive element. The Redeemer Hero in the myths themselves is the deliverer, the savior from chaos, death and evil. In *Stranglers* Fisher taps into these mythological themes, complete with the ancient serpent motif, in a way that reveals more symbolic depth than in his more well known films. In order to assess fully the figure of the Redeemer Hero some other examples need to be considered.

It is not surprising that Fisher's interest in the Redeemer Hero should lead him to the English legendary figure, Robin Hood. During the 1950s Fisher was one of the directors of the popular TV series filmed in England titled *The Adventures of Robin Hood*. Also, one of Hammer's early color films had been *Men of Sherwood Forest* released in 1954. In 1960 Fisher began filming *The Sword of Sherwood Forest* on location in Ireland. Robin Hood would be played by Richard Greene who had essayed the role on television and, ironically, had played Sir Henry Baskerville in the Basil Rathbone version of *The Hound of the Baskervilles*. His co-star would be another actor famous for playing Sherlock Holmes, Peter Cushing, who took the role of the Sheriff of Nottingham. Contrary to the dark pagan atmosphere of *The Stranglers of Bombay*, this next portrayal of the Redeemer Hero would be in a recognizable Christian context.

Just as Fisher and Hammer had done with the classic gothic horror stories, the familiar story of Robin Hood is adapted to an existing outlook which both illuminates aspects of the famous tale while, at the same time, adds some new dimensions to them. *Sword of Sherwood Forest* is, among other things, a very appealing, attractive film. It was filmed in Ireland in Technicolor and benefits from the lush scenery of the Irish countryside which doubles as the Sherwood Forest of the title. The opening shot of the film shows a dramatic waterfall as Fisher's camera pans to the surrounding woods introducing the audience visually to the world of Robin Hood. It is unfortunate that this also is a film that is relatively unavailable and not often seen, since it is one of Fisher's more stunning looking films. In addition, it continues Fisher's cinematic reflection on the figure of the Redeemer Hero.

As is often the case in Fisher's films, the beauty of nature is offset by human cruelty. The opening shot of the film shows a man being taken prisoner. The man is on horseback with his hands tied behind him. Suddenly he spurs his horse and seeks to escape. Several solders pursue him on horseback and one wounds him with the arrow of a crossbow. The man eludes his captors but collapses by a stream in the forest where a beautiful young woman is swimming. Two archers find the man unconscious but alive. A third bowman, Robin Hood (Richard Greene), arrives. The young woman emerging from her swim accuses the men of spying on her. When she sees the wounded man she realizes she has not been the object of their attention. Nonetheless, Robin is clearly intrigued with her. Keeping her distance from him she still gives him her name, Lady Marian Fitzwalter (Sarah Branch).

Marion herself is apparently intrigued with the outlaw so she arranges a special meeting with him and the Sheriff of Nottingham (Peter Cushing, in one of his most sinister roles). The Sheriff is prepared to offer Robin a full pardon on the condition that he turn over the wounded man Robin found in the forest. Distrusting the Sheriff, Robin declines the offer much to the chagrin of Maid Marian. His suspicion is justified when the Sheriff attempts to capture him in spite of the truce which set up the meeting. Robin escapes and makes his way back to his camp in Sherwood. The wounded man dies from his injuries. Just before he dies he mentions the name "Bortry." The only clue he leaves is a medallion showing a falcon seizing a daisy. Robin doesn't know why the Sheriff was so interested in this man or what his dying word signifies. However he suspects that something major is about to happen.

Sensing that the Sheriff will come looking for his escaped prisoner, Robin orders his men to break camp. His suspicions are justified as the Sheriff and his soldiers begin combing the countryside. They find one of Robin's men, Martin of Eastwood. The Sheriff is prepared to have Martin executed but promises him a free pardon if he will reveal Robin's hiding place. Terrified, Martin tells where the outlaw camp is located. The Sheriff has him executed anyway. As Martin lies dying after the Sheriff and his men have left, Maid Marian finds him and he reveals what has happened. Robin also arrives. Martin begs forgiveness for having betrayed Robin. Robin assures him that the outlaws have moved to a new camp and are all safe. With this assurance Martin dies. Robin crosses himself and adds, "We'll see that he has a Christian burial."

Robin goes to visit Friar Tuck (Niall MacGinnis) to inquire about Bortry. The friar tells him it is the name of a small town of no particular importance some distance away. Robin is convinced that something important is going to happen there and plans to go. However, before he can leave a group of soldiers arrive, asking the friar for water. One of them, Melton (Oliver Reed), spies Robin and arrogantly demands that he bring him a drink. Robin deliberately spills the water on him. Outraged, Melton is ready to attack Robin whom he believes simply to be a servant. Melton's Lord, the Earl of Newark (Richard Pasco), suggests that the dispute be settled by an archery competition. Robin easily shoots Melton's falcon. Impressed, the Earl conscripts Robin into his service, having no idea who this archer really is. As Robin turns to follow the Earl, he asks Friar Tuck to go and find out what is happening in Bortry.

The Earl gives Robin several archery tests which of course he passes admirably. His identity is suddenly revealed when the Sheriff unexpectedly appears and recognizes the notorious outlaw. Once again Robin makes his escape. While in the Earl's employ he had noticed the medallion of the falcon and the daisy which the dying man also had. With information from Friar Tuck Robin now begins to put the pieces of the puzzle together. The medallion is the symbol of a secret group led by the Earl of Newark planning to seize control of England. To achieve this, they have plotted, with the Sheriff's help, to assassinate Hubert Walter, the Archbishop of Canterbury (Jack Gwillim). The Archbishop is ruling in the place of King Richard who is away at war. Their first idea had been to gain possession of a castle in Bortry which they would have used as an ideal site to assassinate the Archbishop on his way to London. When that failed they had to seek another opportunity before Hubert could make his way to London.

Robin seeks now to protect Hubert Walter. Maid Marian has also become aware of the threat at hand and warns Hubert. However before Robin can get to him in time Hubert Walter and his men along with Maid Marian are attacked by the Earl's soldiers. Robin and his men come to the rescue late. Some of Hubert's men have been killed but Hubert himself and Marian escape to the refuge of a nearby convent. Unfortunately the Mother Superior is a member of the secret society and a cousin of the Earl. Hearing that Hubert has taken refuge in the convent, the Earl is more than pleased with his good fortune. With his cousin's aid he plans to murder Hubert while he is in the false security of the convent. This is too much even for the Sheriff of Nottingham. It combines treason with sacrilege.

Before he can do anything to oppose the Earl he is stabbed in the back by Melton. His dying words are, "Is this how you treat your friends?" Fortunately, before the Earl can carry out his plans Robin and his men sneak into the convent and, in a fierce battle, defeat the Earl and his followers. After winning the battle they join in a time of prayer in the convent's chapel. The film concludes with Hubert leaving Sherwood in safety for London. In response to Maid Marian's petition for justice for the slain Martin of Eastwood, Hubert grants him a posthumous pardon so that his family can inherit his land. Hubert's final order is that Friar Tuck perform a wedding for Robin and Marian.

The Sword of Sherwood Forest has a number of striking parallels with Stranglers of Bombay. Like Captain Lewis, Robin Hood is often misunderstood and rejected by the official "authorities" in the country. He must also work outside the normal structures of society. Like Lewis he is confronted with a Thugee-like conspiracy to take over his country which has infiltrated itself into every level of society. To save his country he must place himself in situations of extreme risk and danger with no guarantee that his efforts will be appreciated. Unlike Lewis he does not have to work alone. He has the support of his "merry men," not to mention the added benefit of Maid Marian.

Outside of the love of Maid Marian (which is hardly guaranteed), Robin receives no visible benefit from his efforts to save the life of Hubert Walter and, ultimately, his country. Unlike other Robin Hood films he is not pardoned at the end. In answer to Maid Marian's request for a pardon for Robin, Hubert simply says that he must wait for Richard's return from France. Throughout the film, then, Robin risks his life numerous times against a threat which only gradually becomes evident to him. At the end of the film Robin is the same he was at the beginning: an outlaw living in Sherwood Forest (with the not inconsiderable benefit of having Maid Marian as a wife). Fisher's version of the familiar story is distinguished first by strong religious imagery and secondly by a darker, more perverse than in other accounts of the legend. Fisher shows Robin as a devout Christian, crossing himself at appropriate times and praying. The church atmosphere is further strengthened by having the Archbishop of Canterbury as the country's ruler. Robin's foes in the film are not simply the Sheriff of Nottingham nor a political usurper of the throne. The Earl of Newark is the leader of a secret society which has followers in every level of English society, even in the church. The Earl's falcon society then is a close parallel to the Thugees in Stranglers. This society's practices are too perverse even for the Sheriff of Nottingham, who is finally killed by them.

Robin Hood then takes on the familiar cast of the Fisher hero who is "fighting evil" not in some ordinary sense but in an intense and very threatening form. Like Captain Lewis, Robin shows the sacrificial nature of this character. Because the forces of evil in these films are universally present, and not confined to some specific locale like Castle Dracula or Baskerville Hall, there is no escaping them. Their followers are everywhere and so, then, are their victims. The hero who opposes them is risking his life totally. Capt. Lewis and Robin Hood are saviors of their nations. Yet they are largely unknown to most of those whom they benefit. They act out of a higher duty without any need of recognition or reward (at least Sherlock Holmes gets paid for unmasking the "hound of hell"). These heroes then function on a mythical level in the ancient tradition of gods like Marduk and Osiris who sacrifice themselves to free the world of ultimate forms of evil.[7]

One cannot leave a discussion of *The Sword of Sherwood Forest* without mentioning its obvious influence on George Lucas' *Star Wars* (1977). This is immediately apparent in the similarity of Peter Cushing's General Tonk in *Star Wars* to his Sheriff of Nottingham. The scene where General Tonk promises to save the planet Alderon if Princess Leia will reveal the hiding place of the rebels, and then proceeds to destroy it even after she has told him the location, is a direct cinematic "quote" from the Sheriff using the same ploy on Martin of Eastwick in *Sword of Sherwood Forest*. Anyone watching Fisher's film is struck by the similar dress and hair style of Maid Marian to Princess Leia in the later film. More significantly, the whole concept of rebels in hiding fighting against a massive organization of evil power which uses any means to achieve its ends, in a quasi-medieval setting no less, certainly evokes Fisher's Robin Hood film. Clearly, *Star Wars* borrows from many sources, from *Flash Gordon* to *The Searchers* to a host of genre films. However, the strong parallels to *Sword of Sherwood Forest* combined with the presence of Peter Cushing and David Prowse (as the physical Darth Vader) whose previous films include Fisher's *Frankenstein and the Monster from Hell*, certainly show Fisher's influence. The differences lie in the mythic symbolism. Lucas' "force" seems to borrow from Zen Buddhism as opposed to Fisher's Christian orientation. These differences will have to be discussed further after exploring other examples of Fisher's Redeemer Hero.

One of the most frustrating films in Fisher's career has to be *Sherlock Holmes and the Deadly Necklace*. By all accounts this should have been a classic. The film was produced in (what was then) West Germany in 1962. Christopher Lee was signed on to play Sherlock Holmes. Thorley Walters, who appeared in a number of films for Fisher, portrayed Dr. Watson. Hans Sohnker, an excellent German character actor, appeared as Professor Moriarity. Curt

Siodmak, who had scripted many of the Universal Studios horror classics of the 1940s, wrote the screenplay as an adaptation of the Conan Doyle novel *The Valley of Fear*.[8] Terence Fisher was to direct. On paper the project had all the makings of a Holmes classic worthy of rivaling, if not surpassing, Fisher's earlier *Hound of the Baskervilles*. Unfortunately the final film comes nowhere near such lofty expectations. Like John Barrymore's silent film of *Sherlock Holmes*, first-rate talent does not necessarily lead to first-rate results. One major problem in assessing the film available in Britain and North America is the fact the film was subsequently dubbed by actors other than the originals. To see a physically impressive Lee as Holmes speaking dialogue in another voice that has none of the resonance or force of Lee's own is disconcerting at best and terribly frustrating at worst. The musical soundtrack is bizarre at times, more suggestive of a period piece comedy than a mystery thriller. The script is discordant or incomplete. A recent video copy appears to lack some scenes. While some sequences are impressive, others are not. Fisher shares directorial credit with a Frank Witherstein. Who directed what is again unclear although Fisher seems to have done the bulk of the film. Apparently all connected with the project were unhappy with the final result. In spite of these significant drawbacks, the film does have some merits and is a key stage in the development of the Redeemer Hero in Fisher's work.

The film's rambling plot has Holmes engaged in the familiar cat and mouse pursuit of Professor Moriarity, the "Napoleon of crime." Borrowing elements from the Mummy films, the coffin of Cleopatra is found and with it an incredibly valuable necklace worn by the Egyptian queen herself (hence the "deadly necklace" of the title). Moriarity is in pursuit of the necklace. It is in the possession of a James Blackburn whose identity Holmes deciphers from one of his agents who works for Moriarity. Blackburn is apparently shot in the face by an assailant. Holmes investigates and apparently realizes that Blackburn actually had killed his assailant in a struggle and has dressed him in his clothes so he will be thought dead. This comes from the murder investigation at the heart of the Sherlock Holmes film *The Valley of Fear*. Moriarity gains control of Cleopatra's necklace only to have Holmes sneak into his house and steal it out of an Egyptian sarcophagus. Interestingly in this film, Moriarity is an Egyptologist rather than a mathematics professor. An attempt by Moriarity to regain control of the necklace as the police are taking it to an auction is frustrated by Holmes disguised as one of Moriarity's men. At the end of the film Holmes' attempt to link Moriarity to the theft of the jewel fails. He tries to expose Moriarity by showing that his cane is actually a concealed sword with which he had threatened Holmes' life. Holmes' effort is rebuffed when Moriarity demonstrates that his cane contains nothing more than a small flask and a glass

(Moriarity apparently has a whole collection of canes with hidden features). Inspector Cooper of Scotland Yard has maintained throughout the film that Holmes' suspicions of the respected Professor are completely groundless. The film closes with Moriarity offering a ride to a rich Texan who has just purchased the necklace at the auction. Obviously he will not be in possession of it very long. Holmes indicates to Watson that their conflict with Moriarity is far from over.

Fisher's approach to Sherlock Holmes both here and in *The Hound of the Baskervilles* is a distinctive one. As mentioned earlier, Holmes is the only Fisher hero to have been portrayed by both Peter Cushing and Christopher Lee. Peter Cushing's Holmes in Fisher's version of *Hound* had more of a metaphysical cast to his character. Rather than focusing on solving the mystery, this Holmes emphasized the fact that he was "fighting evil." When Holmes and Watson think they have seen Sir Henry's dead body (it's actually the convict who was wearing Sir Henry's clothes), Holmes says, "I will not rest until I've destroyed the thing that killed him." Holmes is avenging the death more than solving the mystery or preventing a crime. This is a very different reading of Sherlock Holmes than had been seen in previous films or even in the original Conan Doyle stories. At the same time, Cushing's arrogant intensity was closer to Conan Doyle's original than was the case with previous screen interpreters like Arthur Wontner or Basil Rathbone.[9]

Christopher Lee's interpretation continues this development but also adds an intriguing dimension to it. Interestingly, this film apparently was a major point of development in Fisher's work with Lee. It is only after this picture that Lee begins to play the Fisher hero in such significant films as *The Gorgon* and *The Devil Rides Out*. Lee maintains the same arrogant intensity that Peter Cushing brought to the role. Unlike Cushing's performance, Lee's Holmes is shown in disguise frequently, especially in the film's climax. Having Holmes confronted by a Professor Moriarity who is an Egyptian scholar and who keeps glass mummies in his study, complete with deadly traps for those who would seek to open them, certainly brings Sherlock Holmes more into the venue of gothic horror than Victorian mystery. When Holmes in disguise breaks into Moriarity's study and opens the glass case of a mummy in which he rightfully believes Cleopatra's necklace is hidden, he comes upon a deadly snake. Holmes adroitly seizes the snake, chokes it and thrusts it back into the coffin. Given Fisher's penchant for snake imagery as a motif for evil, drawing as he admits on the Garden of Eden account in the Bible, this again gives more than an element of Professor Van Helsing to his view of Sherlock Holmes.[10]

The most telling aspect of Holmes, however, in this film is his vulnerability. Holmes' insistence that Professor Moriarity is a master criminal is ridiculed by Scotland Yard. Like Fisher's approach in *The Hound of the Baskervilles*, this takes an element from Conan Doyle's original story and then develops it in a further direction. Holmes in the original novel of the *Hound* does make a reference to combating evil which then Fisher and his Hammer colleagues develop into a dominant motif in the whole film. Likewise, in *The Valley of Fear* there is a scene in which Inspector MacDonald chides Holmes on his fixation on, in the Inspector's mind, an entirely innocent Professor Moriarity. This scene occurs virtually verbatim in the film. Yet, again, Fisher expands on it. Throughout *The Deadly Necklace*, Holmes' warnings about the Professor go unheeded. Simultaneously, Holmes himself is in danger from the Professor not once but several times, narrowly escaping on each occasion. At the conclusion of the film Holmes has definitely been outsmarted by Moriarity who continues his criminal pursuit of the valuable necklace. This is a highly atypical ending to a Holmes film. Yet it is consistent with Fisher's unique view of Holmes' character and role.

Holmes is another version of Fisher's Redeemer Hero. He is putting his life on the line in a cosmic struggle. Like his predecessors he is not only unrewarded in his efforts but actually rebuffed. Holmes struggles not only against Moriarity but also against an unbelieving Scotland Yard which sees him as doing little more than harassing the Professor. At the end of the film his efforts are still neither vindicated nor rewarded. Holmes achieves nothing personally by his pursuit of Moriarity. In reality he has nothing to gain. Like Captain Lewis and Robin Hood he is sacrificing himself to benefit those who not only do not appreciate him but positively resent his interference. It is ironic that an earlier British film version of Conan Doyle's *The Valley of Fear* was titled *The Triumph of Sherlock Holmes*. In Fisher's version Holmes most assuredly does not triumph. He does however sacrifice himself. The success of his efforts up to a point gives one the expectation that he will eventually triumph (apparently a sequel to the film was planned but never made). However in this film it is the nature and cost of his personal sacrifice that is striking. Moriarity is checked temporarily in this version but not defeated. This alone is the vindication of Holmes' efforts. Lee's performance in this very uneven film prepares the way for his role of Professor Meister in the far more developed film of *The Gorgon*. However Fisher's next treatment of the Redeemer Hero in the cosmic sense of a savior of the world would take place in a contemporary science fiction film with Peter Cushing playing the hero.

Island of Terror was one of several science fiction films that Fisher made in the 1960s away from Hammer Studios. It is the most memorable

Toni (Carole Gray) is threatened by the silicone monsters in *Island of Terror*, Universal Pictures (1966).

of the group and one that advances Fisher's theme of the Redeemer Hero. The film takes place on an island off the east coast of Ireland where a scientist has been working on a cure for cancer. A Dr. Philips (Peter Forbes Robertson) is part of a research project on cancer which is also going on simultaneously in Rome, New York and Tokyo. The island's inhabitants know little of his experiments. The first sign that something is wrong occurs when the body of a local inhabitant is found dead without any trace of bone in him. The body is brought to the home of the island's resident doctor, Dr. Landers (Eddie Byrne). Landers is completely mystified so he goes to London to call on a specialist, Dr. Brian Stanley (Peter Cushing). Stanley enlists the aid of a brilliant young doctor named David West (Edward Judd). When Landers and Stanley go to West's apartment they find him in a very cozy situation with his girlfriend, Toni Merrill (Carole Gray). West agrees to come to the remote island with them on the condition that Toni can come as well. They agree after some hesitation.

Back on the island, Stanley along with West and Landers do a thorough analysis of the boneless corpse. None of them can imagine any cause for the complete absence of bone in the body. Stanley asks if there are any other research facilities on the island so that he can do some more tests. Landers suggests the laboratory of Dr. Philips, the cancer research scientist, although he acknowledges that Philips has always worked in secret and might not be amenable to letting them use his lab. Stanley insists that they have to try. Arriving at the secluded mansion where Philips and his team worked they find it apparently deserted. Becoming suspicious they enter and find more boneless bodies. Convinced that something in the research lab may account for the mystery, they take Philips' notes and begin studying them. However, more bodies without bone are being found on the island, including bodies of animals. They decide to return to Philips' laboratory and this time Toni insists on coming with them. The mansion has a castle-like look to it. Returning to the lab in the lower basement they hear a strange sound. Suddenly they are confronted with a tentacle which belongs to a deadly tortoise-like mutant. These mutants, offspring of the failed cancer research, are the cause of the dead bodies whose bones have been literally sucked out.

This is an intriguing, though hardly original, premise. Prowling aliens were a staple of many low budget science fiction films of the 1950s.[11] *Island of Terror* fits into that category. Its tortoise-like creatures are not exactly memorable and the boneless bodies of their victims look all too much like the rubber dummies that they are. What makes the film memorable is Fisher's strong direction. He steadily builds an atmosphere of claustrophobic menace that leads to a tense conclusion. As the island's inhabitants retreat further and further from the "silicone monsters" and David West, with the concurrence of Dr. Stanley, is about to administer Toni with a lethal injection to save her from a radioactive, bone destroying death, Fisher achieves one of his most frightening climaxes. This is quickly dissipated as the counteractive efforts of the scientists suddenly takes effect and the monsters die from the serum that Stanley and West had used to inject the livestock just before they were attacked by the monsters. This again is a conventional resolution, going as far back as H.G. Wells' *War of the Worlds*. The ending of the film, however, is interesting. Dr. Philips, whose original experiments led to the development of the monsters, had mentioned that Rome, New York and Tokyo all had research teams working on the same project. In an epilogue a laboratory in Tokyo with a team of research scientists explodes and the same high pitched signal heard earlier indicates that this experiment has also gone awry and the monsters will be unleashed once again, though not on an isolated island this time, but in the heart of a major metropolis.

The significance of *Island of Terror* resides in the character of Dr. Brian Stanley. Like the other heroes mentioned in this chapter, Dr. Stanley takes the lead as a Redeemer Hero prepared to sacrifice himself here, literally, to save the world. Once again, Dr. Stanley is brought into the conflict from the outside. He chooses to place himself at risk. This happens early on the first time he and Dr. Landers and Dr. West visit the lab of the doomed Dr. Philips. As the three make their way to the basement laboratory they pass a door that says, "Danger. Radioactive materials." Dr. Stanley, nonchalantly, opens the door and steps inside while the other two, quite willingly, wait outside. He exits with the observation, "He was keeping radioactive isotopes there." Needless to say, he has exposed himself to radioactivity. Peter Cushing brings more than an element of Sherlock Holmes to his portrayal, using such Holmesian phrases as, "interesting problem." When the scientists and now the island police are first confronted with a series of the "silicone monsters," Stanley, in an effort to determine whether or not the creatures are radioactive, volunteers to get near them to find out. "Let me go first" is his matter of fact statement. More importantly, Stanley himself is later attacked by the monsters and can only gain his freedom by having Dr. West chop off his hand with an axe! What is striking about this is that Dr. Stanley becomes the only Fisher hero to suffer bodily loss in his struggle against the forces of destruction. Dr. Van Helsing was bitten by a vampire in *Brides of Dracula* but was able to offset the effects by pouring holy water on his neck, thereby not suffering any long-term consequences. In the loss of his hand, Dr. Stanley suffers scars that will never heal. In a straightforward way he has come to the rescue of the world by leading the fight against the radioactive monsters. He undertakes this for no immediate personal benefit (presumably the monsters could have been contained on the island). He places himself at risk again and again in such a natural way that the viewer never focuses on how much he is continuing to expose himself to risk. Even the loss of his hand is just another aspect of the risks necessary to stop the threat of the monsters. Yet without his leadership and his sacrificial courage, the island would never have been saved.

One could argue that there are really only two foundational stories in world literature. The first is the Gilgamesh Epic with its tale of the fruitless quest for eternal life. The second is that of the Redeemer Hero who at the risk of his own life slays the primordial dragon thereby bringing life and hope to the world. These two stories form the basis of much of the mythology, religious epics and literature of the world. They have been reinterpreted and retold from ancient Sumer to the present. Their motifs repeat from the Babylonian creation account to the continuing saga of *Star Wars*. An essential aspect of Fisher's fantasy films is the retelling of these two epics. Fisher's Frankenstein, as already noted, is a contemporary version of the Gilgamesh story with Fisher's insight that Frankenstein never truly comprehends the futility and utter hopelessness of his quest. In showing this Fisher makes Frankenstein into a parable of society's ill-placed, and essentially atheistic, confidence in science and technology. Fisher's other films show his variations on the Redeemer Hero. He is the figure usually portrayed by either Peter Cushing or Christopher Lee, as Van Helsing, Sherlock Holmes, Father Sandor and Professor Meister. However it is only in looking at some of Fisher's non-horror films that the full dimensions of the Redeemer Hero are seen. The films discussed in this chapter, which represent a variety of film genres, have exemplified the universal scope of this character. Comparing the Van Helsing type with these others, Fisher has, perhaps unintentionally, focused on the ancient mythical view of the savior who gives his life for the world. This figure, prominent in so many mythical and religious accounts from Marduk, Baal and Osiris to Hercules, Siegfried and Robin Hood represents an enduring fascination and indeed appeal across the centuries. Indeed Harry Potter today represents just one more variation on this character whom Joseph Campbell called the hero with a thousand faces.

However, as an interpretation of Fisher's worldview this would certainly be incomplete. His essential view of the hero figure is not simply that of a mythical redeemer but, more precisely, a Christian warrior. Fisher's hero has his roots firmly in an English tradition which includes King Arthur and John Bunyan's Christian. It is appropriate at this point to reintroduce the figure of the Duc De Richeleau, Fisher's hero in his masterpiece, *The Devil Rides Out*. This character as portrayed by Christopher Lee is arguably the summation of all Fisher's previous heroes. He sums up not only the gothic heroes like Van Helsing and Professor Meister but Captain Lewis, Sherlock Holmes, Robin Hood and *Island of Terror*'s Dr. Stanley. De Richeleau is intent on saving the soul of the son of a deceased friend. In accomplishing this he confronts a cosmic witchcraft which goes well beyond a specific figure like Dracula, the Mummy or the Gorgon. De Richeleau is confronting Satan himself through his disciple Mocata. He has the determination, energy and occult knowledge of a Van Helsing. Like Holmes he analyzes each minute detail and disappears when necessary to engage in further research. He is a strategic leader like Robin Hood. He has the independence and nerve of a Captain Lewis. Finally he is fully prepared to sacrifice his own life like Dr. Stanley.

The culmination of Fisher's Redeemer Hero occurs in the climax of *The Devil Rides Out* when, confronted with Mocata's intention to sacrifice the daughter of his niece, he offers himself. "Take me," he says and let the child go free. There is no more provocative or powerful moment in Fisher's cinema. In making that statement De Richeleau is offering not only his body but his *soul*. He is giving himself up not just to death but to a satanic blood sacrifice. The question was raised earlier, does Fisher's view of the conflict between good and evil demand a Christian warrior? That question can now be answered with a definite yes. However, viewing the breadth of Fisher's development of this theme, for him, accurately representing the Christian tradition, the Redeemer Hero per se is no more effective than Gilgamesh was in his quest. The validity of the Redeemer Hero for Fisher is his symbolic pointing to Jesus Christ. The myth of the Redeemer Hero invariably presents an unfulfilled task outside of history. This is why the Redeemer myths were repeated and acted out again and again. They expressed death and rebirth as ongoing cycles of life. The conflict with evil, like the Egyptian myth of the conflict between Osiris and Seth referred to in *The Devil Rides Out,* continues endlessly without resolution. For Fisher, however, there is a resolution. It is found in the cross of Christ which brings a cosmic resolution at the end of *Devil Rides Out.*

Christ is not simply a variant of the Redeemer Hero. He is both its historical and spiritual culmination. He is the reality to which the myths imperfectly point. In that sense, but only in that sense, can De Richeleau be invoking Osiris as Mocata invokes Seth. The mythical names point to the realities of Christ and Satan. The implication of Fisher's films is that the Redeemer Hero can sacrifice himself because his sacrifice points to the true and ultimate sacrifice of Jesus Christ. It is that sacrifice, symbolized in the various forms of the cross, running water, light and even a mongoose, which guarantees the victory. This same sacrifice validates too the love of a mother or a wife. Admittedly, Fisher does not give the same prominence to his female heroes but at the same time they are not completely absent (seen also in *The Devil Rides Out*).

The Redeemer Hero is the culminating image of Fisher's films. It is the counterpart to his Frankenstein/Gilgamesh figure. The Redeemer Hero is both validated and fulfilled in the ultimate Redeemer Savior figure of Christ just as atheism underlies the destructive pursuits of Frankenstein. Ultimately then Fisher's cinematic vision is a spiritual one. It is informed by the same Christian commitment that underlies the fiction of C.S. Lewis, Charles Williams and Dorothy L. Sayers.[12] Fisher's outlook is certainly not that of his contemporaries. In a post–Christian, postmodern secular climate Fisher presented a dynamic Christian interpretation rooted both in ancient myth and biblical faith. Fisher's worldview stands in marked contrast not only to many others in the film world but also differs from many of his colleagues at Hammer Studios. Now, however, two decades after his death in a world that is not only postmodern, but increasingly pagan in outlook and practice, it should be no surprise that Fisher's films continue to find an audience. What remains about them is their essential hope that good is not only definable but ultimately triumphant. For Fisher that hope is fulfilled in the cross of Jesus Christ and his promise of resurrection. Fisher then emerges as a unique, engrossing and challenging Christian apologist. A number of prominent contemporary filmmakers are clearly indebted to him. These include George Lucas, Joe Dante, Martin Scorsese and Tim Burton. Unfortunately their films do not evidence his same confidence and hope. In that respect Fisher stands alone.[13]

Notes

1. Eyles, Allen; Adkinson, Robert; and Fry, Nicholas, p. 15.
2. Pirie, David. p. 58.
3. Dundel, Allen, "The Hero Pattern and the Life of Jesus," in *In Quest of the Hero*, pp. 179–216; Campbell, Joseph, *The Masks of God: Occidental Mythology*, pp. 334–375.
4. Baring, Anne, and Cashford, Jules, p. 328.
5. A classic statement on the nature of myth can be found in Mircea Eliade's *Myth and Reality*.
6. Baring, Anne, and Cashford, Jules, pp. 273ff.
7. Campbell, Joseph, *The Masks of God: Primitive Mythology*, pp. 424ff; *The Masks of God: Occidental Mythology*, pp. 72ff.
8. Steinbrunner, Chris, and Michaels, Norman, p. 204.
9. This judgment applies also to the Granada Television series with Jeremy Brett as Holmes. Brett, while often excellent, makes Holmes downright surly and almost nasty at times. This is hardly Conan Doyle's picture of the great detective. I have recently had opportunity to view several of the 1968 BBC-TV series with Cushing as Holmes. These only sustain my high view of Cushing's interpretation.
10. The most ancient view of the mythical hero has him defeating a giant serpent in Campbell, Joseph, *The Masks of God: Occidental Mythology*, p. 79. Hercules as an infant strangles two serpents.
11. Among many examples one can mention *Invaders from Mars* (1953), *The Thing from Another World* (1951), *It Conquered the World* (1956), *Invasion of the Body Snatchers* (1956) and *I Married a Monster from Outer Space* (1958).
12. Examples include Lewis' space trilogy (*Out of the Silent Planet, Perelandra, That Hideous Strength*), Williams' *Descent into Hell, All Hallows' Eve* and Sayers' *The Nine Tailors*.
13. Fisher stands for an older, more classic Gothic tradition which Bruce Lewis Wright summarizes in these words: "The Gothic position, by contrast, is that good and evil do exist, and that men's actions carry a moral weight; that our choices count" (Wright, p. 163).

Chapter Seven

TERENCE FISHER: NARRATIVE STYLE AND THE BIBLE

This analysis of Terence Fisher's cinema would be incomplete without some consideration of the narrative structure of his films. Critics over the years have complained about his supposedly graphic portrayal of violence, his seeming one dimensional characters and the artificiality of his narrative style.[1] In reality Fisher's narrative style closely follows the narrative format of much of the Bible. To put it simply, Fisher is essentially a biblical storyteller using the conventions of film. To say that he follows a biblical narrative pattern is on one level not striking in itself. The Bible is so foundational to Western culture that it can be said to be the prototype of virtually all narratives. Yet the Bible can hardly claim to be the sole model even in Western Europe. Ancient epics from Gilgamesh to Homer have certainly played a role. Literary styles have gone through their own development from *Beowulf* to James Joyce's *Ulysses* on up to such diverse authors as William S. Burroughs and Toni Morrison.

Fisher's style belongs to a specific genre of biblical narrative, a style which is followed in such classic works as Edmund Spenser's *The Faerie Queene* and John Bunyan's *The Pilgrim's Progress*. The clearest way to see this is to compare Fisher's cinematic narrative with specific examples in the Bible. The importance of this consideration will be seen in the fact that Fisher's unique themes, with their strong biblical roots, have a major influence on his narrative approach. To put it simply, the way Fisher tells a story is often as important as the subject or theme of the story itself. Like the works mentioned above, Fisher relies heavily on allegory, but it is an allegory within a very concrete and realistic narrative framework. There are six basic motifs in Fisher's narrative style, each of which can be found

in the Bible. The first can be seen in the way Fisher portrays the characters in his films. To illustrate this compare a major early work of Fisher's
such as *Dracula (Horror of Dracula)* with a biblical example like the Gospel
of Mark, generally believed to have been the first gospel written. It will be
seen that Fisher's film of *Dracula* follows the biblical example of character portrayal more closely than it does either Bram Stoker's original novel
or previous film adaptations of the story.

The Gospel of Mark opens with little introduction. In this respect it
is similar to many of the Old Testament narratives.[2] Its opening scene presents John the Baptist in the wilderness proclaiming the coming of the
Messiah. Nothing is said as to how John came to this time and place. Even
in the other gospels, including the birth narratives of Matthew and Luke,
little is said to introduce the setting and action. Very little is known about
Joseph and Mary and virtually nothing of the childhood and early adult
life of either John the Baptist or Jesus.[3] No one ever discusses John's motivation or decision to go into the wilderness and start baptizing. Even when
there is a prologue it is very spare. It is simply stated, "In those days John
the Baptist appeared" (Matthew 3:1). In Mark's gospel one plunges directly
into the action. The opening scene shows Jesus being baptized by John in
the River Jordan. Nothing of the significance or importance of this event
is told at this point in the narrative. The great importance of this act will
be revealed as the story unfolds. The author completely passes over background issues such as Israel's captivity under Roman occupation, the hope
for a messiah or even the general religious situation in the time of John
and Jesus. All of this is part of the story which will be told only indirectly
as events progress. The initial theme in the Gospel actually is conflict. Following his baptism Jesus immediately enters into conflict with Satan in
the wilderness and John is arrested.[4] Jesus scarcely begins his preaching
message before he is confronted with the demonic. Jesus heals the sick but
these acts of mercy are implicitly challenged by the demons who know
who he really is (Mark 1:21–27, 34).

The propelling narrative of the story is based on action. The characters seem to be in constant motion. In a brief chapter John appears in the
wilderness. The people come out to see him. Jesus comes to be baptized
by him. Following this the heavens are "torn apart" as a voice proclaims
that Jesus is the Beloved Son. Jesus goes to the wilderness then to Galilee
then to Capernaum. He enters and leaves the synagogue. The sick and
demon possessed come to him for healing. Essentially no explanation or
interpretation is given to any of the actions. The writer never tells why Jesus
or anyone else goes here or there. Jesus calls the disciples to follow him.
The text simply states that they leave their nets and follow him. Why?

What do they think is the purpose of this dramatic call? What is their reaction to Jesus? Is this their first encounter with him or had they known him before? What are they like as individuals? These questions are not addressed. At this point only the actions are described.

Eric Auerbach in his classic study of Western narrative, *Mimesis*, comments on the striking difference between biblical narrative and the epics of Homer.[5] He points out that whereas Homer does reveal the motivations and thoughts of his characters the biblical writers say very little. Auerbach discusses the biblical story of God's command to Abraham to sacrifice his son Isaac as an example. He points out that God's motivation for such a strange request is never given. Neither is anything really said about Abraham or Isaac's reactions. As in the opening of Mark's gospel the story unfolds through the action of the characters. Yet the reader of the Abraham story knows how God's promise to Abraham is dependent on his son Isaac. How then can God command Abraham to sacrifice his son? The action of child sacrifice in itself would seem to be contrary to God's nature as a God of "justice and righteousness" (cf. Genesis 18:17–25). More specifically the command to sacrifice Isaac is all the more incomprehensible given what has preceded it. In this whole account occasional speeches of the characters are recorded but very little of their inner thoughts or even their character.[6] According to Auerbach this narrative approach creates "overwhelming suspense."[7] The audience is kept sufficiently in the dark and genuinely does not know what to expect. Because so much of the characters' inner thoughts and motivations are hidden they can truly surprise. This is very different Auerbach argues from Homer's characters in the *Iliad* and the *Odyssey* whose characters are introduced from the beginning and whose motivations of power, revenge or fame are clearly spelled out.[8]

The striking result however is that Homer's characters, once defined, never really develop or change. Achilles is the same character the day he dies as when he is introduced the *Iliad*. Ten years of wandering bring no change to Odysseus. On the other hand biblical characters change dramatically over the course of their lives. Auerbach mentions two notable examples: Joseph, who is a very different character as the elder official in Egypt from the boy with the coat of many colors, and David, who likewise goes through many stages from shepherd boy to old king. This development however is described through the actions of these figures rather than through any discussion of their inner thoughts and personalities.[9] It is this feature of biblical narrative that according to Auerbach provides the element of "overwhelming suspense." A good example of this is the famous story of David and Bathsheba in the Second Book of Samuel, chapters 11 and 12. David sees Bathsheba bathing. He inquires about her and sends for her. Nothing is recorded of his reaction to her. His internal desires are made explicit through his external actions. In addition the narrator offers no analysis or explanation for David's flagrant adultery. Once Bathsheba is pregnant David goes through a series of elaborate actions to cover up his offense. His final effort is to order Bathseba's husband Uriah into battle under such conditions that he will surely be killed. Yet the inner workings of David's mind as he moves from one failed cover-up to another are never described. David's specific motivations are never given to us. With no knowledge of his inner thoughts David's actions are surprising. There is no inkling of what he might do until he does it. The reader may well be shocked to find that David, the "man after God's own heart," finally resorts to murder. The story does become genuinely suspenseful.[10]

Fisher's films follow the biblical narrative pattern rather than the Homeric or any more modern approach. Consider the opening of *Dracula*. There is the voice-over narration of Jonathan Harker coming to Castle Dracula. Harker is introduced entering the castle. There is no introduction to Harker's visit as there is in Bram Stoker's original novel or in the Tod Browning film version with Bela Lugosi.[11] As will be revealed later in Fisher's version there are important antecedents to this visit. Harker has been in collaboration with Professor Van Helsing. His alleged purpose in coming to serve as a librarian is only a pose. In fact he has come to destroy Dracula. All of this is quite different from the original novel and earlier film versions in which Harker is totally unaware of Dracula's true character. Like the Gospel of Mark and the other biblical examples mentioned, the entire opening of the film introduces the story through action. No characters' prior history is given. The protagonists are understood only as they act. No explanation is ever given why Dracula is a vampire or how he even became one. This is very different from more "psychological" treatments of the story beginning with Dan Curtis' 1973 treatment and continuing through Francis Ford Coppola's 1992 version, to say nothing of the vampire novels of Anne Rice. Nor does the audience know anything about the prior history of the vampire woman or even Harker and Van Helsing themselves. Like Mark's Gospel the story unfolds through action. Explanations are neither offered nor even suggested.[12]

The Gospel of Mark proceeds in a similar vein throughout its brief 16 chapters (slightly more than twenty pages in most editions of the Bible). Yet action itself becomes a form of exposition. The identity of Jesus as God's Son is explained by what he does. He heals, teaches, forgives and, consistently, confronts opponents who are both human and demonic. By the time his identity as the Messiah is clearly revealed in the eighth chapter the reader should be prepared for it. Yet aspects of the story remain undefined such as Jesus' insistence that his disciples should tell no one who he is (Mark 8:30). The purpose of Jesus' mission likewise is revealed through the events of the story. Jesus obliquely refers to his task as "serving rather than being served and giving his life as a ransom for many" (Mark 10:45). The disciples play the analogous role of a Greek chorus in that they voice questions which must inevitably be in the mind of the reader. They don't understand Jesus' cryptic references. His displays of spiritual power are not clear to them (Mark 9:10, 32). Even Judas' decision to betray Jesus is offered without any statement of motivation or purpose (Mark 14:10). This makes what follows all the more suspenseful and surprising. The familiarity of the gospel story should not blind one to the impact it must have had (and still has) at a first hearing. The events of the crucifixion follow at a breakneck pace. Throughout the Gospel narrative, the actions of the protagonists provide the sole insight into their character. This applies to Peter's denial of Christ as well as to Pilate's decision to order the crucifixion. (It is stated simply that Pilate wanted to satisfy the crowd. An explanation is never given why and how he hopes to achieve this.) There is no foreshadowing how events will turn out. The cryptic references to the resurrection, interspersed at various points in the Gospel, prepare neither the characters themselves nor the reader for the impact of Easter. We are given a brief glimpse of the women's emotional response in the narrator's description of them being seized by "terror and amazement" (Mark 16:8). The final scene of the original ending of the Gospel briefly describes the women fleeing and not speaking to anyone. The Gospel then ends as it began with an image of action.[13]

In *Dracula* the same elements of character and plot development are defined by fast paced action with a minimum of embellishment. Indeed some critics have commented that Fisher's *Dracula* moves too fast.[14] Yet Fisher here is following the same approach as the biblical narrative. The opening credits set the mood by the way the camera pans along the outside of Dracula's castle to the booming sound of James Bernard's famous music score. The camera is finally led down a staircase to view Dracula's coffin. The music stops and blood suddenly appears on the coffin. A setting has been given with no elaboration or background. This is comparable to the opening of Mark's Gospel which announces its theme simply as "The beginning of the good news of Jesus Christ, the Son of God" and then quotes from the Old Testament prophet Isaiah (Mark 1:1–3). Like the gospel narrative itself the film plunges into action. Jonathan Harker begins to tell of his arrival at Castle Dracula. Compared with all other film versions this is accomplished very quickly. A carriage travels along an autumnal road.

Harker walks toward the bridge that leads into the castle. Next he is in the castle. No one is present but a dinner has been prepared for him, or so a note from Count Dracula informs him. A log thrown on the fire means that he has finished his dinner and some time has elapsed. Harker accidentally knocks over a cover dish. As he bends down to pick it up the hem of a woman's dress enters the frame of the picture. She speaks briefly and then quickly departs. Harker's attention is drawn to a shadowy figure at the top of the stairs. The figure descends, comes toward him and in close-up courteously welcomes him and introduces himself as "Count Dracula."

This opening is a striking illustration of the same type of narrative found in biblical examples like Mark's Gospel. In the course of a few brief shots three characters are introduced, each of whom will play a critical role in the unfolding of the story. Yet very little is known about any of them at this point. This is comparable to the opening of the Gospel story in which John the Baptist, Jesus, Satan and the disciples are introduced without any explanation of what their role or significance in the ensuing story will be. The Gospel likewise opens with a brief series of actions and encounters with virtually no commentary. Events are described in simple, terse statements. In the Stoker novel a good deal about Harker is revealed before he ever comes to Castle Dracula through the narrative device of excerpts from Harker's journal which describe his journey to Castle Dracula. The details of Harker's journey are entirely omitted in Fisher's film. Harker is seen arriving at Castle Dracula without the audience having been given any background information on him at all. This same approach is continued throughout Fisher's *Dracula*. Following the prologue Dr. Van Helsing (Peter Cushing) arrives on the scene inquiring about his friend, Harker. It is in his initial presentation of Van Helsing that it is most clear that Fisher is, unconsciously or not, following the rigid biblical pattern instead of any previous versions of *Dracula*, including the original novel.

There is no introduction to Van Helsing, just as Mark's Gospel gives no introduction to its main characters. In Stoker's novel, Van Helsing is called in by a very puzzled and frustrated Dr. Seward. Seward is unknowingly treating two of Dracula's victims. The same plot development is followed in the Tod Browning version with Bela Lugosi. Van Helsing is an expert in "obscure diseases" and is called in from Amsterdam. Therefore a definite idea is formed of who he is and what his expected role is to be before his introduction. This is true in both the novel and the earlier Browning film. Granted, the audience learns more about him as the story develops. Yet from the outset it is told that he is coming into the story as an expert in the obscure and indeed the occult. Fisher shows no interest in such background information. When Van Helsing enters his film all that is known about him is that he is looking for Harker. The viewer knows that Harker has been killed by Dracula but Van Helsing is unaware of this. In Fisher's film there is no idea initially of who Van Helsing is or what he is up to. By giving no information about Van Helsing, Fisher makes him a more mysterious, and therefore intriguing, character. The audience really only learns about him as he interacts with the other characters. Again following the biblical model, Van Helsing is revealed by what he does rather than by what anyone says.

This approach can be found repeatedly in Fisher's films. Another clear example in a film that parallels *Dracula* is *The Hound of the Baskervilles*. Here again Fisher eschews the approach of both the novel and previous film versions. First of all, Fisher begins the story with the legend of the hound instead of giving an introduction to Sherlock Holmes. This again conforms to the pattern of the biblical gospels, none of which opens with the central character of Jesus but all of which open with a longer or shorter prologue focusing on John the Baptist.[15] All previous (and indeed subsequent) versions of *The Hound of the Baskervilles* begin with Sherlock Holmes in Baker Street demonstrating his powers of deduction through examining Watson in the reflection of a coffee pot or analyzing a walking stick that had been left the night before by a certain Dr. Mortimer. When Mortimer arrives he introduces the problem of the recent mysterious death of Sir Charles Baskerville on the moor. This sets the stage for the hair raising account of the legend of the demonic hound. The reader (or viewer) is then oriented and somewhat prepared for the wildly supernatural account which followers. Fisher allows his viewers no such comfort. With no reference to Holmes he plunges into an action filled account of Hugo Baskerville and the origin of the hell-hound of the title. The viewer is told next to nothing but is shown a great deal. Indeed the introduction to Holmes himself is a piece of action. Following the harrowing narrative Holmes turns to a chess board and triumphantly makes a move. After which (as in the original novel) he dismisses the horror story as a "fairy tale" (or "folk legend"). Again Holmes is defined by action rather than by narrative or description.

There are important reasons for this kind of storytelling which apply equally to biblical narrative and to Fisher's films. It also pertains to certain myths and fairy tales. As Erich Auerbach noted, this approach heightens the suspense of the story. The net result is that the unfolding of the story becomes quite unpredictable. This is a key theme of the gospels. Implied in the events recorded in the story is the question, "Why is Jesus doing this?" The action and its outcome remain unpredictable just as the response of the characters is also unpredictable. Unfortunately, the familiarity of the gospel story has too often obscured this fact. This was not the case with its first time readers to whom the suspense and unpredictability were very real. There is, however, another important reason for this form of storytelling. Biblical narratives, like fairy tales and like Fisher's films, portray a world in which the supernatural is very active. The mundane affairs of what might be called ordinary life are consistently intertwined with a supernatural reality. In fact the use of the term "supernatural" itself is anachronistic.

Biblical narrative has a quite different sense of reality from more modern forms of storytelling. The biblical view of reality is multidimensional. The spiritual realm is just as essential as the natural. This is why the word "supernatural" really doesn't apply. What one would call "natural" in the sense of ordinary physical experience the biblical writers (and indeed many of the ancient myths) would regard as a limited view of reality. Reality for them is much broader. It includes angels, devils and spirits as well as humans. The same would apply to their understanding of history which would include the cosmic and eternal as well as the temporal and the mundane. In this framework witches and devils are as "ordinary" as peasants and kings. In the gospels Jesus communes with Satan, angels and God in the same way he talks to his disciples and Pontius Pilate.[16] When Fisher uses his famous phrase, "fairy tales for adults," he is referring to a kind of storytelling which accepts in a naive and uncritical way (in a modern sense) a belief in a reality which cannot be measured in scientific terms. The myths and legends which lie behind Fisher's stories are not presented as ethereal or fantastic. They are in fact presented in ways that are extremely ordinary. This is the second biblical motif in Fisher. He presents a view of reality that is multidimensional and yet unified.

This can be seen very clearly in the way Fisher presents both the Frankenstein and Dracula themes. Actually the two basic stories are different in the sense that *Frankenstein* is not a story about the supernatural. Frankenstein does not use magic to bring his creation to life. His is rather a warped scientific experiment with disastrous consequences. *Dracula*, on the other hand, is emphatically a tale of what might be called the supernatural. Yet earlier and indeed later versions of both stories present them as examples of fantasy worlds. Earlier film treatments of *Dracula*, such as F.W. Murnau's *Nosferatu* and Tod Browning's 1931 version, portray Transylvania and Dracula's castle as highly fantasized locales. They are clearly on the other side of what one might call reality. This approach extends to the character of Count Dracula himself. Nosferatu is overtly a demonic figure and Bela Lugosi's Dracula is frequently photographed in bizarre close-ups with lights shining on his eyes. Even in scenes where

Lugosi is in social settings his accent and manner all suggest something otherworldly, clearly in distinction from the other characters. The shots in Carfax Abbey in the Browning/Lugosi version carry over the same fantasized style as did the earlier scenes in Castle Dracula. Dracula then in both Murnau's and Browning's version is a fantastic figure who represents an entirely different realm from that inhabited by the so-called ordinary characters in the story. In spite of its alleged scientific theme, James Whale's *Frankenstein* is just as fantastic, borrowing some of the same German Expressionist style so evident in the Murnau and Browning *Draculas*. Actually, the sequels, *Bride of Frankenstein* and *Son of Frankenstein*, are even more fantastic in style. This dichtomy between the real and the fantastic is found repeatedly in horror films.[17] It is notably absent in Fisher's films.

Some have criticized Fisher's style as being pedestrian.[18] Quite simply, it is straightforward. Fisher does not cultivate a sense of the fantastic over against the ordinary, or of a dream world different from day to day life. Fisher's *Frankenstein* and *Dracula* films do not have two different realms of existence. Having established his basic context which, granted, never intends to be realistic in a strict historical sense, Fisher nonetheless adheres to it throughout. Fisher certainly makes use of atmosphere and color effects but never embraces a two-tiered view of reality, one supernatural and the other natural. Frankenstein's house and Dracula's castle, while striking in appearance, are not fantastic locales. They are not different in style from the various other houses, inns and settings found in these films. Baron Frankenstein and Count Dracula are never portrayed as either hysterical or fantastic figures. Rather they are essentially seen as ordinary people. It is only after they are accepted as recognizable human figures that one could meet in ordinary life that they can be seen in their respective outbursts of fury. Yet both Peter Cushing's portrayal of Baron Frankenstein and Christopher Lee's Count Dracula are never figures who exist in some fantastic landscape outside of ordinary experience. This is the same as the biblical narratives along with earlier mythical stories. In the Gospel of Mark Jesus encounters Satan in the wilderness but Satan is also present in the synagogue and among the disciples.[19] Miracles are performed in the day to day world. More importantly, the Resurrection takes place in the same reality as Jesus' arrest and crucifixion. Fisher follows the same pattern. Vampires, mummies and werewolves are not otherworldly characters. They are part of *this* world. This convention of an integrated, single reality is one of the strengths of Fisher's so-called "fantasy" films and a convention he shares with biblical narrative.

The third biblical narrative motif that Fisher follows is that of a world in essential conflict. David Pirie and others have spoken of a dualistic world in Fisher's films.[20] This dualism is not one of physical versus spiritual or natural versus supernatural as noted. It is rather a conflict that is essentially ethical in character. In this respect Fisher is not dealing with metaphysical issues. He is not raising questions of flesh versus spirit in a material sense. His world rather is one of binary opposites, of spiritual actions in conflict with unspiritual ones. This refers back to an important difference between Greek culture and the essentially Hebrew orientation of even the New Testament. For Plato, flesh and spirit are in conflict because they are materially different. They have different desires. The spirit or soul for Plato is a nonmaterial, intellectual substance whose ultimate goal is the contemplation of the ideal, eternal forms which exist independent of time and space. The flesh or body, on the other hand, has no such inclination. Its motivation is to satisfy its physical appetites for food, clothes, comfort, sex and whatever else. Plato then can lament that the soul is imprisoned in the body.[21] Their difference is one of substance. The body's physical appetites are constantly interfering with the soul's desire for contemplation of the eternal.

This is not the dualism of the New Testament. When the apostle Paul speaks of struggling with the "flesh," he is not referring to a struggle with the material or physical aspect of life.[22] In the biblical framework the human person is one. One may distinguish various aspects of body, mind, spirit and soul. However these are not distinct entities as in Plato and the classic Greek tradition. For Paul, "flesh" refers to behavior that is contrary to God's will. That behavior may be mental, physical or spiritual. "Flesh" here is used in a broader sense. It refers to the realm of human life, understood, however, as human life lived on its own, apart from God.[23] Spiritual life then is defined as acting in obedience to God. What are metaphysical distinctions in Plato are purely ethical ones in Paul.

Fisher's outlook, as noted, is clearly Pauline in the New Testament sense. His famous comment on his belief in the "ultimate victory of good over evil."[24] This is the key to his understanding of the reality of conflict. This theme, as already seen, is certainly a major one in his work. Beyond this, it needs to be recognized how closely Fisher's portrayal of conflict follows the Bible's own depiction of this archetypal struggle. In Fisher's cinematic world this essentially ethical as well as spiritual conflict is fundamental to any understanding of his films. When critics miss this point they tend to distort the most pivotal point in Fisher's whole perspective or "world view."[25]

Fisher's handling of this whole subject shows how closely he follows the biblical model. Evil in the Bible is both personal and purposeful. The Gospel of Mark places a major focus on the demonic. Jesus is tempted by

Satan (Mark 1:13). He acknowledges that his ministry represents a continuing battle against Satan (Mark 3:22–27). Jesus warns against Satan's power to distort the truth and even sees Satan motivating a leading disciple like Peter (Mark 4:13-15; 8:33). In other parts of the New Testament Satan is described as disguising himself as an angel of light (II Corinthians 11:14), as physically interfering in the ministry of the Gospel (I Thessalonians 2:18), as launching fiery darts of temptation (Ephesians 6:16) and as a lion prowling around looking for a victim he can devour (I Peter 5:8). Satan's ultimate symbol is that of the serpent. This image has its roots all the way back in the Garden of Eden story in the Book of Genesis (Genesis 3:1; II Corinthians 11:3; Revelation 20:2). These references constitute the backdrop for Fisher's entire motif of spiritual conflict. To put it very simply, Fisher's villains are invariably Satanic figures in the classic biblical sense. The role they play in his films follows the same narrative pattern one finds in Scripture. Once again this can be seen clearly in *Horror of Dracula.*

Christopher Lee's portrayal of Count Dracula is, quite simply, Satan incarnate. Rather than an ominous, fearful character like Nosferatu or Bela Lugosi's Dracula, Fisher initially presents him as an "angel of light." His first appearance in the film is as a refined, polite aristocrat. He gives Jonathan Harker a warm and friendly welcome, belying his real intentions. Dracula is deceitful throughout, seducing his victims and leading Van Helsing on a complicated chase. Yet he is also a devouring demon and has fangs like a serpent. As a spiritual figure he also moves about freely in the world of human beings. More than a character he is a central theme of the narrative. The entire story is built around the opposition and struggle between Dracula and Van Helsing. Dracula is not evil only because he drinks blood. He is evil because he is in essence bent on destruction and is ultimately a form of death itself.

The narrative revolves fully around the two protagonists, one representing spiritual good, the other spiritual evil. This is why uniquely in Fisher's version Van Helsing is introduced before most of the other characters. Even Jonathan Harker is an ally of Van Helsing's and is therefore an entirely different character from the Harker found in Bram Stoker's novel or other film versions. Peter Cushing's Van Helsing character in many ways personifies the apostle Paul in the New Testament. Unlike Stoker's depiction of an elderly Dutch scholar, Cushing's Van Helsing displays the energy, intensity and commitment — not to mention faith — of the Paul of the New Testament.

Outside of the biblical context the apostle Paul, like Fisher's view of Van Helsing, can appear as an obsessed fanatic.[26] In this context, however, that is not the case because the biblical narrative assumes the existence and work of Satan. In the biblical world Satan is a fundamental reality, as concrete and real as God himself (though never as powerful). In the biblical account of Paul's conversion, God tells Paul that he is sending him to turn people from darkness to light and "from the power of Satan to God" (Acts 26:17–18). Satan then is an essential rationale for Paul's whole ministry in Jesus Christ's service. The same assumption is found in Mark as well as the other Gospels. Jesus needs to be a Savior because the world is in the power of Satan. It is only in the driving out of the demonic powers which keep humanity in the grip of death that salvation can come to the human race.[27]

This narrative motif, in all its biblical richness, runs throughout Fisher's cinematic work. All of life is lived in this ethical conflict between choosing to serve God or succumbing to the temptations of Satan. The struggle between flesh and spirit is a result of this larger spiritual battle. As noted above Fisher is not a Platonist. He does not object to physicality per se. It is how physical life is lived out that is centrally important. Personal life in all its aspects—physical, emotional and spiritual—plays into this classic biblical antithesis between God and Satan. One sees this most clearly in the fourth motif which is Fisher's much discussed approach to sexuality.[28]

The observation has been made that Fisher's female characters, especially in the *Dracula* films, often exhibit a dichotomy between sexual repression and sexual indulgence.[29] These females, prior to becoming Dracula's victims, are portrayed in a Victorian primness which oscillates between repression and uncontrollable passion. Once bitten by Dracula, they become lustful, sexually vociferous creatures. This comfortable sexual dialectic has been applied to Fisher's work generally with negative comments. The most notable example is Barbara Shelley's character, Helen, in *Dracula, Prince of Darkness*. In the early scenes of the film she is presented as a repressed, judgmental and ultimately fearful woman. Once bitten by Dracula she becomes sexually voracious until finally she is held down and staked by a group of priests in what has been widely seen as a symbolic, group rape (as discussed in the earlier chapter on *Dracula*). Others have interpreted this scene as a patriarchal punishment of a sexually active woman.[30] Additional examples are often cited in Fisher's work. These include the various "serpent women" in *Stranglers of Bombay* and *Two Faces of Dr. Jekyll*, Cecile in *Hound of the Baskervilles*, Mina in *Horror of Dracula*, Christine in *Frankenstein Created Woman*, among others. The general point seems to be that Fisher subscribes to the old stereotype that good women are docile, subdued and sexually repressed; in other words,

Victorian. Their sexual awakening, on this reading, constitutes a subversive challenge to the established social order. These women then must be staked, killed, or otherwise eliminated in order to preserve the existing, i.e., patriarchal, order.

This reading has received support from examples of more recent horror films in which teenagers engaging in sexual activity are setting the stage for their own doom. This kind of situation has been a cliché ever since John Carpenter's first *Halloween* (1978). Such an interpretation of horror films, whether those of Fisher's or other's, certainly suggests more of a Platonic outlook than a biblical one. The critical point here is that the fault of these women lies in their becoming overtly sexual. In other words it is their physical, sexual nature that leads to their destruction. Once this nature is engaged they become destructive, antisocial agents. It is no wonder that feminist interpreters have deplored this image of women. But this interpretation does not apply to Fisher. A closer examination of Fisher's portrayals of women shows they also follow an essentially biblical narrative pattern. The conflict again is an ethical one. It is not a matter of physical versus spiritual, still less of natural against supernatural.

In the Bible itself women are never identified with sin because of their sex. It is not female sexuality that is sinful. It is rather the misuse of that sexuality that becomes sin. This is contrary certainly to popular views of the Christian Church historically. Yet Western Christianity has often been Platonic as much as biblical.[31] The Bible itself has no inherent misgivings about sex. Here again this is a narrative pattern, more than just a subject. How the Bible talks about sexuality is as important as what it says about it. The Bible is really very matter of fact in its discussions about sexuality and sexual behavior. Sexual desire and sexual activity are normal. The Bible never falls into the false dichotomy of "virgin vs. whore." That distinction predates the writing of the Bible and has more to do with the ancient myths of the goddess than anything in the Bible itself.[32] Feminist scholar Tikva Frymer-Kensky has pointed out that the Bible does not recognize any dichotomy of sexual roles between men and women. Contrary to the Platonic view and to Victorian stereotypes, the Bible portrays men and women as being essentially identical in their sexual desires and behavior. Men are lustful but so are women. Sexual pleasure, seduction, even sexual abuse can be found equally in both sexes.[33] There is nothing inherently sinful in sexual attractiveness or even sexual desire. While there are biblical passages that warn against sexual misconduct there are others that celebrate sexual passion in the context of marriage.[34] The Bible never succumbs to the view that good women (or men) cannot be interested in sex.

Following the biblical model Fisher never equates sexuality with sin. Nor does he ever identify sexual attractiveness with temptation or threats to the established social order. This can be seen in his first gothic work, *The Curse of Frankenstein*. There are two central women in this film. The first is Elizabeth, Victor Frankenstein's fiancée, played by Hazel Court. The second is the chambermaid, Justine, played by Valerie Gaunt. Both of these women are attractive, well endowed and sexual. While Valerie Gaunt's Justine is sexually promiscuous, Hazel Court's Elizabeth is a sexual figure in an appropriate sense. Nothing suggests that Elizabeth, as the counterpoint to Justine, is repressed or fearful. Quite the contrary. She remains in Frankenstein's castle even after several mysterious events have occurred. Her appearances in Victorian evening dress certainly carry none of the repressed quality noted in Helen in *Dracula, Prince of Darkness*. For that matter, Hazel Court's character, Janine, in *Man Who Could Cheat Death* is a model who apparently is seen posing nude in the European version of the film. Yet she is not presented as any kind of immoral or threatening character. In both films Hazel Court is an appealing, sympathetic and, at the same time, sexy heroine. This aspect is even more the case with Yvonne Furneaux's Isobel in Fisher's *The Mummy*.

The character of Isobel is an interesting example in Fisher's work. As noted in the previous discussion of *The Mummy*, Isobel is not the reincarnation of some ancient Egyptian priestess.[35] She only looks like the ancient priestess. On a purely narrative level this is an absurd coincidence. Yet on a thematic level it is quite striking. Isobel saves her husband by, in effect, tricking the Mummy into thinking she is the ancient Princess Anaka. She does this by letting her hair down and thereby exposing her sexuality. In this context doing so saves the life of her husband. Her sexuality then, far from being negative, is a highly positive aspect. Following the ethical line of the Bible, it is not her sexuality that is the issue: It is the use to which she puts it. In this example her sexuality is extremely positive. It is worth noting that Fisher shows the relationship between Isobel and her husband, John, as tender and mutually supportive. Granted, not much of this relationship is seen but it is clearly intended to be positive. Isobel is as attractive and sexual as Fisher's female vampires. The difference lies not in their sexuality but in the way that sexuality is expressed. This follows the same lines as the biblical pattern.

The gothic tradition is far more fearful of sexual issues than the biblical tradition ever was. Thinking in terms of the two archetypal stories, *Frankenstein* and *Dracula*, one can see this clearly. Frankenstein's creation puts women at risk. Justine, the servant girl, is hanged for a murder committed by the monster. Later on, in perhaps the novel's most disturbing scene, Frankenstein's bride, Elizabeth, is killed on her wedding night. The Universal films, particularly *Frankenstein* and *Bride of Frankenstein*, both play up this theme. Elizabeth in both films is threatened and abducted by the monster. While there are other victims, her status as victim is given the greatest emphasis. The implicit theme here is that male creativity can be destructive to women. One wonders to what extent Mary Shelley felt victimized by the creative men around her (including her father). On the other hand Dracula is a threat to men. He is specifically so because of what he does to women. The twin fates of Lucy and Mina form the central focus of Stoker's novel. Where women are threatened by Frankenstein's creature, men are threatened by Dracula's women. It is interesting to note in both Stoker's novel and subsequent films the male heroes are far more concerned about what has happened to their women (and what these women might do) than by Dracula himself. While Fisher certainly deals with these themes they are not central for him. Fisher's primary focus—the spiritual conflict between good and evil—is not presented primarily in sexual terms. The conflict is acted out in Fisher's Frankenstein films by Frankenstein's interaction with either his male associates or the larger community. Certainly the central emphasis of Fisher's *Dracula* lies far more in the struggle between Van Helsing and Dracula than in any of the female vampires. In this respect Fisher again can be seen following a biblical narrative pattern.

To emphasize the distinctiveness of Fisher's approach it may be helpful to make a simple comparison with one of the other directors who worked at Hammer Studios. Roy Ward Baker made three films that deal with some of the same subjects as Fisher: *Scars of Dracula* (1970), *The Vampire Lovers* (1970) and *Dr. Jekyll and Sister Hyde* (1971). These films evidence far more the questionable approach to sexuality which sometimes has been attributed to Fisher. In all three pictures overt sexuality is identified with evil and destruction. Vampire women in Baker's films who act out their sexuality are stabbed, beheaded or otherwise subjected to graphic forms of destruction. There is little of the sense of relief or deliverance found in Fisher's films. The women in Baker's films seem to be clear examples of the equation that to be sexual is to be evil. Like Fisher's movies these are set in a Victorian period. Unlike Fisher, however, a film such as *The Vampire Lovers* seems to equate sexual awakening with vampirism itself. This form of sexuality is clearly seen as threatening to an established, patriarchal social order. Whereas in Fisher's *Dracula* films female vampires are released through the help of lovers or brothers who are peers in some sense, in *The Vampire Lovers* it is clearly the fathers who must expunge the vampirism of their daughters. In a gratuitous nude scene in *Scars of Dracula* it is an outraged father who confronts his naked daughter. The message of such scenes, intentional or otherwise, is that sexuality is a perceived sexual and social evil which must be countered by the patriarchal authority figures. In such a treatment the vampire women can be viewed as symbols of sexual liberation. This is essentially the same approach that is followed later in Francis Ford Coppola's 1992 version of *Bram Stoker's Dracula*. "Sister" Hyde in Baker's inversion of the Robert Louis Stevenson classic is a Romantic Fatal Woman for whom sexuality is the ideal means of seduction and therefore power (as in the ancient myths of Ishtar). The social threat of sexuality is carried to an extreme when this demonic woman puts on male Victorian dress and becomes, in effect, Jack the Ripper.

Whatever interest these films may hold they represent a very different approach to sexuality than that found in Fisher's work and in the Bible itself. The scene in Baker's film where Dr. Jekyll is transformed into a beautiful young woman who examines her newly given breasts in the mirror sets the stage for a story in which sexuality is a seductive and deadly weapon. In Fisher's *Two Faces of Dr. Jekyll* it is the actions of the woman protagonists, not their inherent sexuality, which lead to sin with its deadly consequences. In Baker's films it seems to be the sexual nature itself, as evidenced in the mirror scene, which is both evil and deadly. There has been much valid concern expressed during the past 30 years over the depiction of sexuality in horror films. This disturbing trend has its origin in films like Baker's (and in earlier Hammer imitations like *Horrors of the Black Museum*). It is not found in Fisher's work which follows the biblical narrative approach to sexuality.

The fifth biblical motif found in Fisher's work is the theme of atonement. This is one of the most central ideas in the Bible. It is expressed in the classic phrase, "without the shedding of blood there is no forgiveness of sins" (Hebrews 9:22). This statement is rooted in the Law of Moses which states, "it is the blood that makes atonement" (Leviticus 17:11). The basic idea of atonement is the covering over of sin by the shedding of blood. The idea is a near universal one. The ancient practice of human sacrifice was a form of atonement.[36] Blood was shed to appease the gods or to win their favor. A famous example of this in Greek mythology is the story of Agamemnon sacrificing his daughter, Iphigenia, in order to get the winds that would bring his ships to Troy in the Trojan War.

The Bible forbids the practice of human sacrifice.[37] It does, however, point out that disobedience to God has destructive consequences. Atonement therefore is necessary to pay the consequences of sin. The root idea of atonement is the concept of vicarious sacrifice. Someone must die in the place of the sinner if the sinner is to survive. In classic paganism it might even be the king who must die to atone for the sins of the community so that the community might survive.[38] In ancient Israel bulls and goats took the place of the community on the Day of Atonement (Leviticus 16). It was important that such sacrificial offerings were made to God and not to demonic figures (Deuteronomy 32:17). The celebration of the Passover included the slaughter and eating of a sacrificial lamb (Exodus 12:3–8). In the New Testament the crucifixion of Jesus is seen as the fulfillment of the earlier Israelite practices of atonement. The apostle Paul calls Christ "our Passover lamb" (I Cor. 5:7). The author of the Letter to the Hebrews explains in detail how Jesus' death fulfills the earlier forms of atonement (Hebrews 9–10). The Christian community, like earlier Israel, is warned against sacrificing to the demons as an inverted form of atonement (I Corinthians 10:18–21).

The motif of atonement is a central one in Fisher's films and is grounded in these biblical narratives. Fisher sets off in film after film the idea of blood sacrifice. Like the biblical examples he constantly raises the question, to whom is the sacrifice being offered? Some have commented on the character of ritual in Fisher's films.[39] This ritual really is the practice of atonement. The vampire legend, at least in Western culture, is rooted in the whole idea of blood sacrifice. Here quite clearly it is a sacrifice to a demonic figure. As noted previously, one of the few possible vampire references in the Bible is found in the Book of Isaiah (Isaiah 34:14). Also mentioned in this same context is the "goat-demon" who is warned against in the texts dealing with sacrifice and atonement (Lev. 17:7). The vampire takes the blood of another to sustain its own life and in turn bestows a form of immortality in making its victim a member of the "Undead."

The original novel of *Dracula* stresses the ceremonial aspect of destroying the vampire. The destruction of the vampire is itself a form of atonement. The blood of the vampire is shed in pounding a stake through its heart so that its soul may be put to rest. The crucial symbol of the cross invokes the atonement of Jesus Christ which in Christian belief has the ultimate power to overcome evil. In Fisher's vampire films the staking of a vampire has this character of a ritual. It is a spiritual ceremony as befits its origins in the Day of Atonement observance. While this is implied in certain scenes in *Horror of Dracula* it is made explicit in Fisher's later Dracula films. For example, the staking of Baroness Meinster in *Brides of Dracula* is given all the trappings, complete with music, of a religious ceremony. The same applies to the much discussed scene of the staking of Helen in *Dracula, Prince of Darkness.* The fact that this scene has Father Sandor officiating only underscores the religious note of atonement.

Fisher's focus on atonement is double edged. Following the biblical pattern he not only stresses the importance of the service of atonement, he warns against the sacrificing to demons. Demonic sacrifice is the counter pole of true atonement. This is first seen clearly in the Dracula films. Lucy in *Horror of Dracula* prepares herself as a sacrificial victim awaiting the nocturnal arrival of Dracula. Her final preparation for this role includes removing the cross from around her neck and then lying with arms spread out on her bed in anticipation of Dracula's arrival. There is the suggestion of some kind of demonic activity on the part of Baron Meister which has resulted in his becoming a vampire in *Brides of Dracula*. Most notably, there is the prolonged scene of the reviving of Dracula in *Dracula, Prince of Darkness*. The hapless victim, Alan, is murdered by Dracula's servant Klove and then is hung upside down over Dracula's crypt. His throat is slashed and his shed blood becomes the means of Dracula's rebirth. This is a clear depiction of a demonic blood sacrifice. Throughout these films scenes of demonic sacrifice are offset by images of atonement in which blood is shed for redemption (the staking of the vampire) and by the ultimate symbol of atonement, the cross.

This strong emphasis is certainly not confined to the Dracula films. It is emphatically present in *The Devil Rides Out*. The whole idea of atonement is explicitly dealt with here in the contrast between the satanic cult of Mocata and the Christian rituals of the Duc De Richleau. The final climax is a multilayered view of atonement. Mocata intends to sacrifice the child Peggy. Her intended death is one level of atonement in the ancient practice of child sacrifice. The Duc De Richleau offering of himself to save Peggy is a second dimension of atonement in the sense of one person giving his life to save another. The final image of atonement is the appearance of the cross which destroys Mocata and his cult. Another example actually is *The Hound of the Baskervilles*. In the opening prologue Sir Hugo Baskerville pins his female victim down on a sacrificial slab which suggests Druid origins. His stabbing of her then has a sacrificial overtone. This is not accidental. In a later scene the body of the convict Seldon who has been killed by the hound is found in the same location where the girl was killed in the prologue. Seldon's body has been the object of "some revolting sacrificial rite" performed with Sir Hugo's original dagger. None of this is found in Conan Doyle's original novel. It is however consistent with Fisher's continuing use of the atonement motif.

The idea of atonement also extends to the Frankenstein films. While the image of ritual sacrifice is less apparent in this series, it is nonetheless present. The whole ethos of Frankenstein's laboratories in the various films takes on a ritualistic air. Frankenstein is constantly sacrificing others to form his new "creations." He continually destroys others so that he can have the material for his experiments. These experiments are as much a structured ritual as Mocata's satanic cult. Baron Frankenstein is not unlike a pagan high priest who selects victims to be the next sacrifice. Frankenstein's view of science is as demonic as the "goat-demons" mentioned in the Bible. It is a pursuit of power not unlike the ancient practice of trying to secure the favor of the gods for healthy crops or a strong sailing wind. This pursuit of power is essentially the same quest which Mocata is following. In fact Mocata is not unlike Baron Frankenstein in his style, demeanor and quasi-scientific posture. Frankenstein's demon is his relentless search for the source of life apart from any regard for the true God. This search leads him eventually into a demonic form of sacrifice. Frankenstein then for Fisher is more high priest than scientist, more of a wizard than a doctor. At the end of virtually every Frankenstein film the creation of Frankenstein perishes but the Baron goes on. This perpetual sacrificing of the creature is then an atonement in the most primitive sense. A life is sacrificed in order that the one offering the sacrifice may be empowered with new life.

The sixth and last biblical motif in Fisher's films could be called hope in tension. This is very much a fundamental part of the biblical narrative and is central to Fisher's stated belief in the final victory of good over evil. This final motif underscores the whole of the biblical narrative and yet is also strongly paradoxical. The biblical narrators emphasize that Jehovah, unlike the gods in the classic myths, is the one true God alone and is all powerful. Yet this unique God is opposed by other spiritual beings, chiefly Satan. The figure of Satan evolves over the course of the Bible but is nonetheless present in the opening narrative of the temptation of Adam and Eve in the Garden of Eden in the form of the serpent, a near universal symbol of evil. Following Adam and Eve's disobedience, God says to the serpent,

> I will put enmity between you and the woman,
> and between your offspring and hers;
> he will strike your head,
> and you will strike his heel [Genesis 3:15].

This text has been the subject of multiple interpretations.[40] Christians have traditionally seen it as a prophetic statement anticipating the coming of Christ as the Redeemer from sin and death. A key point in this famous text is the distinction between "head" and "heel." It was generally assumed that a snake bite on one's heel was much less dangerous than being bitten in other parts of the body because there is relatively little blood flow in the heel. On the other hand, a blow to the head is frequently fatal. The Christian interpretation of this verse then sees the serpent or Satan striking Jesus' heel metaphorically in his death on the cross. This death is not ultimately fatal because Jesus rises from the dead. On the other hand, Jesus will destroy the Devil as numerous texts in the New Testament maintain.[41]

More than one Sunday School student has asked the obvious question, why doesn't God if he is all-powerful simply destroy Satan and eliminate the problem of evil in the world? This question has vexed great theologians and its posing has been the occasion of lengthy discussions on everything from human free will to God's inscrutable purposes. The biblical writers never really debate the issue. They assume a two sided reality. First of all, Satan is permitted to act in the world as he does in the Book of Job by unleashing a barrage of calamity on poor Job with God's consent. Why God allows this and where Satan comes from are questions that are never answered.[42] Yet the biblical writers are completely confident that God will eventually destroy Satan and bring peace to a "new heaven and new earth" (Isaiah 65:17; Revelation 21:1). In the meantime however the battle rages. It often appears that Satan has all the power on his side. He is described as a "roaring lion seeking whom he may devour" (First Peter 5:8). Believers are counseled to "put on the whole armor of God" in order to resist "the fiery arrows of the evil one" (Ephesians 6:11).

The biblical writers maintain a confident hope in God's ultimate victory even in the midst of a spiritual struggle in which evil can appear to have the upper hand. This appearance is always deceptive (and it is the nature of the devil to be deceptive) because God's ultimate victory is a foregone conclusion. For the New Testament writers this victory is guaranteed in the death of Jesus Christ on the cross and in his subsequent resurrection.[43] While the spiritual war may continue in the present, the decisive battle has already been won and the final outcome is never in doubt. The practical implication of this view is that the Christian should never lose hope, never surrender in the face of evil and never despair of the final outcome of one's own spiritual struggles. This attitude exists in much Christian literature outside the Bible and is clearly present in Terence Fisher's films.

The biblical theme of hope in tension is in one sense common to the horror genre. Much of gothic literature carries over the biblical idea of God's victory over the forces of evil. Yet this view cannot always be assumed. Nineteenth century literature with its emphasis on Romanticism introduces a different view. Oscar Wilde's *Picture of Dorian Gray*, for example, does not depend on a biblical view of God. Wilde himself would not have subscribed to such a view. A classic horror film like James Whale's *Bride of Frankenstein* mocks a number of Christian themes. Contemporary horror films in many cases do not subscribe to any ultimate hope and indeed border on nihilism. The biblical idea of hope in tension therefore, while certainly a traditional view in Western culture, cannot be taken for granted. Fisher, however, holds to the theme unreservedly. A clear example can be seen in his three *Dracula* films.

Fisher's first *Dracula* film follows the basic orientation of Bram Stoker's original novel in which Dracula is a surrogate for Satan. He is defeated by those who invoke the power of God revealed through Christ's death on the cross. At the conclusion of Fisher's *Dracula* the Count is completely destroyed. The twin symbols of this destruction, the cross and the light, are fundamentally biblical in character. Two years later Fisher made *Brides of Dracula*. The prologue and context of this film is that Dracula, while dead, still has influence through his disciples. In an even more graphic example, the vampire in this film is destroyed by the cross when caught in its shadow. Fisher's third film in this series, *Dracula, Prince of Darkness*, begins with Father Sandor remonstrating another priest for his fears since the source of evil, Dracula, has been destroyed. Yet Father Sandor warns travelers against going near Castle Dracula. Dracula, though destroyed, can still come back to life. The reviving of Dracula, as noted above, requires an elaborate ritual (subsequent Hammer Dracula films would miss this point entirely). However, it can still be done. As mentioned in the earlier discussion of this film the revived Dracula does not have the same powers he previously held. All of this fits the biblical pattern of a tension that acknowledges a decisive defeat over Satan but which nevertheless still looks forward to a final victory.

Fisher's films abound with images of incomplete victories. Sir Henry Baskerville is free from those who sought to destroy him with a pseudo-supernatural hound. Yet since Fisher locates the "curse of the Baskervilles" within the Baskervilles themselves, particularly in their lustful nature, he is not fully delivered. It is not certain at the film's end if he has learned from his close escape. Will his lustful desires bring him into further danger in some other context? Leon's death in *Curse of the Werewolf* has an incomplete feel to it, especially with the final shot of a mourning Cristina in the town square. Professor Petrie, the Phantom of the Opera, dies giving his life for Christine while the real villain, Lord D'Arcy, apparently gets away. Professor Moriarity escapes both Scotland Yard and Sherlock Holmes. Robin Hood still awaits the return of King Richard. Captain Lewis is left with the shortsighted East India Company. The gorgon is killed but why won't the spirit of Megara take possession of someone else? Kharis the Mummy arises out of an English bog and is impervious to gunshots. When he sinks into the bog a second time after being shot again one has to wonder, is he really destroyed?

These incomplete victories never suggest that good and evil are on an equal footing. In every specific encounter the power of God overcomes the power of evil. The cross is never ineffective (as it became in so many later horror films including Hammer's own products of the 1970s). As Fisher maintained, his confidence in the ultimate victory of good over evil remains constant. There are examples of complete victories. In Fisher's unique film world, Dr. Jekyll does overcome Mr. Hyde. The cross delivers the Duc De Richleau and his friends and even brings the dead back to life. The man who could cheat death finally doesn't cheat it. And every vampire is destroyed.

All of this is consistent with the biblical narratives which stress both the final victory over evil and the continuing struggle in the present. Both themes are emphasized in the Bible, and one cannot collapse one into the other. Different narratives pick up different parts of the theme. One has to see the whole to understand the parts. Hence the same biblical book can maintain that Satan has been destroyed and yet still has power in the world (First Epistle of John 3:8; 5:19). This essential tension underlines Fisher's series of Frankenstein films.

Fisher was once asked how the power of good was demonstrated in the Frankenstein series. He replied that it is seen throughout in Frankenstein's inevitable failure. In several films it is Frankenstein's assistant who warns him of transgressing essential moral and spiritual boundaries. The key to the theme of hope in tension in the Frankenstein films is seen in the negative light of Frankenstein's hopeless mythical quest for the secret of life. What is striking about the series as a whole is the fact that Frankenstein always achieves his immediate goal. He creates a human being, transplants a brain (or a soul) or whatever. Yet the end result is never what he intends. The experiment always fails ultimately. The film closes with images of Frankenstein walking blankly through woods, prattling about biochemistry or even starting over as his own creation. The experiment never works and he never learns. This is a classic biblical example of humanity blinded by sin. The Bible gives many illustrations of obsessive pursuits which lead to destruction. These include Pharaoh's continuing refusal to let Israel leave Egypt, Solomon's pursuit of glory mirrored in his accumulation of wives and false gods, Absalom's revolt against his father David, Jezebel's persecution of Elijah, and Israel's incessant practice of idolatry. These failures witness to the fact that God alone determines the final outcome. All of these stories demonstrate a hope that remains firm in the midst of conflict and struggle. Biblical prophets continually call attention to God's coming kingdom, fully realizing that present opposition to such a kingdom remains strong.[44] The greater the idolatry the stronger the faith in God remains. Frankenstein unintentionally testifies to the one true Creator by his incessant failure to be the creator he wants to be.

These six motifs of character, reality, conflict, sexuality, atonement and hope in tension show the extent to which Fisher's cinematic storytelling follows a series of patterns found in biblical narrative. Research reveals that Fisher never claimed to be a student of the Bible. Nonetheless, as a believing Christian his approach to narrative was fundamentally biblical. This is consistent with his overall Christian outlook. The Bible explains the meaning of faith more through storytelling than any other means. For all the poetry and exposition found in Scripture, it is in the Bible's narratives that its essential message is encountered. The Old Testament is dominated by the fundamental narrative of the exodus from Egypt. The New Testament centers on the narrative of Jesus' life, death and resurrection. In approaching his role as a film director Fisher inevitably drew upon these narratives because they clearly had meaning for him. Fisher's primary literary sources are never his only sources. He draws heavily upon myth but even more so upon biblical themes and patterns. It is only when Fisher can finally be recognized as a biblically inspired film director that his full contribution will be appreciated.

Notes

1. Butler, Ivan, pp. 85–87.
2. This approach can be seen as early as the story of Abraham which begins succinctly with the words, "Now the Lord said to Abraham..." (Genesis 12:1).
3. The only story of Jesus' childhood is of his visit to the Temple in Jerusalem when he was twelve years old (Luke 2:41–51).
4. This is stated in the barest terms possible in Matthew 4:1–12.
5. Auerbach, Eric, pp. 7ff.
6. Auerbach, Eric, p. 11.
7. *Ibid.*
8. *Ibid.*, pp. 13–14.
9. *Ibid.*, p. 11.
10. While David's inner motives are not described his desperate actions, including ordering Uriah to return from the battlefield to cover up his impregnating Uriah's wife, only increase the suspense.
11. In both cases an initial insight into Harker is given before he arrives at Castle Dracula. This is accomplished through limited but significant contact with other travelers and with the innkeeper and his wife. In Fisher's version a carriage

is seen but there are no scenes of Harker interacting with anyone before arriving at Dracula's Castle.

12. A recurring question throughout the Gospel narratives is "why?" This of course is implicit in the whole Gothic tradition. The fundamental question, "Why are these things happening?" forms the basis of much of the narrative.

13. Most commentators believe that the original Gospel of Mark ended with the brief picture of the Resurrection which concludes at verse 8 of chapter 16.

14. Peary, Danny. *Guide for the Film Fanatic*, p. 199.

15. In the case of the Gospel of Luke, John's parents are first introduced.

16. Jesus' dialogue with Satan in the temptation scene in the Gospels is just as realistic as his dialogues with the disciples or the religious leaders.

17. This is evident in the whole Expressionist motif of the classic horror films of the 1920s and 30s. It applies also to the stylized dream sequences of more modern horror films like *A Nightmare on Elm Street*.

18. Pirie, David, p. 50.

19. Satan can be referred to metaphorically in the Gospels as when Jesus rebukes Peter by calling him "Satan" (Mark 8:33). Yet demons in the Gospels are clearly presented as part of ordinary life. The Gospels never conceive of some unique haunted sphere which is the domain of the demonic. While demons appear to inhabit the wilderness they are also clearly present in the towns and cities where ordinary people live (Mark 1:32–34; 9:38; Luke 8:27).

20. Pirie, David, p. 51.

21. Plato outlines this view in detail in the "Phaedo."

22. "Flesh" in the biblical sense has the idea of one's whole existence with an emphasis on the tendency to disobey God's will, cf. Romans 7:14–20.

23. Paul says that "the mind that is set on the flesh is hostile to God" (Romans 8:7).

24. Eyles, Adkinson and Fry, p. 15.

25. An example of this is S.S. Prawer's discussion of Fisher in *Caligari's Children*, pp. 241–269.

26. This charge has been leveled at Cushing's Van Helsing by more than one critic. See McCarty, John, *The Modern Horror Film*, p. 29.

27. Beker, J. Christiaan. *The Triumph of God*, pp. 80ff.

28. The most recurring comment usually refers to the sexuality theme in the Dracula films. This is a point Fisher himself acknowledged. Cf. Eyles, Adkinson and Fry, p. 14.

29. Pirie, David, pp. 89–93.

30. Prawer, S.S., pp. 261–263.

31. No less a figure than St. Augustine identified all sexual desire as sin. Women were often the cause of this desire.

32. Campbell, Joseph. *The Masks of God: Primitive Mythology*, p. 412.

33. Frymer-Kensky, Tikva, pp. 118ff.

34. Cf. Song of Solomon, chapts. 7–8; Proverbs 5:18–19; Ezekiel 16:6–8.

35. This again is in contrast not only to the older film versions of the Mummy story but to the newer ones as well.

36. Campbell, Joseph. *The Masks of God: Primitive Mythology*, pp. 405ff. For a discussion of the theatrical aspects of ancient sacrifice, cf. Driver, Tom, pp. 101–104.

37. Leviticus 20:1–4; II Kings 23:10.

38. Baring, Anne, and Cashford, Jules, pp. 160ff.

39. Pirie, David, pp. 90–91.

40. While Christians have historically interpreted this verse as a prophetic reference to Jesus Christ, others have seen it as a reference to humanity in general.

41. Hebrews 2:14; I John 3:8.

42. Christian tradition has read Isaiah 14:12–21 as an account of the fall of Lucifer, an archangel. However the Bible is far from clear on this point.

43. The whole fifteenth chapter of Paul's first letter to the Corinthians is an expression of this hope which concludes with the words, "But thanks be to God who gives us the victory through our Lord Jesus Christ" (I Cor. 15:58).

44. Isaiah the prophet is called to go to a people whose eyes are shut and whose ears are closed (Isaiah 6:9–10).

THE LESSONS OF HORROR: TERENCE FISHER IN CONTEXT

In the years 1957–60 Western culture was entering a period of profound crisis. In England particularly, this crisis was seen as the final dismantling of the British Empire inaugurated by the Suez Crisis of 1956. Yet the crisis existed throughout Europe and North America. The crisis objectively took the form of the Cold War with its nuclear arms race, the emergence of Third World nations from the breakup of Western colonialism, race relations and an increasing materialism. This crisis was reflected in the arts, both popular and classical. The focus of the crisis was variously perceived as social, political or racial. Its manifestations included beat poetry, rock and roll music, science fiction films and the Theater of the Absurd. Within a decade the crisis would be felt by every major Western cultural institution. The years 1957–60 witnessed the onset of this cultural crisis.

The foundation of the crisis lay deeper than any of its manifestations. This emerging crisis was essentially spiritual. It represented a breakdown of fundamental values and beliefs. Western culture's historic reliance on Christian faith had essentially been replaced by a faith in science. The dawn of the nuclear age had served to color science in a more negative light since scientific technology now had the capacity to destroy the world. Nonetheless, the scientific method was still uncritically accepted as the gateway to objective truth. The twin emergence of psychoanalysis and psychiatry as dominant cultural forces in the 1950s had also undermined traditional Christian belief by replacing the concept of sin with that of neurosis. Liberal Christian theology retreated behind an essentially subjective, existentialist interpretation of faith which avoided attempts at truth claims or even historical bases for belief. More conservative, orthodox Christians, both Roman Catholic and Protestant, tended to withdraw from the culture at large into a basically fortress mentality. Faith was celebrated during the 1950s but it was preeminently a subjective, individualistic therapeutic belief rather than a faith in the historic creeds of Christendom.[1]

The net result of this emerging crisis was the search for some ultimate belief which could give coherence and purpose to ordinary life. Science was increasingly questionable as a source of ultimate allegiance. Political ideology and nationalism were also dubious sources in the wake of the McCarthy Era, the Suez Crisis and the Cold War stalemate. Political figures and movements would crumble throughout the West in the 1960s and 1970s, in the wake of the Profumo Affair, the Viet Nam War, urban riots and Watergate. The period of the late 1950s to early 1960s could be described as the beginning of what is now termed "postmodernism." It is a period in which Western culture was becoming essentially atheistic.

Initial warnings of this fundamentally spiritual crisis could be seen earlier in such diverse examples as the plays of Samuel Beckett (*Waiting for Godot, End Game*), the poetry of Allen Ginsburg ("Howl"), the EC horror comics of 1950–54 and a number of science fiction films (*It Came from Outer Space, War of the Worlds, Forbidden Planet, Creature from the Black Lagoon* and *Them!*). The year 1957 nonetheless brought the first signs of a full scale cultural crisis. It was the year in which the launching of the Russian *Sputnik* satellite created a furor in the West over a possible Soviet domination of space. The year saw the passage of the first modern civil rights legislation in the United States. It was also the year in which a counterculture which had flourished in a social underground came alarmingly to the fore. Its disturbing expressions included John Osborne's play *Look Back in Anger*, Jack Kerouac's beat manifesto, *On the Road*, the English translation of Jean-Paul Sartre's seminal work on Existentialist philosophy, *The Transcendence of the Ego*, and the emergence of rock and roll as a symbol of a growing youth culture. Its most significant expression, however, was in film. Nowhere else was the fundamentally spiritual character of the crisis of Western culture clearly articulated as in the cinema.

Ingmar Bergman's film *The Seventh Seal* won the Cannes Film Festival award in 1957. *The Seventh Seal* is a bleak allegory of a knight returning home to medieval Sweden after the Crusades. While the film reflects various social and political images, its fundamental image is that of Death personified in a black robe who stalks the knight and his company throughout the picture. In this film, uniquely, the emerging cultural crisis is presented using overtly religious imagery. The Knight has lost his faith in God so he is confronted only with Death. The Oscar-winning film that year was David Lean's *The Bridge on the River Kwai* which in historical perspective can be seen as a metaphor of the declining British empire. Another striking film of 1957 is Elvis Presley's *Jailhouse Rock* in which the anarchistic image of rock and roll is clearly seen.

Of more interest for the purposes here are the fantasy films of 1957. Perhaps the best American science fiction film of the period was released that year, *The Incredible Shrinking Man*, directed by Jack Arnold with screenplay by Richard Matheson. This film had more than its share of social and religious overtones. The film's hero (Grant Williams) has every apparent material need met. However exposure to a mysterious radioactive cloud causes him to shrink virtually to atomic size. As he continually shrinks his middle class suburban home becomes more threatening. He is attacked by the household cat and almost drowns in a drop of water. The metaphor of a shrinking soul amidst material bounty is apt, especially since his final hope is that, though lost to earthly sight, he is known to God with whom "there is no 'small'."

Even more striking is the resurgence of gothic horror that year. Nonsupernatural vampire films had appeared first in Italy the year before (*I Vampiri* directed by Riccardo Freda) and then in the U.S. (*The Vampire*, directed by Paul Landres). Mexico witnessed a Dracula spinoff in *El Vampiro* directed by Fernando Mendez. Britain saw the release of the excellent *Curse of the Demon* based on a Victorian ghost story by M. R. James and directed by Jacques Tourneur who had also directed such outstanding 1940s horror films as *Cat People* (1942) and *I Walked with a Zombie* (1943) (a classic in spite of its silly title). Actually *Cat People* was partially remade in England as *Cat Girl* in 1957 starring Barbara Shelley, soon to become the reigning queen of British horror. In this light one should also recall Laurence Olivers's bloody staging of Shakespeare's *Titus Andronicus* which was a theatrical sensation both in London and on the continent.

In retrospect such diverse films of 1957 as *The Seventh Seal, The Incredible Shrinking Man* and *Curse of the Demon* all give expression to an essentially spiritual crisis. It is notable that films with overtly supernatural and religious themes were appearing simultaneously in Britain, the United States, Sweden, Mexico and Italy. This was occurring at the same time that leading poets, dramatists, philosophers and even theologians were accepting the demise of religion in any purely supernatural sense.

It is into this context that Terence Fisher emerges with his first major work, *Curse of Frankenstein*. The opening prologue of the film expresses the spiritual crisis beginning to engulf Western culture in 1957. A priest enters the cell of the arch rationalist scientist, Victor Frankenstein, whose first words from the shadows are, "Keep your spiritual comfort for those who think they need it." While *Curse of Frankenstein* is not technically the first modern horror film, it is unquestionably the most famous and influential fantasy film of the late 1950s.[2] The public outrage which greeted the film is often laid to its vivid portrayal of blood and violence. While this is no doubt true on a surface level, one may also wonder whether the film's severely negative depiction of science and materialism did not also contribute to its hostile reaction. With the release of his first masterpiece, *Dracula*, the following year, Fisher introduces his clear Christian symbolism. In effect Fisher's defense of orthodox Christianity is quite simple. Evil is real and has supernatural power. The secularist who denies this is seeking to evade the plain reality of a fallen world. Only the cross of Christ can ultimately overcome the power of evil. Therefore Christianity, understood in an orthodox and conservative sense, is true. This simple thesis is clearly evident in the bulk of Fisher's most successful films. (e.g., *Dracula*, *Brides of Dracula*, *Stranglers of Bombay*, *Curse of the Werewolf*, *Dracula*, *Prince of Darkness* and *The Devil Rides Out*). It is implied to varying degrees in his other films for Hammer, with the Frankenstein series emphasizing the negative view of science.

Fisher nonetheless was responding to a theme of spiritual emptiness which other directors had also picked up. Despite Fisher's success and prominence it is not his theme of Christ's victory over evil which other directors emulated. This accounts for the fact that while the horror film has remained a dominant symbol of the spiritual crisis of Western culture for almost half a century, it has seldom presented the Christian message which Fisher emphasized.[3] Fisher in the context of his period is one voice in the general cinematic response to a spiritual crisis. It is the value of cinema in this period that it is able to see the unfolding cultural crisis as an essentially spiritual dilemma. Where Fisher's films respond to this crisis using Christian symbols, many other films only reflect the crisis. The clarity and focus of Fisher's work enabled other directors to react to a turbulent period in spiritual, moral and indeed supernatural terms. However while Fisher's style, technique and even choice of themes were widely imitated, his Christian orientation was often ignored.

This is clearly evident in three British films made between 1958 and 1960 which are definitely influenced by Fisher. In fact several of the same actors who had appeared in Fisher's Hammer films also appear in these pictures as well. The first was *Horrors of the Black Museum* by veteran director Arthur Crabtree, released in 1959. The film follows the same strong narrative line as Fisher's early films complete with color, blood and sexuality. In thematic treatment, however, this film is totally removed from Fisher's work. *Horrors of the Black Museum* is essentially exploitative with touches of sadism thrown in. The opening scene shows a beautiful young woman receiving a pair of binoculars as a present. When she attempts to adjust them iron spikes cut into her eyes. The film continues on a similar level. Though set in contemporary London, the Black Museum, complete with vat of acid, is clearly borrowed from the laboratory in *Curse of Frankenstein*. In the end of the film everyone dies including the central character, Michael Gough, a sympathetic figure in Fisher's *Dracula*, but here a sadistic villain (and a future leading player in Tim Burton's *Batman* films as Burton's personal tribute to British horror films). In actuality, while Fisher was filming the works of British authors like Mary Shelley, Bram Stoker and Conan Doyle, *Horrors of the Black Museum* seems to have been derived from the Marquis de Sade.[4]

The second film in this series was *Circus of Horrors*, released in 1960 and directed by Sidney Hayers. *Circus of Horrors* retains a cult following to this day and has lost little of its original impact. More than any other single film of the 1957–60 period it is the progenitor of the slasher and sex films of the 1970s and 1980s. Alternately gruesome and almost pornographic, *Circus of Horrors* is a relentless parade of scantily clad circus women dying horrible deaths. This film is clearly about spiritual crisis, exemplified by moral chaos in which the dominant figure is a psychotic doctor. The culmination of this trend was *Peeping Tom* (1960) directed by Michael Powell, one of Britain's finest film artists (*The Thief of Baghdad*, *The Red Shoes*). *Peeping Tom* is one of the most debated films in British history, hailed as a masterpiece by some and damned by others. The film presents the story of a psychologically disturbed young man who murders prostitutes and simultaneously photographs them in the act of dying. While the film is well made and well acted its sordid theme cries out for fuller development. *Peeping Tom* invites comparison with Hitchcock's *Psycho*, released the same year. Yet in virtually every respect *Psycho* appears superior both in its restraint and its sense of moral boundaries, limited as those are.

By 1960 a major horror film character had emerged who was absent from Fisher's work. This was the deranged, psychotic killer who murders without clear motive or purpose. Other British studios leapt to portray this character who had more in common with the purposeless killers of German cinema (*The Cabinet of Dr. Caligari*, *M*) than with previous British or American film (some exceptions would include *Night Must Fall* [1937], *Love from a Stranger* [1937] and *The Stranger on the Third Floor* [1940]). The team of Robert Baker and Monte Berman released *Flesh and the Fiends* (1959) with Peter Cushing, based on the real life Scottish murderers Burke and Hare. They also released a sensationalistic *Jack the*

Ripper in 1960 (in other respects such films of theirs as *Blood of the Vam-pire* and *The Hell Fire Club* seem clearly inspired by Fisher's *Dracula* and *The Hound of the Baskervilles*, respectively).

The psychotic killer is a dominant film figure of the past 40 years. He appears as the mad doctor who kills to preserve the beauty of his daughter in the atmospheric and excellent *Eyes Without a Face* (or *Horror Chamber of Dr. Faustus*) directed in France by Georges Franju. He also appears in a number of Hammer films obviously trying to cash in on the success of *Psycho* (*Maniac* [1963], *Paranoiac* [1963], *Nightmare* [1964], *Hysteria* [1965]). Hammer was more successful with thrillers with former Hollywood leading ladies such as Tallulah Bankhead (*Fanatic* [or *Die! Die! My Darling!*]) and Bette Davis (*The Nanny*). None of these films, however, had anything to do with Fisher. John Carpenter claims to have been strongly influenced by Fisher but his *Halloween* (1979), while directed as an interesting series of cat-and-mouse sequences, draws again on the psychotic killer image.[5] With the 1980s this figure takes on a supernatural character in *Halloween II* (1980) and *Nightmare on Elm Street* (1985). The culmination of this trend is the cannibalistic Dr. Lector (Anthony Hopkins) in the highly acclaimed *The Silence of the Lambs* (1991). The psychotic killer continues to appear on the screen in such manifestations as the ex–CIA agent turned presidential assassin in *In the Line of Fire* (1993), the various *Scream* films and in the sequel *Hannibal* (2001). The psychotic killer, like the authoritarian masterminds in pre–World War II German cinema, is an important cultural symbol. The fact that this figure appears in major films like *Peeping Tom*, *Psycho* and *The Silence of the Lambs*, not to mention scores of lesser films, over a 40-year period is a striking point. Insofar as the origin of this trend can be found in *Horrors of the Black Museum* and *Circus of Horrors*, both of which seem stylistically dependent on Fisher, one might wonder if there is any trace of such a figure in Fisher's work. The answer actually must be yes. The closest link is Fisher's portrayal of Baron Frankenstein. Frankenstein is not purposeless, nor is he psychotic. He is, however, ruthless and capable of murder. It is not an overly long step from Frankenstein, the nineteenth century scientist, to Hannibal Lector, the twentieth century psychiatrist.

Cannibalism was a theme in Fisher's *Revenge of Frankenstein* (1958). The critical difference, however, between Fisher's Frankenstein and the Peeping Toms, Norman Bateses and Dr. Lectors lies in the fact that Frankenstein is a rebel in a world ultimately ruled by God. Frankenstein inevitably fails because he is limited by a spiritual and moral authority which ultimately frustrates him even without his knowing it. Conversely, the psychotic killers from *Horrors of the Black Museum* to *The Silence of the Lambs* inhabit a spiritually vacuous world in which chaos predominates. These films portray a violent world of spiritual desperation which is all too clearly seen on the evening news. Fisher would agree with these films to a point. He never accepted a spiritually empty world. However, he would argue that to attempt to live apart from God is to live in chaos. The image of the psychotic killer symbolizes a world turned away from God in which there is no restraint. This is hardly a "modern" or even "postmodern" view. The fearful consequences of seeking to live apart from any divine restraint are portrayed again and again in the Bible.[6]

Another contemporary derivation of Fisher can be seen in the occult or demonic film. Witchcraft and black magic appear in a number of Italian films of the 1960s, most notably *Black Sunday* starring the haunting Barbara Steele and atmospherically directed by Mario Bava. The 1960s witnesses a variety of supernatural films including the Edgar Allan Poe series directed by Roger Corman (*House of Usher, Tales of Terror, The Tomb of Ligeia, Masque of the Red Death*) as well as several intriguing ghost films both in Britain and America (*The Innocents, The Haunting*). However, these films, while invoking the supernatural, present little of the spiritual conflict between God and Satan so central to Fisher's work. The ambiguous supernatural quality of films like *Black Sunday* and *The Innocents* really don't touch on the spiritual issues in Fisher's films.

A significant change occured following the filming of Fisher's *The Devil Rides Out*. Fisher was scheduled to direct a new Dracula film with the obviously religiously derived title, *Dracula Has Risen from the Grave*. Fisher's plans to direct the film were halted by his being struck twice by automobiles and breaking his leg (one is tempted to think of a demonic influence!). The film was eventually directed by Freddie Francis. Ostensibly the film has strong religious imagery including a climax showing Dracula impaled on a cross. Francis introduces significant differences however. The warfare against Dracula in this film depends more on the faith of those fighting the vampire than on the symbols themselves. Staking Dracula is ineffective for example without prayer. The implication here is that faith itself is the source of spiritual power rather than the symbolic presence of Christ. The protagonists are a young atheist and a priest with a lapsed faith. Dracula is only defeated when the atheist converts and the priest regains his faith. This is very different from Fisher's *Dracula, Prince of Darkness* for example in which Diana and Charles discover the power of the cross even though they are not clearly believers.

The setting of *Dracula Has Risen from the Grave* prefigures *The Exorcist* five years later. A year earlier Roman Polanski had parodied Fisher with his *Fearless Vampire Killers*, which presents a Van Helsing character as a bungling old fool. In 1968 Polanski introduced the modern Satanist film genre with *Rosemary's Baby*. Here in an even more severe step the doctor-figure is actually part of the witches' coven. Ray Bradbury is certainly right in seeing this film as a major departure from the gothic tradition.[7] In this film, Satan is triumphant. This film opens the flood gates of a new cinematic vision in which evil conquers good, or worse, good is nowhere to be found. This approach is not confined to the horror genre but can also be found in a number of Westerns over the years from Kirk Douglas' *Posse* (1974) to Clint Eastwood's *Unforgiven* (1992). The trend, though, is most clearly seen in the horror film with endless examples like *The Omen* (1976), *The Sentinel* (1976), *Friday the 13th* (1980) and *The Awakening* (1980).

In actuality this trend is not surprising because the years 1968–80 demonstrate a near fatal collapse of confidence in Western cultural values (including Christianity). These years witnessed the assassinations of Martin Luther King and Robert Kennedy, the resigning in disgrace of Spiro Agnew and Richard Nixon, the collapse of South Vietnam, the rise of the feminist movement, the legalization of abortion, extensive drug use with the suicidal deaths of several prominent rock music stars and an alarming increase in divorce. One does not need to view all these elements negatively to recognize that in various ways they represent an overturning of a traditional Christian ethic and belief system. For good or ill, Western culture by 1980 had abandoned much of the Christian structure which had undergirded it in various forms since Medieval times. No alternative spiritual direction has yet arisen to replace Christianity in spite of various attractions to Eastern mysticism, astrology and New Age spirituality.

In the late 1960s Fisher saw himself fighting a losing battle even at Hammer Studios. The decline of Christian values had opened the door to sexual activity devoid of any clear guiding ethic. By 1969 nudity mixed with violence had become common in many French and Italian horror films. Fisher was ordered to add a rape scene to *Frankenstein Must Be Destroyed* to enhance its commercial appeal. He refused and walked off the set.[8] His career was effectively over. He would make only one film in the final decade of his life, the bleak *Frankenstein and the Monster from Hell*. Hammer opened the gates to nudity in the early 1970s, combined with elements of sadism, in films like *Countess Dracula*, *Lust for a Vampire* and *Scars of Dracula* which hark back more to *Circus of Horrors* than to Fisher's original *Dracula*. (They even made a *Vampire Circus* in 1971.) Some Hammer films of distinction were made after 1970 but most were increasingly sensationalistic and the studio soon collapsed. Fisher himself died in 1980, and his death was barely mentioned in the press.[9]

The dominant figure in horror films and literature of the past three decades is clearly Stephen King. A number of prominent films have been made based on King's works including *Carrie, The Shining, Cujo, Christine* and *Children of the Corn*. King's recent television drama, *The Storm*, portrays a virtually invincible demon who demands a child of a terrified and isolated New England community. The demon identifies himself as "Legion" after the unclean spirit in the Bible (Mark 5:9).[10] Yet, unlike the biblical account, there is no casting out of the demon by Jesus Christ or any representative of Christian spirituality. In fact the minister in the story is as powerless as any of the other characters. Evil is triumphant.

The dominant image in the horror film now is chaos and disintegration which actually can be traced all the way back to *Horrors of the Black Museum*. In various ways directors such as George Romero (*Night of the Living Dead*), Joe Dante (*The Howling, Gremlins*), John Landis (*An American Werewolf in London*), Tobe Hooper (*The Texas Chainsaw Massacre, Poltergeist*), David Cronenberg (*The Dead Zone, The Fly*), Wes Craven (*The Hills Have Eyes, A Nightmare on Elm Street*) and Tim Burton (*Sleepy Hollow)* have presented variations on a symbolic image which frankly is quite frightening. Western culture, now largely divorced from its spiritual foundations of the past millennium, is drifting more and more into a violent neo-paganism, a direction predicted in the last great British horror film, *The Wicker Man* (1973) and further evident in Francis Ford Coppola's revision of *Bram Stoker's Dracula* (1992). This trend in cinema is paralleled in literature with, for example, the modern vampire "Chronicles" of Anne Rice.[11] The increasing celebration of goddess worship today is also a sign of this neo-pagan orientation. However, one wonders if those enamored of the goddess as a symbol of feminism are prepared to come to terms with her ancient practices of human sacrifice and ritual prostitution.[12]

The horror film bears study as a symbolic statement of the spiritual crisis of Western culture. This culture is passing through a transition into directions not yet clearly seen. The dominant images of chaos and disintegration found in the horror film are unfortunately not encouraging. As part of this study Terence Fisher demands attention. He perceived instinctively the coming spiritual crisis of Western society. He gave expression to that crisis using the conventions of the nineteenth century gothic novel. The fact that *Frankenstein* and *Dracula*— along with *Dr. Jekyll and Mr. Hyde, The Hound of the Baskervilles* and *The Phantom of the Opera*—continue to be dramatized on film, television and in the theatre testifies to the resiliency of these stories even in a time of cultural change. Even after September 11, 2001, these stories exert a power to shock and fascinate. The most recent expression of this tradition, Wes Craven's *Dracula 2000*, moves more in the direction of Christian orthodoxy than other recent horror films but with dubious results. The attempt to "explain" Dracula by making him into Judas Iscariot in a variation on the Wandering Jew legend is far from satisfying. The heroine of this film turns out to be Van Helsing's daughter, Mary, who in spite of being a generation–Xer seems far more resolute and grim than any of Fisher's Christian heroes. The film's literalness and excessive violence only make one yearn for the mythical approach of classic horror. (A far more effective and interesting approach is found in the 1999 Canadian musical version of *Dracula*.)

Fisher's lasting contribution lies in the way he envisioned a Christian response to Western culture's continuing spiritual crisis. He rejected the twin alternatives of a blind faith in either science or religion. He acknowledged the seductive beauty of evil and the weakness of the flesh. He showed the reality of both human cruelty and demonic power. Yet he held up the image of a spiritual redeemer hero: rational, eccentric, even scientific, but above all firm in faith. More than this, he portrayed an objective God of goodness symbolized by the cross of Christ. In spite of some of the Victorian trappings of his own understanding of Christian faith, he resolutely and vividly presented a spiritual universe in which good is ultimately victorious over evil. In a world of increasing chaos and disintegration, the cinematic vision of Terence Fisher is still very much needed.[13]

Notes

1. One of the most famous statements of the era was that of President Dwight D. Eisenhower: "Our government makes no sense unless it is founded in a deeply felt religious faith — and I don't care what it is."

2. Hardy, Phil, p. 107.

3. Religious references in films such as *The Exorcist* inevitably point toward weakened or compromised Christian leaders. Worse, in examples like *Carrie* Christian faith is identified with fanaticism.

4. David Pirie even refers to these films as "Sadian Movies." Pirie, pp. 99ff.

5. Carpenter's *Halloween* includes a number of references to *Psycho*. See Hardy, Phil, p. 329.

6. The apostle Paul gives a strong summary of this in Romans chapter 1 verses 18–32.

7. Bradbury, Ray. "A New Ending to *Rosemary's Baby*," in Huss, Roy, and Ross, T.J., *Focus on the Horror Film*, pp., 149–151.

8. Hallenbeck, Bruce G. "Veronica Has Risen from the Grave: An Interview with Veronica Carlson," *Scarlet Street*, No. 9 Winter 1993, p. 68.

9. *Little Shoppe of Horrors*, No. 10/11 July 1990, p. 6.

10. So named because he is in fact many demons.

11. Anne Rice can be credited with the dubious distinction of introducing a more sympathetic vampire figure in the character of Lestat.

12. Young, Dudley, pp. 153–155.

13. The fact that more and more of Fisher's films are becoming available on video and DVD is an encouraging sign.

FILMOGRAPHY
(IN CHRONOLOGICAL ORDER)

The Astonished Heart (1949) Gainsborough
Directed by Terence Fisher and Anthony Darnborough
Screenplay by Noel Coward
Stars: Noel Coward, Celia Johnson, Margaret Leighton

So Long at the Fair (1949) Gainsborough
Directed by Terence Fisher and Anthony Darnborough
Screenplay by Hugh Mills and Anthony Thorne; Photography by Reginald Wyer
Stars: Jean Simmons, Dirk Bogarde, David Tomlinson, Marcel Ponchin, Cathleen
  Nesbitt, Honor Blackman, Francis De Wolff

Stolen Face (1952) An Exclusive Production/Hammer
Directed by Terence Fisher
Screenplay by Richard H. Landau and Martin Berkeley; Photography by Walter
  Harvey; Edited by Maurice Roots; Music by Malcolm Arnold; Produced by
  Michael Hinds
Stars: Paul Henreid, Lizabeth Scott, Mary Mackenzie, Andre Morell, John Wood,
  Susan Stephen

Four-Sided Triangle (1953) Hammer
Directed by Terence Fisher
Screenplay by Paul Tabori and Terence Fisher from a novel by William F. Temple; Photographed by Reginald Wyer; Edited by Maurice Rootes; Art Direction
  by J. Elder Wills; Music by Ivor Slaney; Produced by Michael Carreras

The Curse of Frankenstein (1957) Hammer
Directed by Terence Fisher
Screenplay by Jimmy Sangster from the novel by Mary Shelley; Photography by
  Jack Asher; Art Direction by Ted Marshall; Edited by James Needs; Music by
  James Bernard; Executive Producer: Michael Carreras; Associate Producer:
  Anthony Nelson-Keyes
Stars: Peter Cushing, Christopher Lee, Hazel Court, Robert Urquhart, Valerie Gaunt

Dracula (Horror of Dracula) (1958) Hammer
Directed by Terence Fisher
Screenplay by Jimmy Sangster from the novel by Bram Stoker; Photography by
    Jack Asher; Art Direction by Bernard Robinson; Edited by James Needs and Bill
    Lenny; Music by James Bernard; Produced by Anthony Hinds
Stars: Peter Cushing, Christopher Lee, Michael Gough, Melissa Stribling, Carol
    Marsh, Olga Dickie, John Van Eyssen, Valerie Gaunt, Miles Malleson

The Revenge of Frankenstein (1958) Hammer
Directed by Terence Fisher
Screenplay by Jimmy Sangster with additional dialogue by H. Hurford Janes; Pho-
    tography by Jack Asher; Art Direction by Bernard Robinson; Edited by James
    Needs and Alfred Cox; Music by Leonard Salzedo; Associate Producer: Anthony
    Nelson-Keys; Executive Producer: Michael Carreras; Produced by Anthony
    Hinds
Stars: Peter Cushing, Francis Matthews, Eunice Gayson, Michael Gwynn, John
    Welsh, Lionel Jeffries

The Hound of the Baskervilles (1959) Hammer
Directed by Terence Fisher
Screenplay by Peter Bryan from the novel by Sir Arthur Conan Doyle; Photogra-
    phy by Jack Asher; Art Direction by Bernard Robinson; Edited by James Needs;
    Music by James Bernard; Executive Producer: Michael Carreras; Associate Pro-
    ducer: Anthony Nelson-Keys; Produced by Anthony Hinds
Stars: Peter Cushing, Andre Morell, Christopher Lee, Marla Landi, Ewen Solon,
    Francis De Wolff, Miles Malleson, John Le Mesurier, David Oxley

The Mummy (1959) Hammer
Directed by Terence Fisher
Screenplay by Jimmy Sangster from the screenplay of *The Mummy* (1932) by John
    L. Balderston from a story by Nina Wilcox Putnam and Richard Schayer; Pho-
    tography by Jack Asher; Art Direction by Bernard Robinson; Edited by James
    Needs and Alfred Cox; Music by Frank Reizenstein; Associate producer:
    Anthony Nelson-Keys; Produced by Michael Carreras
Stars: Peter Cushing, Christopher Lee, Yvonne Furneaux, Felix Aylmer, Eddie
    Byrne, Raymond Huntley, George Pastell

The Man Who Could Cheat Death (1959) Hammer
Directed by Terence Fisher
Screenplay by Jimmy Sangster from the play *The Man in Half Moon Street* by Barre
    Lyndon; Photography by Jack Asher; Art Direction by Bernard Robinson; Edited
    by James Needs; Music by John Hollingsworth; Executive Producer: Michael
    Carreras; Associate Producer: Anthony Nelson-Keys; Produced by Anthony
    Hinds
Stars: Anton Diffring, Hazel Court, Christopher Lee, Arnold Marle, Delphi
    Lawrence, Francis De Wolff

The Stranglers of Bombay (1959) Hammer
Directed by Terence Fisher

Screenplay by David Z. Goodman; Photography by Arthur Grant; Art Direction by Bernard Robinson and Don Mingaye; Edited by James Needs and Alfred Cox; Music by James Bernard; Associate Producer: Anthony Nelson-Keys; Executive Producer: Michael Carreras; Produced by Anthony Hinds

Stars: Guy Rolfe, Allan Cuthbertson, Andrew Cruickshank, Marne Maitland, George Pastell, Marie Devereux

The Curse of the Werewolf (1960) Hammer
Directed by Terence Fisher

Screenplay by John Elder (Anthony Hinds) from the novel *The Werewolf of Paris* by Guy Endore; Photography by Arthur Grant; Art Direction by Bernard Robinson and Thomas Goswell; Edited by Mames Needs and Alfred Cox; Music by Benjamin Frankel; Associate Producer: Anthony Nelson-Keys; Executive Producer: Michael Carreras; Produced by Anthony Hinds

Stars: Oliver Reed, Clifford Evans, Hira Talfrey, Catherine Feller, Yvonne Romain, Anthony Dawson, Richard Wordsworth

The Brides of Dracula (1960) Hammer
Directed by Terence Fisher

Screenplay by Jimmy Sangster, Peter Bryan and Edward Percy; Photography by Jack Asher; Art Direction by Bernard Robinson and Thomas Goswell; Edited by James Needs and Alfred Cox; Music by Malcolm Williamson; Associate Producer: Anthony Nelson-Keys; Executive Producer: Michael Carreras; Produced by Anthony Hinds.

Stars: Peter Cushing; Yvonne Monlaur, Freda Jackson, David Peel, Martita Hunt, Andree Melly, Miles Malleson, Mona Washbourne, Henry Oscar

The Two Faces of Dr. Jekyll (House of Fright; Jekyll's Inferno) (1960) Hammer
Directed by Terence Fisher

Screenplay by Wolf Mankowitz from the novel *The Strange Case of Dr. Jekyll and Mr. Hyde* by Robert Louis Stevenson; Photography by Jack Asher; Art Direction by Bernard Robinson; Edited by James Needs and Eric Boyd-Perkins; Music by Monty Norman and David Heneker; Associate Producer: Anthony Nelson-Keys; Produced by Michael Carreras

Stars: Paul Massie; Dawn Addams, Christopher Lee, David Kossoff, Francis De Wolff

The Sword of Sherwood Forest (1960) Hammer
Directed by Terence Fisher

Screenplay by Alan Hackney; Photography by Ken Hodges; Art Direction by John Stoll; Edited by James Needs and Lee Doig; Music by Alun Hoddinott; Executive Producer: Michael Carreras; Produced by Richard Greene and Sidney Cole

Stars: Richard Greene, Peter Cushing, Richard Pasco, Niall MacGinnis, Jack Gwillim, Sarah Branch, Nigel Green, Oliver Reed

The Phantom of the Opera (1962) Hammer
Directed by Terence Fisher

Screenplay by John Elder (Anthony Hinds) from the novel by Gaston Leroux; Photography by Arthur Grant; Art Direction by Bernard Robinson and Don

Mingaye; Edited by James Needs and Alfred Cox. Music by Edwin Astley; Associate Producer: Basil Keys; Produced by Anthony Hinds

Stars: Herbert Lom, Edward De Souza, Heather Sears, Michael Gough, Thorley Walters, Ian Wilson

Sherlock Holmes and the Deadly Necklace (1962) CCC/Criterion/NCEI
Directed by Terence Fisher and Frank Winterstein
Screenplay by Curt Siodmak from the novel *The Valley of Fear* by Sir Arthur Conan Doyle; Photography by Richard Angst
Stars: Christopher Lee, Thorley Walters, Senta Berger

The Gorgon (1964) Hammer
Directed by Terence Fisher
Screenplay by John Gilling from a story by J. Llewellyn Devine; Photography by Michael Reed; Art Direction by Bernard Robinson and Don Mingaye; Edited by James Needs and and Eric Boyd Perkins; Music by James Bernard; Produced by Anthony Nelson-Keys
Stars: Peter Cushing, Christopher Lee, Barbara Shelley, Richard Pasco, Michael Goodliffe, Patrick Troughton, Jack Watson

Dracula, Prince of Darkness (1966) Hammer-Seven Arts
Directed by Terence Fisher
Screenplay by John Sansom from an idea by John Elder (Anthony Hinds) based on characters created by Bram Stoker; Photography by Michael Reed; Production Design by Bernard Robinson; Art Direction by Don Mingaye; Edited by James Needs and Chris Barnes; Music by James Bernard; Produced by Anthony Nelson-Keys
Stars: Christopher Lee, Barbara Shelley, Andrew Keir, Francis Matthews, Suzan Farmer, Charles Tingwell, Thorley Walters

Island of Terror (1966) Planet
Directed by Terence Fisher
Screenplay by Edward Andrew Mann and Alan Ramsen; Photography by Reg Wyer; Produced by Tom Blakeley
Stars: Peter Cushing, Edward Judd, Carole Gray, Niall MacGinnis, James Caffrey, Ian Bellows, Syd Kydd

Frankenstein Created Woman (1967) Hammer-Seven Arts
Directed by Terence Fisher; Screenplay by John Elder (Anthony Hinds); Photography by Arthur Grant; Production Design by Bernard Robinson; Art Directed by Don Mingaye; Edited by James Needs and Spencer Reeve; Music by James Bernard; Produced by Anthony Nelson-Keys
Stars: Peter Cushing, Susan Denberg, Thorley Walters, Robert Morris, Duncan Lamont

The Devil Rides Out *(The Devil's Bride)* (1968) Hammer
Directed by Terence Fisher
Screenplay by Richard Matheson from the novel, *The Devil Rides Out* by Dennis Wheatley; Photography by Arthur Grant; Art Direction by Bernard Robinson;

Edited by James Needs and Spencer Reeve; Music by James Bernard; Produced by Anthony Nelson-Keys

Stars: Christopher Lee, Charles Gray, Nike Arrighi, Leon Greene, Patrick Mower

Frankenstein Must Be Destroyed (1969) Hammer

Directed by Terence Fisher

Screenplay by Bert Batt, from a story by Anthony Nelson-Keys and Bert Batt; Photography by Arthur Grant; Art Direction by Bernard Robinson; Edited by Gordon Hales; Music by James Bernard; Produced by Anthony Nelson-Keys

Stars: Peter Cushing, Veronica Carlson, Simon Ward, Freddie Jones, Thorley Walters, Maxine Audley

Frankenstein and the Monster from Hell (1973) Hammer

Directed by Terence Fisher

Screenplay by John Elder (Anthony Hinds); Photography by Brian Probyn; Art Direction by Scott MacGregor; Edited by James Needs; Produced by Roy Skeggs

Stars: Peter Cushing, Shane Briant, Madeline Smith, John Stratton, Bernard Lee, David Prowse, Patrick Troughton

BIBLIOGRAPHY

Books

Baring, Anne, and Cashford, Jules. *The Myth of the Goddess: Evolution of an Image.* London: Arkana Penguin Books, 1993.

Barth, Karl. *Protestant Theology in the Nineteenth Century.* Valley Forge, Pa.: Judson Press, 1973.

Beker, J. Christiaan. *Paul the Apostle: The Triumph of God in Life and Thought.* Philadelphia: Fortress Press, 1980.

_____. *The Triumph of God: The Essence of Paul's Thought.* Translated by Loren T. Stuckenbruck. Minneapolis: Fortress Press, 1990.

Bell, Robert E. *Women of Classical Mythology.* New York and Oxford: Oxford University Press, 1991.

Boot, Andy. *Fragments of Fear: An Illustrated History of British Horror Films.* London and San Francisco: Creation Books, 1995.

Borst, Ronald V. *Graven Images: The Best of Horror, Fantasy and Science Fiction Film Art.* New York: Grove Press, 1992.

Brasnan, John. *The Horror People.* New York: Plume Books, New American Library, 1977.

Brode, Douglas. *The Films of the Fifties.* Secaucus, N.J.: Citadel Press, 1976.

Bulfinch, Thomas. *Bulfinch's Mythology.* New York: Modern Library.

Butler, Ivan. *Horror in the Cinema.* New York: Paperback Library, 1970.

Campbell, Joseph. *The Hero with a Thousand Faces.* Princeton, N.J.: Princeton University Press, 1968.

_____. *The Masks of God: Creative Mythology.* New York: Viking Press. 1968.

_____. *The Masks of God: Occidental Mythology.* New York: Viking Press, 1964.

_____. *The Masks of God: Oriental Mythology.* New York: Viking Press, 1962.

_____. *The Masks of God: Primitive Mythology.* New York: Viking Press. 1969.

Clarens, Carlos. *An Illustrated History of the Horror Film.* New York: Capricorn Books, 1967.

Cushing, Peter. *An Autobiography and Past Forgetting.* Baltimore: Midnight Marquee Press, 1999.

Davies, David Stuart. *Holmes of the Movies.* London: New English Library, 1976.

Dixon, Wheeler Winston. *The Charm of Evil: The Life and Films of Terence Fisher*. Metuchen, N.J.: Scarecrow Press, 1991.

Douglas, Drake. *Horror!* Toronto: Collier Books, Macmillan, 1966.

Driver, Tom F. *The Magic of Ritual*. San Francisco: Harper San Francisco, 1991.

Edwards, Carolyn McVickar. *The Storyteller's Goddess*. San Francisco: Harper, 1991.

Eisner, Lotte H. *The Haunted Screen*. Berkeley: University of California Press, 1973.

Eliade, Mircea. *Myth and Reality*. New York: Harper Colophon, 1963.

Everson, William K. *Classics of the Horror Film*. Secaucus, NJ.: Citadel Press, 1974.

_____. *More Classics of the Horror Film*. Secaucus, N.J.: Citadel Press, 1986.

Eyles, Allen; Adkinson, Robert; and Fry, Nicholas. *The House of Hammer: The Story of Hammer Films*. New York: The Third Press, 1973.

Florescu, Radu. *In Search of Frankenstein*. New York: Warner Books, 1976.

Frymer-Kensky, Tikva. *In the Wake of the Goddesses: Women, Culture and the Biblical Transformation of Pagan Myth*. New York: Fawcett Columbine, 1992.

Graves, Robert. *The Greek Myths*. Mount Kisco, N.Y.: Moyer Bell Limited, 1960.

Grimal, Pierre. *The Penguin Dictionary of Classical Mythology*. London: Penguin Books, 1991.

Hardy, Phil, editor. *The Overlook Film Encyclopedia: Horror*. Woodstock, N.Y.: Overlook Press, 1993.

Higham, Charles. *The Adventures of Conan Doyle*. New York: Pocket Books, 1978.

Hogan, David J. *Dark Romance: Sexuality in the Horror Film*. Jefferson, N.C.: McFarland, 1986.

Houston, Jean. *The Hero and the Goddess*. New York: Ballantine Books, 1992.

Hughes, Pennethorne. *Witchcraft*. Baltimore: Penguin Books, 1965.

Huss, Ray, and Ross, T.J. *Focus on the Horror Film*. Englewood Cliffs, N.J.: Prentice-Hall, 1972.

Hutchinson, Tom. *Horror and Fantasy in the Movies*. New York: Crescent Books, 1974.

Jones, Stephen. *The Illustrated Frankenstein Movie Guide*. London: Titan, 1994.

_____. *The Illustrated Vampire Movie Guide*. London: Titan, 1993.

Kracauer, Siegfried. *From Caligari to Hitler: A Psychological History of the German Film*. Princeton, N.J.: Princeton University Press, 1947.

Landy, Marcia. *British Genres: Cinema and Society, 1930–1960*. Princeton: Princeton University Press, 1991.

Lee, Christopher. *Tall, Dark and Gruesome*. London: W.H. Allen, 1977.

Lewis, C.S. *Christian Reflections*. Grand Rapids, Mich.: Eerdmans, 1967.

_____. *Essays Presented to Charles Williams*. Grand Rapids, Mich.: Eerdmans, 1966.

_____. *God in the Dock: Essays on Theology and Ethics*, edited by Walter Hooper. Grand Rapids, Mich.: Eerdmans, 1970.

_____. *Mere Christianity*. New York: Macmillan, 1960.

Luhr, Willam, and Lehman, Peter. *Authorship and Narrative in the Cinema: Issues in Contemporary Aesthetics*. New York: Capricorn Books, G.P. Putnam's Sons, 1977.

Mank, Gregory William. *It's Alive! The Classic Cinema Saga of Frankenstein*. London, England: Tantivy Press, 1981.

Maxford, Howard. *Hammer, House of Horror*. Woodstock, N.Y.: Overlook Press, 1996.

McCarty, John, editor. *The Fearmakers: The Screen's Directorial Masters of Suspense and Terror.* New York: St. Martin's Press, 1994.

_____. *The Modern Horror Film.* New York: Citadel Press, 1990.

McNally, Raymond, and Florescu, Radu. *In Search of Dracula.* Greenwich, Conn.: New York Graphic Society, 1972.

Michelet, Jules. *Satanism and Witchcraft: A Study in Medieval Superstition.* New York: Citadel Press, 1939.

Miller, David. *The Peter Cushing Companion.* London: Reynolds and Hearn Ltd., 2000.

Miller, Mark A. *Christopher Lee and Peter Cushing and Horror Cinema. A Filmography of Their 22 Collaborations.* Jefferson, N.C.: McFarland, 1995.

Milne, Tom, editor. *Time Out Film Guide.* London: Penguin Books, 2000.

Murphy, Robert. *Sixties British Cinema.* London: British Film Institute, 1962.

Nollen, Scott Allen. *Sir Arthur Conan Doyle at the Cinema.* Jefferson, N.C.: McFarland, 1996.

Paglia, Camille. *Vamps and Tramps.* New York: Vintage Books, 1994.

Peary, Denny. *Guide for the Film Fanatic.* New York: Simon and Schuster, 1986.

Pirie, David. *A Heritage of Horror: The English Gothic Cinema 1946–1972.* New York: Avon Books, 1973.

Pohle, Robert W., Jr., and Hart, Douglas C. *Sherlock Holmes on the Screen.* London: A.S. Barnes, 1977.

Prawer, S.S. *Caligari's Children: The Film as Tale of Terror.* New York: Da Capo Press, 1980.

Ricoeur, Paul. *The Symbolism of Evil.* Boston: Beacon Press, 1967.

Rigby, Jonathan. *English Gothic: A Century of Horror Cinema.* London: Reynolds and Hearn, 2000.

Ronay, Gabriel. *The Truth About Dracula.* New York: Stein and Day, 1972.

Rousseau, Jean-Jacques. *The Confessions.* Middlesex, England: Penguin Books, 1954.

Russell, Bertrand. *A History of Western Philosophy.* New York: Simon and Schuster, 1945.

Sandars, N.K. *The Epic of Gilgamesh.* London: Penguin, 1972.

_____, translator. *Poems of Heaven and Hell from Ancient Mesopotamia.* London: Penguin, 1971.

Sayers, Dorothy L. *Creed or Chaos?* Manchester, N.H.: Sophia Institute Press, 1949.

Schneider, Kirk J. *Horror and the Holy: Wisdom Teachings of the Monster Tale.* Chicago: Open Court, 1993.

Schwarz, Hans. *Evil: A Historical and Theological Perspective.* Translation by Mark W. Worthing. Minneapolis: Fortress Press, 1995.

Silver, Alain, and Ursini, James. *The Vampire Film, Revised.* New York: Limelight Editions, 1993.

Skal, David J. *The Monster Show: A Cultural History of Horror.* New York: Penguin Books, 1993.

Soren, Dr. David. *The Rise and Fall of the Horror Film.* Baltimore: Midnight Marquee Press, 1977.

Steinbrunner, Chris, and Michaels, Norman. *The Films of Sherlock Holmes.* Secaucus, N.J.: Citadel Press, 1978.

Steinem, Gloria. *Revolution from Within: A Book of Self Esteem.* Boston, Toronto, London: Little, Brown, 1992.

Summers, Montague. *The History of Witchcraft and Demonology*. New York: University Books, 1956.

_____. *The Vampire: His Kith and Kin*. New Hyde Park, N.Y.: University Books, 1960.

_____. *The Vampire in Europe*. New Hyde Park, N.Y.: University Books, 1961.

Tropp, Martin. *Images of Fear: How Horror Stories Helped Shape Modern Culture (1818–1918)*. Jefferson, N.C.: McFarland, 1990.

Twitchell, James B. *Preposterous Violence: Fables of Aggression in Modern Culture*. New York: Oxford University Press, 1989.

Van Franz, Marie-Louise. *Shadow and Evil in Fairy Tales,* revised. Shambhala, Boston and London, 1995.

Vermilye, Jerry. *The Great British Films*. Secaucus, N.J.: Citadel Press, 1978.

Volta, Ornella. *The Vampire*, translated by Raymond Rudorff. New York: Award Books, 1962.

Wink, Walter. *Engaging the Powers*. Minneapolis: Fortress Press, 1992.

Wolf, Leonard. *A Dream of Dracula: In Search of the Living Dead*. Boston: Little, Brown, 1972.

_____, editor. *The Essential Dracula*. New York: Plume, 1993.

Wolkstein, Diane. *The First Love Stories*. New York: Harper Perennial, 1992.

Wollen, Peter. *Signs and Meaning in the Cinema*. Indiana University Press, Bloomington and London, 1969.

Wright, Bruce Lanier. *Nightwalkers: Gothic Horror Movies: The Modern Era*. Dallas: Taylor, 1995.

Young, Dudley. *Origins of the Sacred: The Ecstasies of Love and War*. New York: St. Martin's Press, 1991.

Articles

Dundes, Alan. "The Hero Pattern and the Life of Jesus," in *In Quest of the Hero,* edited by Robert A. Segal. Princeton: Princeton University Press, 1990; pp. 179–223.

Fisher, Terence. "Horror Is My Business." *Films and Filming* (July 1964) 7–8. Transcript of interview conducted by Raymond Durgnat and John Cutts.

Leggett, Paul. "The Filmed Fantasies of Terence Fisher." *Christianity Today* Vol. XXV, No. 2; January 23, 1981; pp. 32–33.

_____. "Of Heroes and Devils: The Supernatural on Film." *Christianity Today* Vol. XXII, No. 4; November 18, 1977; pp. 19–21.

McDonald, T. Liam. "The Horrors of Hammer: The House That Blood Built" *Cut! Horror Writers on Horror Film*, edited by Christopher Golden. New York: Berkley Books, 1992; pp. 151–160.

Raglon, Lord. "The Hero: A Study in Tradition, Myth, and Drama, Part II," in *In Quest of the Hero*, edited by Robert A. Segal. Princeton: Princeton University Press, 1990; pp. 89–175.

Rank, Otto. "The Myth of the Birth of the Hero," in *In Quest of the Hero* edited by Robert A. Segal. Princeton: Princeton University Press, 1990; pp. 3–86.

Ringel, Harry. "Hammer Horror: The World of Terence Fisher." *Graphic Violence on the Screen*, edited by Thomas R. Atkins. New York: Simon and Schuster, 1976.

_____. "Terence Fisher: The Human Side." *Cinefantastique* 4, No. 3 (1975); pp. 5–16.

Periodicals

Christianity Today. Carol Stream, IL
Cinefantastique. Oak Park, IL
Hammer Horror. Marvel Comics, London, U.K.
Little Shoppe of Horrors. Des Moines, IA
Midnight Marquee. Baltimore, MD
Phantasma: Cinema Beyond Reality. Albany, NY
Scarlet Street: The Magazine of Mystery and Horror. Glen Rock, NJ
The House That Hammer Built. Suffolk, U.K.

INDEX